Sabers and Utopias

Sabers and Utopias

VISIONS OF LATIN AMERICA

Mario Vargas Llosa

TRANSLATED FROM THE SPANISH
BY ANNA KUSHNER

FARRAR, STRAUS AND GIROUX
NEW YORK

Farrar, Straus and Giroux
175 Varick Street, New York 10014

Library of Congress Cataloging-in-Publication Data
Names: Vargas Llosa, Mario, 1936– author.
Title: Sabers and utopias : visions of Latin America / Mario Vargas Llosa ;
    translated from the Spanish by Anna Kushner.
Other titles: Sables y utopías. English.
Description: New York : Farrar, Straus and Giroux, 2018. | "Originally
    published in Spanish in 2009 by Santillana Ediciones Generales, Spain, as
    Sables y Utopías." | Includes index.
Identifiers: LCCN 2017038306| ISBN 9780374253738 (cloth) | ISBN
    9780374708917 (ebook)
Subjects: LCSH: Latin America—Politics and government—1948–1980. | Latin
    America—Politics and government—1980– | Latin American Literature—
    History and criticism. | Arts, Latin American.
Classification: LCC F1414.2 .V394513 2018 | DDC 980.03—dc23
LC record available at https://lccn.loc.gov/2017038306

Designed by Jonathan D. Lippincott

www.fsgbooks.com
www.twitter.com/fsgbooks • www.facebook.com/fsgbooks

1   3   5   7   9   10   8   6   4   2

Contents

Foreword:
The Instinctive Struggle
for Freedom

Every April 23, on the date of Cervantes's death, we celebrate Spanish Language Day in Spain, a tribute to the tongue we share with inhabitants of about twenty countries, more than 450 million people. In keeping with tradition, cultural events are organized to promote literature written in Spanish. Illustrious representatives of Iberian and Latin American culture are also usually asked to select, from among the thousands of words making up the language, that which they like best. Each time Mario Vargas Llosa has been asked this question, his answer has been the same: *freedom*.

Freedom is Vargas Llosa's favorite word, not only because in Spanish—*libertad*—it is a melodic, three-syllable term, but also because it is a value that from very early on allowed him to orient himself in the turbulent modern world and undertake varied cultural, social, and political battles. A very close concept, liberal, is the one that best defines his political positions. Although it is true that depending on the country, a liberal person could be progressive, a defender of the free market, or even a socialist, Vargas Llosa is comfortable with that definition. To him, freedom is indivisible and should be an essential value in an individual's private sphere as well as in a country's public life. In the same way that he defends free trade and open markets, he is also in favor of legalizing drugs, gay marriage, and a woman's right to have an abortion. His liberalism is one that places above other values the freedom of the human being to think, opine, believe, live, and produce without the coercion of external powers, taking as its only limit the legal framework that governs coexistence in societies.

The path that led him to the positions he maintains today has been long. It began in the most complex years of Latin American history, years in which military dictatorships suffocated democracy and armed revolutions promised to bring heaven on earth. A period of sabers and utopias in which the right as well as the left fought intense battles, but none of these for democracy or individual freedom.

In this atmosphere, Vargas Llosa began to forge his political thinking and his visions of Latin America. All have been captured, like the rings inside a tree, in an enormous quantity of essays, chronicles, letters, and conference papers that began to accumulate at the beginning of the 1960s. This volume seeks to illustrate this journey, bringing together essays written over the course of more than fifty years that not only reveal Vargas Llosa's intellectual journey but also touch on the major events that have marked Latin America's recent history. They are organized not by chronological order but by theme, showing the battles that Vargas Llosa has fought for freedom, from his head-on opposition to dictatorships, his hope for and later disillusionment with revolutions, his criticism of nationalism, populism, intolerance, and corruption—the greatest threat to the credibility of Latin American democracies—all the way to the discovery of liberal ideas, the unmitigated defense of the democratic system, and his passion for Latin American literature and art.

Just like the characters in his novels, who tend to be the embodiment of one of those blind forces in nature that lead the human being to carry out great feats or cause terrible cataclysms,

Vargas Llosa has been an instinctive defender of freedom, always conscious of the ideas, systems, or social reforms encroaching on the contours of individual autonomy. His criterion for measuring the climate of a society's freedom has always been the same: the space that is given to writers to freely express their ideas. In the 1960s, when Latin American stories were revolutionizing things and he defined himself as an engaged intellectual, his first forays into public debates were guided less by political doctrines than by literary intuitions. Although he was influenced by Sartre's ideological positions, his youthful ideas regarding what a free and just society should be came, in great part, from reflections regarding the job and social role of the writer.

It was always very clear to Vargas Llosa that freedom, that requirement without which the novelist cannot develop his interests and obsessions, was vital for a rich cultural world where the debate of ideas would facilitate Latin America's transition toward modernity. Only with full freedom to criticize, love or hate the government, nation, or political system that took him in, could the writer give form to that personal product, so largely irrational, and always fermented by passions, desires, individual loves and phobias, that was the novel. The results of bowing down meekly before external powers or political causes could only be servile praise for the tyrant of the moment or the skillful burden of engagement. In "The Role of the Intellectual in National Liberation Movements," an article that was published in 1966, he expressed the tensions that should be borne by a novelist whose conscious engagement tied him to a political cause. If personal demons and public causes coincided, it was a happy coincidence for the creator. In the opposite case, the novelist should assume the internal tearing apart and remain loyal to his literary vocation.

In the 1950s, a decade in which Vargas Llosa's youthful flirtations with literature were becoming a marital engagement, the symbol of the oppression of the spirit and the reduction of freedom was the dictator. In Peru alone, in the first half of the twentieth century, there had been five military coups d'état, which, together with six more that would bloody the country's political life in the following decades, until the untimely attempted escape of Alberto Fujimori, would yield a total of almost sixty years under authoritarian regimes. This foul and sordid atmosphere, causing frustrations, skepticism, and moral apathy, had an overwhelming presence in Vargas Llosa's first three novels. *The Time of the Hero*, *The Green House*, and *Conversation in the Cathedral*, published, respectively, in 1963, 1966, and 1969, were great fictional constructions in which he made a detailed analysis of Peruvian society, revealing the consequences of militarism, machismo, religious dogmatism, or any other form of irascible power that held sway over people. Whether it was in military academies, brothels, missions, jungle areas, or bourgeois surroundings, it always ended badly for Vargas Llosa's characters, who were spiritually weak, submerged in the most abject mediocrity, or turned into something they didn't want to be.

Although these novels were great imaginative creations, inspired more by formal and literary ideals than by ideological engagement, in them you can see the mental and moral universe with which Vargas Llosa interpreted Latin American reality in the 1960s. The essays that he wrote in those years were a conscious echo of the revolutionary longing brewing in his narrative works. If in "Toma de Posición," a 1965 manifesto, he expressed his support for national liberation movements, in his novels he allowed one to make out that only the collapse of the capitalist system and the corrupt bourgeoisie could break the vicious circles that prevented Peru's advance toward modernity.

This explains the euphoria with which he greeted the Cuban Revolution, the first attempt to found a society under the socialist banner. His hopes, however, did not last long. When the dream began to become reality, and Fidel Castro, the fireproof giant who had impressed Vargas Llosa with his receptiveness to intellectuals' criticism, adopted the same type of censorship that had been common among dictatorships, the hopefulness began to fall apart. Two events sealed his break with the revolution. The first of these was the repression the regime carried out against homosexuals—among them, several writers—discriminating against them, locking them up, and "reeducating them." The second was the famous and crucial Padilla Affair, which divided the continent's intellectuals on the left.

In 1971, the poet Heberto Padilla was accused of "subversive activities" following the publication of a book of poems—*Fuera del juego* (*Sent Off the Field*)—in which the Cuban authorities saw counterrevolutionary criticism. Padilla was forced to make a retraction and to carry out a self-criticism that revived the most obtuse practices of Stalinism. That farce did not go unnoticed. Vargas Llosa, who knew Padilla and noticed that the spectacle had been orchestrated from the highest levels, mobilized the most prestigious intellectuals on the left to make manifest, through signing a letter directed to Fidel Castro, a repudiation of the treatment inflicted upon Padilla and other Cuban writers (see "Letter to Fidel Castro"). It was not the first time that Vargas Llosa made clear his opposition to censorship. In 1966, the authorities of the Soviet Union had sentenced two Russian writers, Yuli Daniel and Andrei Sinyavsky, for similar reasons, and the Peruvian had reacted with anger, publishing "A Permanent Insurrection," an essay in which he pulled no punches and criticized the curtailment of freedom of expression in the Soviet Union. The great virtue that Vargas Llosa saw in the Cuban Revolution was, precisely, that of having harmonized justice with freedom. Although Castro had justified the Soviet invasion of Czechoslovakia, his leadership in Cuba seemed "exemplary in his respect for the human being and in his struggle for freedom." But the Padilla Affair removed the veil from the ghost and left on display the hidden face of that "model within socialism" that Vargas Llosa saw—or wanted to see—in the previous trips he had made to the island. The utopian society that Castro proposed had claimed its first victim, freedom of expression, and, with it, literature, journalism, and any type of intellectual activity went into quarantine. After a decade of enthusiasm, the two maxims with which Vargas Llosa had organized his life, literature and socialism, saw themselves in a face-off. Before the dilemma of choosing between his vocation and political engagement, Vargas Llosa ultimately chose the former.

The evidence that Cuba was not the materialization of a utopia, but rather a giant trap for writers and those opposing the regime, forced Vargas Llosa to revisit his ideas regarding the revolution and democracy. His mental world nonetheless remained the same: his values remained immutable and his diagnosis of Peru's ills continued. The writer persisted in thinking that the priority for Latin America was to take the path of Western countries and modernize (he suggested this for the first time in 1958, after a trip to the Peruvian jungle that showed him a world of violence and abuse, foreign to Western civility, and that would inspire *The Green House*, *Captain Pantoja and the Special Service*, and *The Storyteller*), correct its inequalities, and repair the injustices suffered by Peru's minority populations. What changed were the methods, not the goals, and this is reflected in the essays he started to publish in the late 1970s.

In a conference at Acción Popular, in 1978, Vargas Llosa stated that the spectacle of poverty and exploitation reigning in his country continued to horrify him just as before, but he emphasized the mistrust he now felt toward Marxism as a method for correcting inequalities and injustice. Liberal and democratic doctrines had proven to be more efficient, "in other words, those who do not sacrifice freedom in the name of justice," and countries such as Switzerland and Israel had managed to balance individual freedom and systems of social justice. This change in position was the result of new intellectual explorations. The collapse of faith in socialism had forced Vargas Llosa to leave aside

Sartre and look for new models with which to judge global events. This search had led him to revise the early interpretations he had made of Camus, and to read or reread under a different lens the books of Raymond Aron, Jean-François Revel, and Isaiah Berlin, authors who were very different from one another but who had a common objective: the defense of the democratic system and of freedom as the guarantors of pluralism and tolerance.

Revel, a trained philosopher but a journalist by vocation, was, along with Aron, one of the few voices in France who confronted Marxism and the pro-Soviet tide encouraged by Sartre. Beyond theories, facts mattered to Revel, and as such, he didn't hesitate in criticizing the intellectuals who, in order to defend ideology, justified the excesses of Stalinist totalitarianism. Aron denounced something similar in one of his most famous books, *The Opium of the Intellectuals*. The ideological blindness obscured the fact that it wasn't the socialist countries who had led the great social revolutions, but rather capitalist democracies, where women, young people, and sexual and cultural minorities rebelled against the orthodoxy of institutions, demanded rights, and pressed changes upon society. Democratic reforms proved to be the shortest and most efficient path to improving living conditions, not the total revolutions that sought to reconstruct society brick by brick. The great paradox of the twentieth century was proving to be that, while socialist dictatorships atrophied, the internal mechanism of capitalism demanded a constant revolution in ways, customs, tastes, tendencies, desires, and lifestyles to survive.

The thinking of Isaiah Berlin was also fundamental for Vargas Llosa. Although as a writer and public intellectual Vargas Llosa was closer to the controversial Revel than to the circumspect Berlin, the latter's ideas were vital to his understanding why, in art and literature, absolute ambition and the dream of human perfection were praiseworthy but in reality tended to lead to collective massacres. The gut-wrenching idea of Berlin is that perfect worlds do not exist. The dream of enlightenment, according to which societies travel the upward route of progress guided by science and reason, was based on an erroneous premise. Neither science nor reason offers unique and definitive responses to the human being's basic questions. How to live, how to make assessments, and what to desire are questions without specific answers, or at least not comparable to scientific truths. He who rises above his equals and states that he has higher knowledge of human nature and, as such, the best form of life, ends up, generally, submitting his confreres to the tyranny of reason. The integral solutions that enthused the philosophers of the eighteenth century do not exist, and anyone who says he possesses them should be feared, since what he proposes is a fiction, an ideal model that stokes pristine fantasies of a lost paradise but in reality denies human ambiguity and difference. The outward goals around which individuals and cultures organize their existences cannot be reduced to one sole project. Life is fed by a diversity of ideals and values, and, unfortunately, it is impossible for them all to be in frictionless harmony. If you want to avoid oppression, there is no other solution than to foment pluralism, tolerance, and freedom, or, more precisely, what Berlin calls negative freedom: a sphere of life in which no external power can block human action.

Berlin's ideas had a powerful effect on Vargas Llosa's thinking. If in 1975 he still held hope that Velasco's socialist dictatorship would combat the horror and barbarism of underdevelopment, in 1976, with the palace coup by General Francisco Morales Bermúdez, his hopes had completely evaporated. Of the revolutions, there was only left a "noise of sabers," and, once again, instead of equality and justice, the Peruvian people had received new restrictions on the freedom of expression.

Neither the leftist revolutions nor the right-wing coups; neither utopia nor a perfect society: from 1976 on, Vargas Llosa would defend the ballot box as the only legitimate path to power.

Only the democratic system tolerates contradictory truths; that is why it is the one implying the fewest risks to coexistence, the one that tolerates choices among different lifestyles, and the one that not only allows but also demands debate and the free circulation of ideas. From this new angle, the revolution is observed no longer as a solution, but as a symptom. There is a deeper ill, embedded in the gut of Latin America, that does not have anything to do with injustice or inequality. Left-wing revolutionaries, right-wing soldiers, religious visionaries, fanatical and racist nationalists of all stripes have a certain common base: contempt for the democratic rules of the game. The ideas of each group have folded over on themselves until degenerating into fratricidal fanaticisms. This is also the history of the continent. All of the collectivist ideologies, from the Catholic faith to socialism, going through different forms of indigenism, populism, and nationalism, have sprouted robust roots and have defended themselves with a weapon in hand and a blindfold over the eyes.

Vargas Llosa clearly saw these problems thanks not only to Isaiah Berlin and Karl Popper (the other liberal philosopher, a critic of closed societies and historic determinism, whom Vargas Llosa carefully read in the late 1980s), but also to Euclides da Cunha, a Brazilian journalist and sociologist who witnessed one of the most absurd and tragic slaughters in Latin America, the War of the Canudos. *Os Sertões*, the book in which da Cunha explains how ideological blindness distorted reality and led the Brazilian army to eliminate a peasant uprising—behind which they insisted on seeing the British Empire—not only inspired Vargas Llosa's most ambitious work, *The War of the End of the World*, but also showed him that great Latin American tragedies have been born from lack of communication, mutual ignorance, and the different temporalities that separate and generate mistrust between sectors of the population.

Vargas Llosa began to write *The War of the End of the World* in the late 1970s, without suspecting that just around the corner, on May 17, 1980, Sendero Luminoso would burn the ballot boxes in the Ayacucho town of Chuschi and declare one of the bloodiest and most fundamentalist revolutionary wars in Latin America's modern history. Reality seemed to be confused with fiction. As the writer re-created episodes of religious fanatics who saw in the nascent Brazilian Republic the work of Satan, Maoist revolutionaries were hanging dogs from Lima's poles to denounce the betrayal by that "dog" Deng Xiaoping of the Chinese Cultural Revolution.

It was the 1980s, the Berlin Wall was tottering, that great democratic alliance that is the European Union was being plotted, and Latin America was wavering between fanaticism, authoritarianism, and revolution. In Chile, the iron fist of Augusto Pinochet still ruled; Argentina had handed power over to the military junta of Videla, Massera, and Agosti; Brazil was under military rule; Bolivia had suffered the same fate between 1964 and 1982; Paraguay was the domain of Alfredo Stroessner; Ecuador, following two military dictatorships, was involved in a territorial dispute with Peru; Colombia, though lacking dictators, endured an internal struggle with various guerrilla movements, among them the M-19, the EPL, the ELN, and the FARC; Venezuela had enjoyed the democratic bases set down by Rómulo Betancourt, but in 1989, it was facing the Caracazo, and in 1992, Hugo Chávez's (thwarted) military coup; in Panama, there was Noriega; in Nicaragua, the Sandinista revolution was toppling Somoza; Honduras was coming out of the dictatorship of Paz García; in El Salvador, a civil war was beginning between soldiers and warriors from the Frente Farabundo Martí para la Liberación Nacional; Guatemala was in the middle of an atrocious armed conflict; Mexico remained under the "perfect dictatorship" of the PRI; in Haiti, there was Baby Doc; and in Cuba, Fidel Castro. The panorama was far from encouraging. Between coups d'état and revolutions, democracy was a rare species in a habitat dominated by populist caudillos, strongmen, corrupt politicians, fanatical revolutionaries, and tyrants covered in military insignia.

In Peru, however, despite the threat that Sendero Luminoso and the MRTA (Movimiento Revolucionario Túpac Amaru) represented, the democratic system seemed to consolidate itself again with the governments of Belaúnde Terry and his successor, Alan García. Seven years of constitutional stability were restoring faith in institutions, until July 28, 1987, when, in a speech before Congress, García threatened to nationalize banks and insurance and finance companies. That measure sought to give the government control over credits, leaving the industrial sector, including the media, at the mercy of the president and the APRA (American Popular Revolutionary Alliance). The legitimate power that the ballot box had given García could have overflowed and the shadow of authoritarianism was circling back around the fragile Peruvian democracy (see "Toward a Totalitarian Peru").

If García didn't manage to take over the banks, it was because Vargas Llosa and a group of businessmen led protests and a multitudinous march in the Plaza San Martín that, supported by thousands of citizens, finally forced the law's repeal. On the basis of this mobilization, the Movimiento Libertad came about, an organization of citizens that would remain politically active and that, in alliance with Acción Popular and the Partido Popular Cristiano, would put forward Vargas Llosa as a contender in the 1990 presidential elections. That implied a big change—and also a great adventure—for the writer. He was not only going to write opinion columns, debate ideas, and face abstractions; now he would have to subject himself to the judgment of public opinion, make electoral proposals, and deal with daily problems.

Given that his leap into politics was motivated by García's economic policies, it was clear that Vargas Llosa's plan for governing would have to distinguish itself on the same terms. A solid position in economic matters would imply consulting with experts on the subject, intellectuals whose ideas would be in tune with the notion of an open society, but whose reasoning would be coded in specialized terms. The liberalism of Aron, Berlin, and Popper could give general ideas about how to organize a country's productive life, but it would be difficult to translate them into concrete proposals to alleviate the inflation rate or reanimate the business sector. In contrast, the ideas of the economist Friedrich August von Hayek, the fiercest critic of centralized economies, were of great use to counteract the damage of decades of state control, mercantilism, and bureaucratic drowsiness.

If in the sixties it had been Sartre, Camus, and Bataille who served as points of reference against which Vargas Llosa contrasted his ideas, by the end of the eighties and the beginning of the nineties, it was Aron, Berlin, Popper, and Hayek. While the first two gave serious reasons to combat nationalism, fascism, Marxism, populism, indigenism, and all ideologies seeking to enclose the individual within a larger body (whether it be the nation, the party, race, history, or any form of flock supported by caudillos, visionaries, or revolutionaries), Hayek asserted that state planning of the economy, on the rise during the years in which he published *The Road to Serfdom* (1944), concentrated economic power in the state, reduced the space for citizen participation, and, consequently, established a relationship of dependency that undermined individual freedom. If fascism and communism were alike in any way, it was in this point: both systems concentrated the means of production in the hands of the state. In this way, they not only weakened individual initiative and economic freedoms, but expanded the tentacles of state power into the private realm.

After reading Hayek, Vargas Llosa was left persuaded that the defense of individual freedom passed through the defense of free enterprise. Freedom was one and indivisible. Political freedoms and economic freedoms could not be differentiated since one kind depended on the other. The stateism preached by Juan

Perón in the forties, by Castro and General Velasco in the sixties, by Alan García in the eighties, by Hugo Chávez and Evo Morales in 2000, and by the Mexican PRI throughout its history reproduced the mercantilist system that gave government unchecked power, put freedoms on a tightrope, opened the doors to clientelism and corruption, shaped a rentier mentality, had a soporific effect on initiative and economic dynamism, and fomented centralism—all endemic ills of Latin American public life.

During his presidential campaign, Vargas Llosa promoted privatization, fiscal discipline, and foreign investment, and managed to convince a large part of the Peruvian electorate that the path to overcome poverty was to follow the example of countries that, like Japan, Taiwan, South Korea, Singapore, or Spain, had inserted themselves in global markets and had taken advantage of globalization. But in the final stretch, when everything seemed to point to his victory at the ballot box, the demons that Vargas Llosa had tried to exorcise from political life reemerged, and the engineer Alberto Fujimori, wielding the weapons of populism and demagoguery—and, later, racism—forced a second electoral round that sentenced the writer to defeat.

Fujimori's victory not only signified a stumbling block in the personal and collective efforts to transform Peru's reality through liberal ideas. Two years later, in 1992, Fujimori would shut down Congress, the Supreme Court, and the Court of Constitutional Guarantees; would suspend the constitution; and would begin to govern by decree, effecting a self-directed coup d'état that gave him control over justice, legislation, the economy, and the military forces. The plague of authoritarianism, seemingly purged from public life twelve years before, was again rampant in the Peruvian democratic system. Besides, it was leaving a precedent that would impose itself in the following years as a damaging style in Latin America: that of pruning legality from the branches of power, accessing the executive by democratic means to later betray the rules of the game, remake constitutions, compromise judicial

powers, ensure parliamentary majorities, and intimidate the opposition and the media. Breaking his promise not to opine for
Peru, Vargas Llosa forcefully protested and asked for the international community to condemn the situation. His efforts were
in vain. On top of the Sendero Luminoso and MRTA attacks
was now authoritarian rule, and Peru, once again, went back and
forth between dictatorship and revolution.

Despite the fact that Fujimori's regime made sure to tarnish
Vargas Llosa's image and portray him as an enemy of the country's
working-class foundation, Vargas Llosa won the battle in the long
run. The corruption scandals caused by the "Vlad-videos," tapes
on which the strongman of the regime, the former captain Vladimiro Montesinos, was seen handing out bribes left and right,
caused great malaise among citizens. In November 2000, taking
advantage of a trip to Japan, Fujimori prepared the lair where he
would hibernate during his dictatorial hangover, and sent a letter
to Congress communicating his resignation.

Democracy was returning to Peru, but political stability
did not follow. A new wave of revolutionary populism had spent
years, ever since the electoral victory of Hugo Chávez in Venezuela, dragging thousands of people toward new forms of authoritarianism. Reviving the myth of Simón Bolívar and Fidel Castro,
of the anti-imperialist struggle and Bolivarian unity, Chávez had
initiated a process of taking over and bringing down Venezuelan
democratic institutions, borrowing Fujimori's tactics to control
the Supreme Court of Justice, govern through decrees, take control of the most profitable companies (oil, especially), create Bolivarian militias, close media outlets, and create a climate of social
confrontation. This replica of Guevarism inside the democratic
system did not take long to become an export product. Chávez
tried to make his Bolivarian revolution take root in several countries in Latin America, among them Peru, supporting the presidential candidacy of the former soldier Ollanta Humala.

When it entered the public stage, the Humala dynasty, led

by its patriarch, Isaac Humala, advocated a nationalist and xeno-phobic discourse, whose proposals went from a hierarchical orga-nization of society based on race (only Peruvians of "copper-colored skin" would have full rights; whites would be second-class) to the persecution of homosexuals and the public lynching of "neo-liberal traitors." On January 1, 2005, demonstrating that they were not joking, Antauro, brother of Ollanta and leader of the ethno-hunting movement, took a commissary by force in the Andean city of Andahuaylas to demand the resignation of Presi-dent Alejandro Toledo. Although such nonsense should have denied him any political career, Humala won the first round of the 2006 elections. Before knowing who his opponent would be in the second round—Alan García or Lourdes Flores—Vargas Llosa promoted an alliance of democrats to avoid the victory of the ethno-hunter. García's history didn't leave much room for optimism, but, at that moment, to allow Humala's victory would have implied not only Chávez's direct interference in Peru but also the consolidation of a regime of a nationalist bent, animated by the rankest demagogic, xenophobic, homophobic, and bel-ligerent causes. Facing that possibility, Vargas Llosa didn't hes-itate: he gave his vote to García and celebrated his victory as the lesser evil.

No one thought that, five years later, Peru would find itself at an even more complex crossroads and that Vargas Llosa would end up supporting the presidential candidacy of Ollanta Humala to block the return of Fujimorism to power. Despite the Supreme Court of Peru sentencing the former dictator Alberto Fujimori to twenty-five years in prison for crimes committed during his regime, Fujimorism remained strongly rooted in society. It was one more proof of the fragility of democracy in Latin America and the nostalgia that persisted in the population for caudillos and strongmen. For the 2011 elections, Fujimorism was revived through Keiko Fujimori, the daughter of the former dictator and heiress of the corruption framework drawn up by her father during the ten years he was in power. Because of errors by the democratic opposition, the candidate that passed to the second round was, for the second consecutive time, Ollanta Humala. For Vargas Llosa, it was a difficult moment. If in past elections it had been risky to support Alan García, this time the situation was more uncertain. In his opinion columns, Vargas Llosa had been as critical of Fujimori as of Humala's political entourage and ideas. To vote for Keiko Fujimori was to legitimize a corrupt and criminal dictatorship, and very probably to open the doors of the former dictator's jail cell so he could come back to assume control of the country from the shadows. On the other hand, a candidate like Humala represented the possibility that Peru could become a satellite of Venezuela, and that the country would renounce ten consecutive years of economic progress and a reconquest of freedoms.

The reasoning that finally led Vargas Llosa to choose Humala was that he was already familiar with Fujimorism. The dictatorship was an "absolute bad" and he was convinced that with Keiko in the presidency, autocracy would return. With Ollanta Humala, in contrast, there was a possibility that the responsibilities of government would force him to moderate his discourse and be pragmatic. In the end, it was thus. Humala won the elections and, distancing himself from Chavism, he hewed closer to the Brazilian model of Lula and Dilma Rousseff.

Although the current climate in Latin America is less turbulent than in prior decades, the countries of the region are still far from reaching the social and political consensus that will guarantee governmental stability. There are intense controversies over whether Latin America should follow the path of Uruguay and Brazil, countries where a pragmatic and de-ideologized left has taken giant steps toward development, or that of Cuba and Venezuela, where omnipotent caudillos bearing the robes of revolution repeat economic formulas and demagogic rhetoric that have proven since the 1940s to be ineffective. The economic numbers and real data make the answer clear, but the temptation of utopia continues to be an irrepressible vice in the Latin American mind-set. Paradises lost—biblical, Bolivarian, indigenist, Peronist, Guevarist, Castrist, Pinochetist—continue feeding hopes up and down the continent. In politics this tendency to live in unreality and build fictitious worlds where everything is perfect has been disastrous. In the arts, by contrast, it has inspired great literary and artistic works whose imaginative excesses have amazed with their exuberance. That is the other face of Latin America, that of García Márquez, of Borges, of Cortázar, of Frida Kahlo, of Cabrera Infante, of Szyszlo, of Vargas Llosa himself. The fictitious worlds that have come from their hands have been favored in that effort by denying reality. In creative art, the artist can impose her criteria on events and make everything fit together, make logic and illogic coexist, as in Macondo, make reality arbitrarily take on other dimensions, as in Botero's paintings, make fiction sneak into the world and transfigure it, as in Borges's stories. In reality, on the other hand, those attempts to force events into a prefabricated model tend to end tragically. Vargas Llosa's battles for freedom have sought for creators to give free rein to their fantasies and create utopian worlds, as impossible, disastrous, bloody, or perfect as their imaginations allow, so that no ideologue tries to bait and switch them and jail an individual in a similar project. While artists can try out mythical and irrational forms, can be deicides and fantasize about a custom-made world, politicians should come down from the clouds, take reality's pulse, and lay down the base of that imperfect and mundane system, as humble as it is efficient, that is democracy.

Carlos Granés
Madrid, November 2008–October 2014

Part I

The Fall of Somoza

This time, the fall of Anastasio Somoza seems inevitable and imminent. It will likely have happened already by the time this article is published. It is an event that can only produce joy and relief around the world, since it embodies a satrapy that has been one of the most abject in a story that, as is well known, is full of them. Somoza's dictatorship was already an anachronism in our day, full as it is of institutional and ideological dictatorships, a somber manifestation of modernity firmly rooted in Latin America, as can be seen with a quick glance, for example, at the Southern Cone. The regimes of a Pinochet and a Videla, of the Uruguayan military or that which was presided over by Banzer in Bolivia, are of a different nature than those of the "brutal caudillos" described by Alcides Arguedas and Francisco García Calderón and who gave the shameful image of our countries to the rest of the world as little republics governed by gunmen. The institutional and ideological dictatorships are not, incidentally, less bloody or less prone to corruption (inseparable from any system made immune to criticism) than the folkloric ones.

The difference is that they commit their crimes in the name of a philosophy, of a social and economic project they seek to carry out, albeit through fire and blood.

Somoza's regime has been more rudimentary, less brutal and abstract, than the technological dictatorship of our time: its troglodyte predecessor. It belongs to that variety of whose prototypes were a Trujillo, a Papa Doc, a Pérez Jiménez, and of which we still see a Stroessner and a Baby Doc. In other words, individual dictatorship, the crooked, uniformed kind, lacking in pretensions and historical alibis, whose motives are simple and clear: stay in power by any means and ransack the country until it is bled dry.

The New York Times estimates that the Somoza family fortune in land, agrarian, maritime, commercial, and urban businesses, in Nicaragua, amounts to about five hundred million dollars. It's not bad at all, as an operation, if you consider that the country is one of the poorest on the planet, that without a doubt the family has a similar amount in safekeeping abroad, and that the first one in the dynasty to take power—Tacho Somoza, the current Somoza's father—was a poor devil half a century ago, scraping by in the picturesque job of latrine inspector in Managua, something that earned him the pompous nickname "Toilet Marshal."

The history of the dynasty follows a model that has turned out to be classic. Like Trujillo in the Dominican Republic, Tacho Somoza began his political career in the shadow of U.S. military intervention, serving first as a translator for the Marines, and later as an officer and head of the National Guard, created by the occupying forces to implement the policy they imposed on Nicaragua. Somoza the elder was a diligent executor of this policy and his first notable exploit consisted of the treacherous murder of Sandino, when the latter had agreed to disarm the forces with which he confronted, over the course of six years, the occupying troops. Shortly after, in 1936, he deposed President Juan Bautista Sacasa and, in grotesquely rigged elections, was elected in his place. From then until 1956, when he was assassinated by four bullets at a dance, Tacho Somoza was the absolute lord of lives and ranches, and he used those twenty years, relentlessly, to tyrannize the former and take over the latter. His heirs—Luis, for a period of eleven years, and Anastasio, from 1967 until now—were worthy followers of his villainous acts and, besides holding power, they continued to increase the family's spoils.

The responsibility of the United States in the martyrdom that almost half a century of Somozas has represented for Nicaragua should not be downplayed by those who, like this writer, want democratic regimes for Latin American countries, based on elections, in which political parties and freedom of the press are respected. Washington's policies vis-à-vis Nicaragua were exceptionally petty and obtuse. Satisfied with their ally, who supported them unquestioningly in international bodies, seven U.S. presidents—three Republicans and four Democrats—maintained a friendship with the Somozas, to whom, in exchange for obsequiousness, they lent financial assistance, whom they armed, decorated, and even educated at West Point (of which the current Anastasio and one of his sons are graduates). In those same years, by contrast, Washington broke the nonintervention principle—which was respected to Somoza's favor—by intervening in Guatemala, in 1954, to depose the Arbenz government, and in the Dominican Republic, in 1965, to squash the popular uprising against the military dictatorship that overthrew Juan Bosch. These policies were petty because they placed the advantage of a guaranteed vote in the United Nations on all matters and the certainty that, in that country, the interests of a few U.S. companies would not be affected above the interests of a people tormented by a regime of malfeasants above basic norms of justice and ethics. And it was obtuse because when you roll around in the mud, sooner or later you end up dirty. And that's what has happened to Washington in Nicaragua.

The true interests of the U.S. people do not consist of having henchmen of Somoza stock, tyrants hated by their people, who, logically, will extend this hate to anyone associated with their goons, but rather in fomenting the establishment of regimes that put into practice the principles of freedom, tolerance, equality, and representation enshrined in the Constitution of the United States. Governments in this spirit that truly represent their people are the only efficient alternative to the proliferation of Marxist theses, for whom tyrannies turn out to be excellent breeding grounds. These governments need to be treated as equals, respected in their decisions, listened to. But Washington has almost always preferred a servile gorilla to a sovereign and democratic ally.

The Somoza regime would've fallen long ago, as desired by the overwhelming majority of Nicaraguans, without the damages of this civil war, if the United States had, simply, withheld the financial, diplomatic, and military support that served to sustain it. For many years now, the country's finest men tried again and again to replace the tyranny with a civilized regime and they never had the support Washington gave to those—Tacho, Luis, or Anastasio—who imprisoned them, exiled them, or—in the case of the journalist Pedro Joaquín Chamorro—murdered them. Now it's true, what could have been done with help from the United States has been done by the Nicaraguan people on their own (and, clearly, with the help of other countries), and it is not strange that many of the combatants who defeated tyranny believe that they have also defeated those who supported it and whom it served. It is not difficult to piece together the political consequences of this.

What will happen to Nicaragua with the fall of the dictatorship? The Frente Sandinista de Liberación Nacional is an alliance of many, with tendencies spanning from liberal and social democratic to different variations of Marxism, and it is obvious that, once the dictatorship has been defeated, a goal that made possible their union, these different options could battle with one another and perhaps enter into open conflict. In the end, once again, these will be reduced to the inevitable alternative of all people who free themselves of their gorillas: authoritarian socialism or representative democracy. What we can say at least is that, with its policies, the United States has made the task extremely difficult for Nicaraguans to defend the second option. And it has facilitated the work of those who will maintain that the only true defense against imperialism and the quickest way to reconstruct a country flattened by tyranny is the Soviet, Chinese, or Cuban model.

In any event, the important thing is that the Nicaraguan people—with all freedoms—be the ones to decide what to do with their country, the way to heal its wounds, and how to undertake the enormous task of defeating the still lingering beasts: hunger, ignorance, unemployment, inequality. Its decision, whatever it may be, must be respected by others, starting with Washington.

Even more disastrous than the mistake of having supported the Somozas for forty-three years would be, in the interest of freedom and democracy on the continent, for the United States to once again give in to the temptation of intervening militarily in Nicaragua to impose a custom solution of its own, in other words, a new Somoza . . .

Madrid, July 1979

Toward a Totalitarian Peru

The decision by Alan García's government to nationalize banks, insurance, and financial companies is the most important step taken in Peru to keep this country underdeveloped and in poverty, and to ensure that the incipient democracy it has been enjoying since 1980, rather than perfecting, devolves, becoming a lie.

According to the regime's reasons for this divestment, which will turn the state into the owner of credits and insurance, and allow the state to use the shares of the nationalized entities to extend its tentacles through innumerable private industries and businesses, it is being carried out to transfer those companies from "a group of bankers to the Nation," and begs the response: "That is demagoguery and lies." This is the truth. Those companies are seized—against the letter and spirit of the Constitution, which guarantees property and economic pluralism and prohibits monopolies—from those who created and developed them, to be entrusted to bureaucrats who, at some point, as happens with all bureaucracies of all underdeveloped countries without a single exception, will manage them for their own gains and those of the political power under whose shadow they operate.

In all underdeveloped countries, like in all totalitarian countries, the distinction between the state and the government is a legal mirage. It is a reality only in advanced democracies. In those countries, the laws and constitutions, as well as official rhetoric, aim to separate them. In practice, they are as interchangeable as two drops of water. Those who hold positions of government take over the state and use its resources at will. What better proof than that of the famous Sinacoso (Sistema Nacional de Comunicación Social/National Social Communication System), built by the military dictatorship and, since then, a docile ventriloquist for the governments that have followed? Does that chain of radio stations, newspapers, and television stations by chance in any way speak directly to the state, in other words, to *all* Peruvians? No. That media publicizes, flatters, and manipulates information exclusively in favor of those who govern, colossally ignorant of what the rest of Peru thinks and believes.

The inefficiency and immorality accompanying them, as a twin, to the state takeovers and nationalizations mainly come from the servile dependence in which the company transferred to the public sector finds itself in political power. We Peruvians know it all too well since the time of Velasco's dictatorship, which, betraying the reforms we all longed for, through expropriations and confiscations, managed to break industries—such as fishing, cement, or sugar mills—that had reached a level of notable efficiency, and made us importers of even the potatoes that our industrious ancestors created to the world's joy. Extending the public sector from fewer than 10 to almost 170 companies, the dictatorship—alleging, as justification, "social justice"—increased poverty and inequality and gave an irresistible boost to the practice of bribery and illicit business. Both have proliferated since then like a cancer, becoming the greatest obstacle to the creation of wealth in our country.

This is the model that President Garcia has made his brand on our economy, with the nationalization of banks, insurance, and financial companies, a level of state control that places us immediately after Cuba and almost on a par with Nicaragua. It is clear that I have not forgotten that, in contrast to General Velasco, Alan García is a legitimately elected leader at the polls. But I have not forgotten, either, that Peruvians elected him, overwhelmingly, as we are aware, so that he would consolidate our political democracy with social reforms; not so that he would make a quasi-socialist "revolution" that would do away with it.

For there is no democracy that could survive with such an exorbitant accumulation of economic power in the hands of political power. Just ask the Mexicans, where a nationalization law will grant the American Popular Revolutionary Alliance (APRA) government vast control over the public sector if approved.

Its first victim will be freedom of expression. The government will not need to proceed as Velasco did, attacking, gun in hand, newspapers and radio and television stations, although we cannot rule it out: we have already confirmed that their promises are gone with the wind, like feathers, echoes . . . Converted into the country's premier announcer, it will be enough for it to blackmail them with advertisements. Or, to bring them to their knees, to close off the lines of credit without which no company can operate. There is no doubt that faced with the prospect of dying of consumption, many in the media will choose silence or submission; the dignified will perish. And when criticism disappears from public life, the full-throttle congenital vocation of growing and becoming eternal has the means to become reality. Once again, the ignored silhouette of the "philanthropic ogre" (as Octavio Paz has called the PRI) can be made out on the Peruvian horizon.

The progress of a country consists in the extension of property and freedom to the greatest number of citizens and in the strengthening of the rules of the game—legality and customs—that value effort and talent; stimulate responsibility, initiative, and honesty; and penalize parasitism, rentierism, apathy, and immorality. All of this is incompatible with a multiheaded state in which the main actor in economic activity is the government official instead of the businessman and the worker; and where, in the majority of its fields, competition has been replaced by a monopoly. A state of this kind is demoralizing, crushes any business initiative, and makes the traffic of influence and professional favors more desirable and profitable. This is the path that has led so many third-world countries to drown in stagnation and to turn into ferocious satrapies.

Peru is still far from this, fortunately. But measures such as the one I criticize could catapult us in this direction. We must say so loudly so that the poor—who will be its scapegoats—hear us and try to prevent it through all of the legal means within our reach. Without being frightened by the tirades launched currently against government critics by mercenaries in the press or by "the masses" that the APRA party, speaking through its secretary-general, threatens to bring to the streets to intimidate those of us who protest. Both things disquietingly foreshadow what will happen in our country if the government concentrates absolute economic power in its hands, which is always the first step toward political absolutism.

As citizens, institutions, and democratic parties, we should try to avoid letting our country—which already suffers so many misfortunes—become a pseudo-democracy led by incompetent bureaucrats where only corruption will prosper.

Lima, August 1987

The Perfect Dictatorship

Because I called the PRI's political system "a perfect dictatorship" in the Meeting of Intellectuals that *Vuelta* magazine organized in Mexico in September 1990, I was chastised quite a few times, including by someone such as Octavio Paz, whom I admire and have much affection for, but, really, I keep thinking that the qualifier is defensible. Created in 1929, by General Plutarco Elias Calle, the Partido Revolucionario Institucional established a society where, from the revolutionary convulsions of 1910, political affairs were settled by bullets, and it took possession of a state that, from then on, has modeled and managed to its benefit, confusing the two in a way as subtle as the three famous beings in the Holy Trinity.

For all practical purposes, Mexico is now the PRI, and what the PRI is not, including its most vocal critics and challengers, also serves, in a mysterious, brilliant, and horrifying way, to perpetuate control of the PRI over political life and Mexican society. For a long time, the PRI fabricated and subsidized its opposition parties, such that those extraordinary happenings in the country's life—elections—would have some semblance of democracy. Now it doesn't even need the effort of that wastefulness, since, as Eve came from Adam's rib, it has generated a rival excrescence, the PRD, under Cuauhtémoc Cárdenas, a party that, with prodigious blindness, has incorporated all of the ideological scourges and imperfections—populism, statism, socialism, economic nationalism—of which the chameleonic PRI needed to rid itself with the goal of showing itself renewed—democratic, internationalist, pro-market, and liberal—and permeable to the prevailing winds. If this is the alternative presented to the Mexican people—the old PRI camouflaged under the name of the PRD or that of the modernized face embodied by Salinas de Gortari, it is no wonder that the party in power didn't need to fix the recent elections in order to win them.

I won't deny that this system has brought some benefits to Mexico, such a stability that other Latin American countries have not had and freedom from the anarchy and brutality of military caudillism. And it is also a fact that, thanks to the Revolution and the education policy that has followed, Mexico has integrated its pre-Hispanic past into the present and made advances in social and cultural *mestizaje* more than any other country on the continent (including Paraguay). But the disadvantages are enormous. In six and a half decades of absolute hegemony, the PRI has not been able to take Mexico out of economic underdevelopment—despite the gigantic resources with which its soil is blessed—nor of reducing to even presentable levels social inequalities, which are still more ferocious there than in many Latin American countries, such as Argentina, Chile, Uruguay, Venezuela, or Costa Rica. In contrast, the corruption resulting from this political monopoly has been internalized by institutions and normal life in a way that has no comparison, which has created one of the most implacable obstacles to the country's genuine democratization.

The regime's policy toward intellectuals is often cited in favor of the PRI's system, since it has always known how to recruit them and put them in its service without demanding in exchange the politesse or abject servility that a Fidel Castro or

Kim Il-sung ask of theirs. On the contrary, within the exquisite Machiavellism of the system, the intellectual is tasked with a role that is, besides simultaneously perpetuating the swindle that Mexico is a pluralist democracy and that freedom reigns there, meant to free him from scruples and allow him a good conscience: that of criticizing the PRI. Has anyone ever met a Mexican intellectual who *defends* the Partido Revolucionario Institucional? I never have. Everyone criticizes it and, especially, those whose livelihood comes from it, such as diplomats, functionaries, editors, journalists, academics, or those benefiting from phantom positions created by the regime to subsidize them. Only in cases of extreme disobedience, like that of José Revueltas, are they sent to jail. Generally, they are bribed, incorporating them into the magnanimous and flexible despotism such that, without their having to debase themselves too much and at times without even realizing it, they contribute to the essential objective of perpetuating the system.

Considerable benefits have also come out of this "concern for culture" by the PRI: publishing houses, magazines, academic institutions, and an intellectual and artistic activity that is significantly more intense than in other Latin American countries under governments that are almost always semiliterate. But the compensation has been a notorious reduction in the sovereignty and authenticity of the intellectual class, which, for reasons of guilty conscience and because of the invisible pressure of the ruling system, still continues today, after the collapse of totalitarianism in three-quarters of the world, living in fiefdom to those "revolutionary" stereotypes—socialism, collectivism, nationalism, the Benefactor State, anti-imperialism, et cetera—that, for several decades, have been its best alibi, the smokescreen that served to conceal their condition as an instrumental piece of one of the most astute and efficient antidemocratic creations in all of history.

I write these lines under the effects of a book that I recommend to all who, like me, are amazed (while also being terrified) by the case of Mexico: *Textos heréticos*, by Enrique Krauze. It is a collection of articles and essays that appeared in the magazine *Vuelta*, which Octavio Paz runs and where Krauze is lieutenant, in which a liberal tradition is reclaimed, contemporary to that of the Revolution, whose starting point is the government of Francisco Ignacio Madero, whose hidden trail Krauze follows through all the years of the PRI's hegemony, and in which he sees the only acceptable alternative to the present regime. That tradition, although it was displaced from political power after the years of the revolutionary cataclysm, has had periodic resurgences in the intellectual world, in figures such as those of Daniel Cossío Villegas or Paz himself, who, even in the moments of the worst ideological populist obscurantism, did not hesitate to go against the grain and defend democratic values and the reviled "formal" freedoms. This has been the editorial position of *Vuelta*, a true oasis in genre publications in Latin America, where it is no coincidence that in recent years, from the pens of Paz, Gabriel Zaid, Krauze, and others, the most original analyses have appeared about historic events of the last decade.

The book includes Krauze's very severe criticism of Carlos Fuentes—"The Mexican Comedy of Carlos Fuentes"—which, as is known, has unleashed a controversy that keeps popping up all over the place, the most recent of which was the scandal arising a few months ago, on the basis of an intellectuals' meeting supported by the regime and by intellectuals of the opposition of his majesty the PRI, from which, as a reprisal, Paz, Zaid, Krauze, and the rest of the heretics were excluded. Although many of the observations that Krauze makes of Fuentes's political positions seem well-founded—like that careful symmetry of abjurations of democracy and socialism, the United States and the defunct USSR, and the recognition of the Sandinista regime from a democratic position—there is an aspect of that criticism with which I do not agree: the reproach that Fuentes is not very Mexican and that this is reflected in his novels.

Literature does not describe countries: it invents them. Perhaps the provincial Rulfo, who rarely left his country, had a more intense experience of Mexico than the cosmopolitan Carlos Fuentes, who moves through the world as if it were his own house. But that does not make Rulfo's oeuvre less artificial and created than that of Fuentes, even if only because authentic peasants from Jalisco have not read Faulkner while those in *Pedro Páramo* and *The Plain in Flames* have. If it were not so, they would not speak as they speak nor would they appear in fictitious constructions that owe their consistency more to formal skill and a resourcefulness that led to the influence of authors of many languages and countries than to Mexican idiosyncrasy. That said, Krauze's essay is far from being a diatribe. I recall having envied Carlos Fuentes when I read him: if only, in the great garbage dump of challenges that my books have warranted, there were one that revealed as scrupulous and attentive a reading, as much effort to speak with informed consent and not out of envy and hate, effervescent stimulants of the critical vocation in our lands.

The rest of the texts in the book cover a vast array of themes, written to show the deep alienation that the Mexican political system has caused in the country's cultural establishment. Krauze was not content merely with reviewing and noting what the media said during the Gulf War, for example, in which some came to the revolutionary idolatry of Saddam Hussein; he also has expurgated what they said half a century ago about Hitler and Stalin and the way that, in all these years, those who represent thinking and culture guided public opinion about what was happening inside and outside Mexico's borders. The conclusions end up being astonishing because, once again, we see, with concrete examples, how high culture can be at odds with lucidity and common sense, and intelligence can furiously focus on defending prejudice, crime, and the most ignoble political frauds. Steiner said it: humanities do not humanize.

A student and admirer of the great Isaiah Berlin, Krauze

knows that even tolerance and pluralism are dangerous, if no one refutes them, if they don't face opposition and permanent challenges. As such, although he proclaims himself a liberal, a fan of the market, of civil society, of private businesses, of the individual before the state—a matter to which he devotes the most creative study in the compilation *Plutarch Among Us*—he longs for the existence of a new Mexican left, like the one that in Spain contributed to modernizing the country and strengthening democracy. A left that breaks the isolation to which it is confined and goes from ventriloquist soliloquys to controversy and dialogue, which instead of ukases and excommunications relies on reasons and ideas to fight the adversary and renounces authoritarian temptations forever.

I greatly fear that the democratic left which Krauze longs for will take longer to arrive in his country than in other Latin American countries. Because in Mexico, for that to be reality, there exist, besides the well-known obstacles that his book autopsies with a surgeon's hand, the impediment of the PRI and what Salinas de Gortari's government is doing right now. It has carried out a very advanced privatization and deregulated the economy, while simultaneously lowering tariffs, opening the country to international competition, and negotiating Mexico's incorporation into the free-trade treaty with the United States and Canada. All of them are positive measures that have brought a notable breath of fresh air and economic impulse to Mexico. With the automatic traditional reflex, the opposition on the left rejects that whole process of liberation in the name of old populist idols: sovereignty threatened by multinationals, the homeland sold out to the empire, et cetera. In this way, it establishes a Manichaeism in Mexican political life that favors only the regime, which, before such anachronistic positions, can rightfully boast that it embodies progress.

No, the real alternative to the PRI cannot come from that left which is, in truth, the handiwork and expression of the regime.

But rather from those who, like Krauze, are not afraid to defend economic freedom, although the PRI now seems to put it in practice, because they know that, seen through to its full consequences, it would burst the mercantilist frame that contains all the force of what he calls the Mexican "soft dictatorship." Without sinecures to hand out, with a genuine market economy in which political power is incapable of determining the economic success or failure of people and companies, the PRI system would come down like a house of cards. This is the insurmountable limit of the reforms that Salinas de Gortari has initiated, and if he continues along the path he is on, very soon we will see the tragic dilemma of having to liquidate the PRI or of being liquidated by the pachyderm that his policies push to a dangerous precipice. This could be a miraculous moment for democracy in Mexico. As long as there are then many other Mexicans who are convinced, like Krauze, that freedom is one and indivisible, and that political freedom and economic freedom are like the heads and tails of a coin.

Berlin, May 1992

Death in Haiti

There is no more tragic case in the Western Hemisphere, or perhaps the world, than that of Haiti. It is the poorest and most backward of the countries on the continent and its history is a series of bloody dictatorships, cruel and corrupt tyrants, murders and injustices that seem to be the product of a perverse and apocalyptic imagination. Now that there's an air of progress and optimism running through Latin America regarding the consolidation of democratic regimes and economic reforms that will attract a great influx of investment to the region, Haiti continues to drown in political savagery and overwhelming misery.

Who is to blame for Haiti's dismal fate?

There is no dearth of political commentators and sociologists who rely on cultural reasons to explain the phenomenon: voodoo and other beliefs and syncretic practices with African roots, firmly entrenched in the country's rural population, would constitute an insurmountable obstacle for its political and economic modernization and would make Haitians easy prey to the manipulations of any nationalist demagogue, the ready victims of leaders ever prepared to justify remaining in power as the guarantors of what Papa Doc called "Haitianism" or "noirism."

And nonetheless, when one takes even the most cursory look

at Haiti's modern history, you can discern, like a current of clear water running between the daily massacres and bloodbaths, an inspiring constant: each time they were given the opportunity to express their wants in relatively clean elections, that nation of the poor and illiterate chose well, voting in favor of those who appeared to represent the fairest and most honorable option, in opposition to the goons, the corrupt, and the exploiters. That is what happened—although it now seems like a grotesque parody—in 1957, in the island's first elections with universal suffrage, following nineteen years of North American occupation (1915–1934), when the population overwhelmingly chose someone who appeared to be an honorable and idealist doctor—François Duvalier—and a defender of the rights of the black majority (90 percent of the population) against the mulatto minority, who were then the owners of wealth and political power, as well as shameless accomplices in colonial intervention. No one could have suspected, at that moment in which Haiti was believed to be on the threshold of a new era of progress, that Dr. Duvalier would soon become the raging Papa Doc, in other words, a revived version of his revered role models in despotic outrages: Dessalines and Christophe.

But, above all, following the collapse of the Duvalier dynasty (although not of the military, police, and gangster-like structures that maintained it), we have seen the immense majority of Haitians send unmistakable signals to the whole world of their will to live peacefully within a regime of freedom and legality. This is the deep meaning of the development of the Se Lavalas movement, from the most marginalized and orphaned social stratum of Haitian society, which, starting in 1986, would impose an irresistible democratizing dynamic on the whole country.

This popular movement of peasants, workers, artisans, and the unemployed was an admirable civic gesture of epic proportions that, let's not forget, was created in the most adverse conditions, defying the implacable military repression and criminal groups of the former regime, which had been barely impacted by the removal of Baby Doc. Despite the preventive murders and punishment—fires, bombings, kidnappings, torture, in the poorest neighborhoods and villages—Haitians arrived en masse to sign up for the electoral registers and approved the new Constitution by a crushing majority in the March 3, 1987, referendum. And, in the most beautiful and highly attended elections in Haiti's history, those taking place on November 29, 1990, they elected Jean-Bertrand Aristide as president by a plebiscitary majority: 67 percent of the votes.

It is worth remembering that it was this popular civic movement that, in a way, cured the former little Salesian priest of his whims and made him a democrat. Before that referendum, between miraculous escapes from attacks on his life and quarrels with the Catholic hierarchy, Father Aristide preached for direct action—the Revolution—and demonstrated complete skepticism about peaceful and democratic ways to reform the country. The civic mobilization that made Se Lavalas a formidable political force with wide support throughout the country, which lifted the dreams of an entire nation for peaceful change like a wave, convinced him of the possibilities of democracy—of the law—to carry out the radical transformation with which he dazzled the listeners of his sermons.

Despite everything that has been said—and the truth is that unfair attacks and slander have rained down on him since he was removed from office—President Aristide respected democratic legality, and tried to do away with corruption, political crimes, narco-trafficking mafias, economic privileges, and the exploitation of the peasants, following the mechanisms dictated by the Constitution. It was the reformist nature of these changes, and not the excesses and popular chaos—which also happened—of the first months of his government that unleashed against him the conspiracy of the army and the plutocratic elite, which culminated in the September 1991 coup d'état that brought General Raoul Cédras to power.

What has happened since then in Haiti should fill all Western democratic countries with regret and shame, but especially the United States, which, with a bit of good faith and decision, had the ability to end the operations of a true genocide with which the military dictatorship tries to squash Haitians' resistance. It's difficult to understand the logic that allowed the American government to send the Marines to Grenada and Panama, alleging that the tyrannies there were a danger to the entire hemisphere, and, in contrast, to withdraw those same Marines when they were going to disembark in Haiti to guarantee the Governors Island agreement, sponsored by the United Nations and signed by Aristide and by Cédras, because a handful of the dictatorship's goons threw rocks at the ship on which they arrived. There's a dangerous asymmetry and incoherence to this as a precedent for the continent's future attempted coups d'état.

Not even the reason of complicity with Noriega's drug mafias, which served as the excuse for invading Panama, is valid in this case. Since everybody knows—and all the reports about the situation in Haiti confirm it—that one of the main reasons for Cédras's coup was to maintain the narco-trafficking monopoly that the Haitian army held unlawfully—and which, all things considered, was their main source of revenue—and which takes all of its earnings from intercepting the transit of Colombian cocaine to the United States.

Naturally, an armed invasion cannot be unilateral and always implies very serious risks, which should be carefully evaluated. But if there is a single actual case in the world in which the United Nations can and should consider this extreme recourse for putting an end to the crimes against humanity committed by a criminal tyranny against a defenseless people, it is that of Haiti. What is happening there is difficult to describe, because testimonies go beyond realism and what is believable and even transcend the magical-political horrors dreamed up by Alejo Carpentier about Haiti's past in *The Kingdom of This World*. As such, regarding the embargo decreed against the regime by the international community as a means of pressure, it is mocked daily by the Dominican border, a sieve that, besides, allows smugglers—that is, all of them, the military and politicians—to multiply their revenues; the dictatorship, calmed by Washington's declarations that it will not recur to armed force in any case to reestablish democracy, persists in complete comfort to physically exterminate the most visible members of Se Lavalas, in a policy of mass terror and scare tactics with the goal of eradicating from Haitian consciousness the dream of a return to democracy.

To this end, the regime has created a more modern and efficient organization—better paid and better armed—than Papa Doc's right-hand men (the Tonton Macoutes): the FRHAP (Haitian Front for Advancement and Progress). Under the bloody rule of Lieutenant Colonel Michel François, chief of police, the men of the FRHAP exterminated whole families every night in the neighborhoods and villages known for their Aristide sympathies, and burned down the houses of his supporters or kidnapped them and subjected them to atrocious torture to then release them, mutilated, so that they serve as living examples of what can be expected by those who still dare to dream of a return to a legal regime. Thus many of the ministers who, with the goal of favoring an agreement negotiated for his return to Haiti, had been named by President Aristide in the framework of the Governors Island Accords perished or were terribly mistreated. And, although it may seem like a lie, there are still declarations heard in certain U.S. media according to which the Haitian problem cannot be solved by the intransigence of Jean-Bertrand Aristide, who had not made enough concessions to the genocidal army (even the very petty ones of guaranteeing impunity for their

SABERS AND UTOPIAS

crimes and allowing them to retire to their winter barracks undisturbed).

Just as the approval of NAFTA (the free-trade treaty with Mexico and Canada) has been the great success of Latin American policy by President Clinton's government, its great failure to date is Haiti. Inefficiency, contradictions, confusion have characterized all of its initiatives in the face of this problem, which, if it ends with the consolidation of Cédras's dictatorship, will always cast an ominous shadow over the international policy credentials of the Democratic Party's return to power, a party, let's not forget, that used to wave respect for human rights and the promotion of democracy as one of its priorities in regard to Latin America.

Fortunately, at the heart of these same American Democrats, there is a current of opinion that grows ever more forceful criticizing the government for its actions vis-à-vis Haiti. In this vein, the Congressional Black Caucus just denounced the administration for its ineffectiveness and demanded more forceful action to return President Aristide to power. And a respected human rights leader, also black, Randall Robinson, just initiated a hunger strike in front of the Capitol Building with the same objective. These are just drops in the bucket, without a doubt, but perhaps others will pour down, more and more, until a great torrent of public opinion is unleashed and develops an effective solidarity effort that helps the Haitian people to emerge from the barbarism that Cédras, François, and company want to perpetuate.

Washington, D.C., April 1994

Fidel and His "Melancholy Whores"

Concealment does not figure among Fidel Castro's defects. In the forty-five years he has been in power—the longest dictatorship in the history of Latin America—he has never attempted to mislead anyone about the nature of his regime or about its foundational principles.

Cuba exists in a "Communist" system (his words) that, according to him, is more just, more egalitarian, and more free than the putrefied capitalist democracies that are the target of his extreme contempt, as the "comandante" always manifests in his cacophonous speeches, and which he predicts will come down sooner rather than later beneath the weight of their corruption and internal contradictions. It's possible that Castro is the only person in Cuba who still believes this nonsense, but without a doubt, he believes it, and since vertical totalitarianism reigns on the island in which the Maximum Leader has absolute power and is the only source of truth, the system functions on the basis of such convictions, crushed by the one-dimensional propaganda as if they were unveiled axioms. (It is for this reason that Reporters Without Borders just placed Cuba 166th out of 167 countries studied regarding freedom of the press, in other words, second to last, just in front of North Korea.)

The "comandante" has made it known ad nauseam: since the Cuban Communist regime is superior to Western democracies, it is not going to be so weak as to carry out that which its enemies request with the sole purpose of destroying it; in other words, allowing free elections, freedom of expression, of movement, independent courts and judges, changes in leadership, et cetera. These institutions and practices are the smokescreen for the exploitation and discrimination that proliferates in the "social-idiotic" democracies, a rarefied vulgarity invented by Castro to denigrate the socialists and social democrats who criticize him and are the constant targets of his diatribes.

Why would a government supported by 99.9 percent of the population call for free elections? To sow division and chaos in that limitless, beautiful unity that guarantees the one-party regime? What those who demand those electoral inquiries, freedom of political parties, an independent press, and things of that nature actually want is to open Cuba's doors to the imperialists who want to do away with the great "social achievements" of the Revolution—should we include, among those, having sent homosexuals along with common criminals to concentration camps in the times of the UMAP?—and turn Cuba into a pseudo-liberal, neocolonial, and social-idiotic democracy, where 11 million Cubans will be mercilessly exploited by a handful of Yankee capitalists.

Those who ask for these types of changes are thus, pure and simple, enemies of the Revolution, agents of imperialism, and should be treated like troublemakers, criminals, and traitors. These are not merely the words of a paranoid megalomaniac but rather a conviction supported by forty-five years of rectilinear conduct in which Castro has not taken a single step back in this profession of faith. This has materialized over and over again in massive incarcerations, a systemic, brutal, and disproportionate repression in the face of the slightest display of dissidents, with periodic purges in which real or supposed critics of the system are judged and sentenced, in trials as grotesque as those carried out in the Stalinist USSR, bordering on ferocious when, from time to time, execution by firing squad makes an appearance. Despite this policy of systematic terror and utter disregard for the most basic of human rights, that there are still Cubans, such as the poet Raúl Rivero and his seventy-five colleagues jailed in the last wave of repression, who maintain, in cells where they are rotting alive, their fighting spirits is not only surprising and awe-inspiring: it demonstrates, besides, as Václav Havel highlighted in the tribute he just dedicated to them, that even within societies devastated by the most extensive darkness and the most abject horror, freedom always finds a way to survive.

That this regime still has supporters abroad should not be surprising. The hate that open societies inspire in many leads them to prefer a "social" dictatorship to democracy, and that is why they deplore the fall of the Berlin wall, the dissolution of the Soviet Union, and the transformation of the People's Republic of China into unbridled and "savage" capitalism (the expression can be allowed here). Of course, I believe that those who think this way are mistaken and that many of them would not be able to withstand twenty-four hours in a society like the one they defend, but, if they believe that, it's logical that they show their solidarity with a satrap who embodies their own ideals and political aspirations. You have to concede that they have an undeniable coherence in their approach.

In contrast, there is nothing but incongruence and confusion in the way that intellectuals, politicians, or governments who claim to be democratic serve the interests of a regime that is the number one enemy of the Western Hemisphere's democratic culture and, instead of showing solidarity with those who, in Cuba, go to prison, live like outcasts, are subject to all kinds of privations and outrages or lose their lives for freedom, support their executioners and agree to play the lamentable role of matchmakers, accomplices, or "melancholy whores"—to use a current term—of the Caribbean dictatorship.

It insults the intelligence to aim to make anyone who has summarily followed the almost half century of the Cuban regime believe that the most effective way to obtain "concessions" from Castro is via appeasement, dialogue, and displays of friendship with his tyranny. And it is so because Fidel Castro himself has definitively taken care of dissipating any misunderstanding in this regard: he has accomplices, courtesans, and servants who collaborate with his policies, his plans, his government, and his social-political model, from which none of his numerous "friends" have ever made him stray by a millimeter. It is true that, at times, some of those carpetbaggers of convenience or intellectuals seeking their credentials as progressive who go to have their picture taken with him and to give him a hand with publicity receive a political prisoner like a gift, whom they later exhibit as an alibi for their duplicity. But that disgusting treatment of prisoners, rather than demonstrating the soft side of the regime—which nearly immediately replaces those given away with new ones—is actually a flagrant symbol of its vileness and inhumanity.

Why talk about this now? Rodríguez Zapatero's Spanish government just made public its intention to join together with the European Union, which, following the executions and sentences of the seventy-five dissidents, had chosen to adopt a policy of firmness in the face of the Cuban dictatorship as long as there was no real human rights progress on the island, and move to reverse this, opting instead for rapprochement and friendly dialogue with Castro, in other words, to cut all ties with and support for his opponents. The pretext is that "firmness" has not yielded any results. What have been the results of cowardice and complicity with the Cuban regime by all of these Latin American "democracies" who vote in favor of Fidel Castro at the United Nations and increase friendly gestures toward him, reasoning that it is necessary to show solidarity with "their continental brother"?

At least the policy adopted by the European Union has sent a clear message to the millions of Cubans who cannot protest, who cannot vote, who cannot escape, that they are not alone, that they have not been abandoned, and that Western democracies are morally and civically on their side in this battle which they, like the Czechs, the Poles, the Romanians, the Russians, and so many others in the past, will win sooner or later.

Rapprochement, dialogue, private diplomacy are lying euphemisms for what is, in clear terms, a shameful abdication by a government that, in obvious contradiction to its origins and its democratic nature, decides to contribute to the survival of a dictatorship as ignominious and ignoble as that of Franco, and is a terrible blow to the countless Cubans who, like millions of Spaniards under Franco, dream of living in a country without censorship, or torture, or executions, and without the suffocating monotony of one party, lies, surveillance, and the omnipresent caudillo.

What inspires the most criticism in this case is that Spanish leaders, unless they have fallen victim to a sudden plague of childish naïveté, know perfectly well that the change they propose to their European allies with respect to Cuba, should it move forward, would not obtain the slightest opening from the regime, but, quite the opposite, would inject its failing lungs with oxygen (Fidel Castro already publicly said that the decision of the Spanish government was "the correct one"). So why do they do it? For internal consumption. To prove that in this sphere as well there is a radical break with the previous government. Or to give a little bit of encouragement to those remaining third worldists and Stalinists who, while they are happily a minority, still exist within Spanish socialism, real stragglers in this regard compared with their British, French, German, and Nordic fellow travelers, where socialists don't have the slightest inferiority complex vis-à-vis the Cuban tropical Gulag.

My hope is that these magnificent European "social idiots"

prevent this lamentable initiative from materializing. It should be denounced and fought for what it is: a demagogic and irresponsible act that will serve only to strengthen the longest Latin American dictatorship. We cannot allow democratic, modern, and European Spain, in so many ways an example for Latin America, to turn into Fidel's "melancholy whore."

Madrid, October 27, 2004

Funeral Rites for a Tyrant

Chance has willed it that I find myself in Santiago, Chile, for General Augusto Pinochet's funeral rites. Following solid criteria, Michelle Bachelet's government denied him a state funeral and the former dictator was honored only by the armed forces, as the former commander-in-chief of the army. But not even the Chilean armed forces have wanted to fully identify with the former dictator, as proven by the fact that they immediately dismissed Pinochet's grandson, Augusto Pinochet Molina, for having delivered a speech, unauthorized, at his grandfather's funeral.

Although several thousand people, nostalgic for the seventeen years that the dictatorship lasted, went to show their respects before the remains displayed at the Military School, all surveys prove that a great majority of Chileans today condemn this regime now, because of the human rights violations, corruption, and illicit enrichment that characterized it. Just like in the rest of the world, here also there are many lamenting that Pinochet died without having been sentenced for any of the crimes he committed. More than three hundred open cases for murder, torture, abuses of power, and illicit trafficking, which his attorneys managed to delay and delay, must now be dismissed, although this

will not exonerate his subordinates, accomplices, and those involved in the exactions.

But the bulk of Chilean public opinion, and international
opinion, had already sanctioned him, and Pinochet will go down
in history, not for being "the general who saved Chile from communism" (thus said the signs held by some of his fans), but as the
caudillo of a tyranny that murdered at least 3,500 opponents,
tortured and jailed many thousands, forced countless more into
exile, and throughout seventeen years governed with unmitigated brutality a country that had a tradition of legality and
democratic coexistence that was rare in Latin America. The myth
according to which he was an "honorable" dictator was eclipsed
long ago, when it was discovered that he had secret accounts
abroad—at Riggs Bank in Washington—totaling almost $28
million and that, as such, he perfectly fit into the prototypical
mold of Latin American dictators, as a murderer and thief.

The violent incidents that took place on the day of his death
on the streets of Santiago between his supporters and his adversaries are flagrant proof of the wounds and divisions that the
military dictatorship has left in Chilean society and how slow its
healing and reconciliation will be. Even now, when Chile is a very
different country from the one in which Pinochet took power
through a military coup, a modern and prosperous democracy, in
full expansion, the spite, bitterness, and underground hate that
grew during his government—some of these, before, during the
Unidad Popular—continue to fragment the country and threaten
to come to the surface with any pretext.

The firm and unequivocal sentence of the tyrant who Pinochet was, and of his cruel system, should not signify, however,
justification or oblivion of the most serious mistakes committed
by the Unidad Popular under Salvador Allende, without which
there would have never come to be a climate of misrule, violence,
and demagoguery that led many Chileans to support Pinochet's
putsch. Allende presided over a legitimate government, born from

impeccable polls, but supported by only a little more than a third of the Chilean electorate. His mandate was not authorized to carry out the radical socialist revolution he attempted, following the Cuban model, and this produced hyperinflation that generated insecurity and fury among the middle classes, and a political polarization that, in contrast to other Latin American countries, Chile had not known until then. This explains why the military coup was not rejected by the bulk of a society that until then seemed to have solid democratic convictions and a good part of which, nonetheless, crossed their arms and supported the uprising soldiers.

It is also true that Pinochet's shameful dictatorship unexpectedly opened a path for Chile's economic recovery and modernization. It bears repeating, once and again, that this happened not *because of*, but *despite*, the dictatorial regime, owing to a series of circumstances specific to Chile that allowed something inconceivable under any military satrapy: that the regime would hand economic management over to a group of civilian economists—the Chicago Boys—and let them make radical reforms—opening borders, privatization of public companies, integration into global markets, dissemination of property, fomenting investments, reforms in work and social security—that put Chile on a path to the prosperity it now enjoys.

Nonetheless, Chile's true modernization began later, with the fall of the dictatorship, when the first democratic government of the Concertación (Coalition of Parties for Democracy), in 1990, while taking apart Pinochet's entire censorship and repression apparatus, maintained the economic model at its core while perfecting its details. When the Chilean electorate ratified that sensible policy with its votes and, in fact, a national consensus was established regarding guidelines—political democracy and market economy—Chile began to at last leave that underdevelopment behind in which the majority of Latin American countries were still wading.

There are fools who still believe that a Pinochet is necessary for a backward country to begin to progress. This was, for example, the reasoning of Peruvian Pinochetists, who are Fujimorists. It is true that Fujimori made some economic reforms. But all of them—without a single exception—were thwarted by the dizzying theft and raging abuses that went along with them. The same, in different versions, can be said of all the regimes that have sought inspiration in the "Pinochetist" model.

There is no Pinochetist model. A country does not need to experience a dictatorship to become modern and to reach wellbeing. The reforms of a dictatorship always carry a price in atrocities and have ongoing ethical and civic repercussions that are infinitely more expensive than the status quo. Because there is no real progress without freedom and legality, and without clear support for the reforms of a public opinion convinced that the sacrifices they demand are necessary if they want to come out of stagnation and take off. The lack of being convinced of this and the passive resistance by the population to the shy, or awkward, attempts at modernization explain the failure of so-called neoliberal governments all over Latin America, and phenomena like the thunderous Comandante Chávez in Venezuela.

If Pinochet's nonagenarian corpse is already an archaeological figure, what will, sooner or later, Fidel Castro's be? The horrific breed of which both are emblematic figures, will it end with them? Nothing would make me happier, but I am not so sure. It is true that today, in Latin America, with the exception of Cuba, all of the governments have a legitimate origin, even Chávez's. And also that the grand majority of the governments on the left in power respect the democratic game and cling to constitutional uses. This is a positive development, without a doubt.

The problem is that political democracy without economic development does not last. Poverty, unemployment, and marginalization lessen the popular support for a democracy without social successes and provoke so much frustration and bitterness that they can make it collapse. The populism that several of these governments flaunt is an insurmountable obstacle to true progress, even in countries that have been blessed by providence with black gold, like Venezuela.

Let's hope that the tragic story of Allende and Pinochet does not repeat itself, in Chile or anywhere.

Santiago, December 2006

Warning to Dictators

The former dictator Alberto Fujimori's sentencing to twenty-five years in prison for human rights crimes handed down by Peru's Supreme Court goes well beyond Peruvian borders and now hangs over all of Latin America as a warning to those who, from one end of the continent to the other, seek to attain power by attacking it and govern under the auspices of force. Leaders who trample all over the constitution and laws, and use torture and murder, now know that their crimes will not go unpunished, as had nearly always happened before, but rather that sooner or later, they can be judged and condemned by their own people. This sets an unparalleled historical precedent to those of us who dream of a Latin America forever emancipated from the scourge of authoritarianism.

The former dictator has been sentenced for two kidnappings and two particularly cruel murders of the many that were perpetrated during his regime, but not for the greater crime he committed: having destroyed, on April 5, 1992, through an act of military force, the democracy by which he had been legitimately elected president. The two kidnappings—of the journalist Gustavo Gorriti and the businessman Samuel Dyer—coincided with the coup. The first of the murders had been carried out a few months before, in November 1991, in a central Lima neighborhood—Barrios Altos—where a death squad known as the Grupo Colina, made up of soldiers and assembled with Fujimori's consent, murdered fifteen people, an eight-year-old boy among them, who were at a neighborhood party. The pretext—which was false—was that they were supporters of Sendero Luminoso and that they were trying to collect funds for the terrorist movement. One of the factors leading to the putsch was, as such, guaranteeing impunity for the crimes that the new government had already been committing, not only crimes against humanity but also economic crimes, since the sacking of public tills had already begun, something that, in the years to follow, would reach its climax under the lead of the president's right-hand man and expert in larceny, Vladimiro Montesinos.

The other murder took place in July 1992. By night, gunmen from the Grupo Colina invaded the Universidad de La Cantuta, which was besieged and surrounded by military forces, and kidnapped nine students and a professor, whom they murdered in a vacant lot with shots to the head. There they buried them, and sometime later, when independent journalists, despite the regime's concealment maneuvers, discovered evidence of the crime, they disinterred them, burned them, and reburied the bones in another place. The international scandal unleashed when this macabre story was made public and the bloody inner workings of the system were made known was one of the most damaging episodes for the dictatorship in the eyes of the Peruvian people, a percentage of which, until then, embraced the erroneous belief that an authoritarian government could be more efficient than a democracy in combating Sendero Luminoso and Movimiento Revolucionario Túpac Amaru terrorists. In reality it wasn't the dictatorship's death squads who defeated Abimael Guzmán and the Senderistas, but rather an event that signaled a qualitative change in the antisubversive struggle: the capture of its leader and of almost the entire Central Committee of Sendero Luminoso, thanks to the systematic search by a small group of police who were struggling against Vladimiro Montesinos and the regime's intelligence services.

Fujimori's trial lasted almost seventeen months, was televised, was attended by journalists and international observers, and the accused enjoyed all the guarantees to a defense. The three-member court, presided over by a prestigious criminal attorney, magistrate, and university professor, Doctor César San Martín, whose conduct throughout the proceedings was of a calmness and uprightness recognized by all sides, issued a sentence that should be published and read in schools across Latin America—abridged, because it is almost 700 pages long—so that new generations learn, through concrete events and identified people, about the tragedy of human suffering, public insecurity, criminality, distortion of values, lies, and contempt for the most basic civil rights in modern society in a country, and within the corruption and degradation of institutions of a dictatorship like the one Peru experienced between 1992 and the year 2000, when Fujimori, failing in his attempts to be reelected in rigged elections, fled to Japan and quit the presidency via fax.

As long as borders exist, countries urgently need armed forces, and, for the same reasons that society entrusts them with the responsibility to oversee its security and the weapons that allow them to fulfill their mission, it is indispensable that the institution work within the strictest legality and be a bastion of civil society, not its enemy. Fujimori did incalculable damage to the army by forcing upon it as its true mentor Vladimiro Montesinos, a captain whom the Peruvian Army had expelled and sentenced as a traitor to his homeland and his uniform, and who, since then, via manipulations and blackmail, had ignominiously abused the power conferred on him. Montesinos passed over capable, upright officers, sometimes forcing them to ask for their leave, while he promoted and placed his accomplices and servile collaborators in key positions to protect his excesses—a vast catalog of horrors ranging from arms trafficking to narco-trafficking operations—for his own benefit.

One of the most enlightening aspects of the sentence is the uncontestable proof that, contrary to Fujimori supporters' aim to exonerate the former dictator under the reasoning that it was Montesinos who committed crimes while Fujimori was an ingénue who had no idea what was happening right under his nose, there was an absolute symbiosis between the dictator and his adviser, the kind that exists between a person and his shadow or between a puppet and the ventriloquist who makes him speak. Both shared a job in which, on the one hand, the men in power got rich up to their ears, eliminated adversaries, bought and intimidated judges, and swept public offices, and on the other hand, through bribery or blackmail, controlled the media to manipulate public opinion with ad hoc television campaigns and to discredit their critics by relying on the tabloid journalists they financed or the hosts of reality shows.

Only in such an environment, completely devoid of legality and political decency, where ukase and arrogance reign, is it understood that the Grupo Colina would prosper and that in a couple of years they would assassinate, in nine perfectly planned and executed operations, about fifty people. Those who joined their ranks knew that what they were doing had been ordered and sanctioned by the highest authorities and, as such, they received the logistical assistance necessary from military institutions and the due political and judicial protection—including an amnesty law—when their dark deeds were discovered and decried. What they didn't know was that the dictatorship would fall—they always fall—democracy would rise from its ashes, and, for the first time in Peru's history, a former dictator and his main accomplices would be brought before a court.

We Peruvians who live abroad tend to see our country appear in the newspapers, radios, and television stations of the places where we are because of a coup d'état, a terrorist attack, an earthquake, or quintuplets—in other words, always some catastrophe or anomaly, political or social. It is so strange and so beautiful, what has happened to us in recent days, to notice that the Peru spoken about in the press and by the people on the street with respect and admiration is a civilized nation facing its past with dignity and courage and where a civil court judges and condemns the crimes of a dictator. Yes, an example for Latin America. And for the entire world.

Madrid, April 15, 2009

The Leader's Honor

The president of Ecuador, Rafael Correa, just won an important legal battle against freedom of the press in his country and has taken one more step in turning his government into an authoritarian regime. The National Court of Justice, the highest court in the judiciary, has sentenced the daily *El Universo*, a beacon of the Ecuadorian press with more than ninety years in existence, for slander against the president with a very severe penalty: $40 million and three years in jail for those in charge of it—the brothers Carlos, César, and Nicolás Pérez.

The case against *El Universo* began a little under a year ago, on the basis of an article by Emilio Palacio, who, commenting on the president's actions in a confusing police raid in September 2010 in which he was implicated, stated, "The dictator should recall, finally, and this is very important, that despite a pardon, in the future, a new president, perhaps an enemy of his, could take him before a criminal court under charges of having ordered a shooting without prior notice against a hospital full of civilians and innocent people." Rafael Correa considered this phrase damaging to his honor.

Celebrating the court's verdict, while his followers burned copies of the incriminated daily on the streets, the Ecuadorian head of state said that three objectives had been achieved: "that *El Universo* lied, that you can judge not the clowns, but the owners of the circus, and that citizens can react to abuses of the press."

He did not say whether he felt that he had been indemnified for his abused honor, and for a very simple reason: because it is only now, as a result of this legal decision that the international press, journalists' and human rights organizations, and democratic parties and governments from around the world consider a cynical and outlandish blow to freedom of expression with tragic consequences for Ecuador, that his honor—and his good name and the reputation of his government—have been discredited. Especially when you take into account that this is not the first nor will it be the last time. A few days ago, two other Ecuadorian journalists, Juan Carlos Calderón and Christian Zurita, were sentenced to pay $2 million for the supposed "moral damages" they caused the president in a book describing his family's business deals.

It goes without saying that the sentence from the National Court of Justice of Ecuador places a sword of Damocles over all communications media and the government's adversaries, warning them that any criticism of power can lead to reprisals as ferocious as this one, which, in practice, is equivalent to closing this body of the press (since the fine exceeds the newspaper's assets), and long prison sentences for the disobedient journalists.

The intimidation and threats that seek to place self-censorship in the information world, forcing journalists and correspondents to become censors of themselves and to look over their shoulders while they write, is a method that all modern dictators exercise— the most conspicuous example in Latin America, after the obvious case of Cuba, is that of Commander Hugo Chávez in Venezuela, followed by his excellent Argentine student, Cristina Kirchner—and is more hypocritical but also more effective than anachronistic prior censorship or the mere police closure of media that is indomitable and resistant to political obsequiousness.

The disappearance of a free press and its replacement by media that has been neutered and is incapable of exercising criticism is the dream, also, of demagogic pseudo-democracies devastated by populism, of which the prime example is the government of Rafael Correa.

Its regression into demagogic populism and the horrifying and coarse rhetoric it now employs—to watch him go off on rampages, eyes looking at the heavens, with his swollen neck veins, drunk on his own self-admiration, is a priceless spectacle—is unfortunately not an infrequent diversion in Latin American politicians. And, in his particular case, is rather sad. Because the truth is that, when he began the rise to prominence in April 2005, right in the middle of a constitutional crisis, this Catholic economist, with degrees from the Universities of Louvain and Illinois and a distinguished academic career, encouraged many hopes. He seemed motivated by generous and idealistic feelings, and it was believed that his governmental administration would serve to reinforce democratic institutions, social justice, and Ecuador's modernization.

It has been exactly the opposite. Dizzied by power and an obsession to retain control, a foot soldier of the socialist and Bolívarian delirium of Commander Chávez along with the Bolivian Evo Morales and the Nicaraguan Daniel Ortega, the government of Rafael Correa, with its short-term policies, fiscal irresponsibility, multiple instances of corruption, hostility toward private businesses, foreign investments, and his outdated leftism, have impoverished and left Ecuadorian society off-kilter, irritating and infuriating it. As such, his popularity has systematically declined in recent times. The indigenous movements, which at first supported him, are now among his most tenacious critics.

This is the context that explains the desperate blows to freedom of expression by President Correa in recent months and the brutality of the sentence against *El Universo*. With it, the head of state and his government got rid of one of the few democratic credentials they could still brandish and assumed, unconcealed, the Chavist authoritarian system that they always took as a model.

That said, no one can deny that journalism, in Ecuador as well as in the rest of Latin America, is far from always being a paragon of integrity, harmony, and objectivity. Of course it sometimes succumbs to tabloid journalism, in other words, exaggeration, slander, and libel, and an upright and independent judicial system should protect citizens against those excesses. But decapitation is not the most appropriate remedy for headaches. The penalty against *El Universo* by Ecuador's National Court is scandalous, among other things, because of how disproportionate it is compared with the supposed offense, and the outlandish nature of it is the best demonstration that it is not about undoing a wrong of which a person has been a victim, but rather that it is a political act, aimed at finishing once and for all with those pillars of democracy that are freedom of expression and the right to criticize.

In any event, this is a pyrrhic victory for Rafael Correa. His popularity will continue to decline, and even more so if he achieves his goal of gagging the press entirely in his country, which, despite everything, does not appear to be that easy. What happened has served to demonstrate, on the one hand, how unreliable Ecuadorian courts are in matters of justice because of how indebted they are to those who hold political power, and, on the other hand, the courage and uprightness of *El Universo*'s owners and journalists and many Ecuadorian colleagues who have acted in solidarity with them. The limitless efforts by the government to divide and break them have been useless. They have all fought together, businessmen, journalists, administrators, and graphic designers, without making any concessions, proudly defending their independent position with dignity, such that they have gained the world's admiration and have become the very symbol of the resistance of the Ecuadorian people against the authoritarian night, which has in turn come down on them.

It is certain that, in the short or long term, it is they and not the dictator's apprentice or the prevaricating judges who will have the final word. This is one more of the many stumbling blocks that history has thrown at this old newspaper, and there's no doubt that *El Universo* will once again survive the very hard test and will soon return to take its position in the vanguard of the fight for civilization and against barbarism. By then, Rafael Correa will already be a shadowy, half-faded silhouette in the crowd of little caudillos and carpetbaggers that mark the worst tradition of Latin America.

New York, February 2012

Part II

Letter to Fidel Castro

Comandante Fidel Castro
Prime Minister
of Cuba's Revolutionary Government:

We believe it is our duty to communicate our shame and anger to you. The deplorable text of the confession that Heberto Padilla has signed could only have been obtained by means that are a denial of revolutionary legality and justice. The content and form of said confession, with its absurd accusations and delirious statements, as well as the ceremony held at the National Union of Cuban Writers and Artists in which Padilla himself and his comrades Belkis Cuza, Díaz Martínez, César López, and Pablo Armando Fernández submitted to a pitiful masquerade of self-criticism, recalls the most sordid moments of the Stalinist era, its prefabricated verdicts, and its witch hunts. With the same vehemence with which we have defended the Cuban Revolution from the first, which seemed exemplary in its respect for the human being and the struggle for his freedom, we exhort you to spare Cuba dogmatic obscurantism, cultural xenophobia, and the repressive system that Stalinism imposed on socialist countries, and of which events similar to those occurring in Cuba were flagrant

manifestations. The contempt for human dignity implied by forcing a man to ludicrously accuse himself of the worst treason and
vile acts does not alarm us because it concerns a writer, but because
any Cuban comrade—peasant, worker, technician, or intellectual—
could also be the victim of similar violence and humiliation. We
would like the Cuban Revolution to return to what it was when we
considered it a model within socialism.

Sincerely,

Claribel Alegría

Fernando Benítez

Italo Calvino

Fernando Claudín

Roger Dosse

Giulio Einaudi

Francisco Fernández Santos

Jean-Michell Fossey

Carlos Fuentes

Ángel González

André Gorz

Juan Goytisolo

Rodolfo Hinostroza

Monti Johnstone

Michel Leiris

Joyce Mansour

Juan Marsé

Plinio Mendoza

Ray Milibac

Marco Antonio Montes de Oca

Maurice Nadeau

Pier Paolo Pasolini

Jean Pronteau

Alain Resnais

Rossana Rossanda

Claude Roy

Simone de Beauvoir

Jacques-Laurent Bost

José María Castellet

Tamara Deutscher

Marguerite Duras

Hans Magnus Enzensberger

Darwin Flakoll

Carlos Franqui

Jaime Gil de Biedma

Adriano González León

José Agustín Goytisolo

Luis Goytisolo

Mervin Jones

Monique Lange

Lucio Magri

Dacia Maraini

Dionys Mascolo

István Mészáros

Carlos Monsiváis

Alberto Moravia

José Emilio Pacheco

Ricardo Porro

Paul Rebeyroles

José Revueltas

Vicente Rojo

Juan Rulfo

Nathalie Serraute   Jean-Paul Sartre
Jorge Semprún   Jean Shuster
Susan Sontag   Lorenzo Tornabuoni
José Migel Ullán   José Ángel Valente
                    Mario Vargas Llosa

The initiative for this protest came about in Barcelona, when the international press made known the ceremony at the National Union of Cuban Writers and Artists in which Heberto Padilla emerged from the cells of the Cuban police to make his "self-criticism." Juan and Luis Goytisolo, José María Castellet, Hans Magnus Enzensberger, Carlos Barral (who later decided not to sign the letter), and I got together at my house and wrote, each of us separately, a draft. Later, we shared them and picked mine based on a vote. The poet Jaime Gil de Biedma improved the text, adding an adverb.

The Logic of Terror

"No one is innocent," cried Ravachol the anarchist as he threw a bomb at the stupefied diners of Café de la Paix in Paris, blowing them to pieces. A similar thought must have gone through the mind of the anarchist who, from the balcony, threw another bomb at Barcelona's Teatre del Liceu's unsuspecting spectators in the stalls, right in the middle of an opera.

Terrorist attacks are not, as some believe, the product of lack of reflection, blind impulses, a temporary lapse of judgment. On the contrary, they follow rigorous logic, a strict and coherent intellectual formula in which dynamite and gunfights, kidnappings and crimes, all seek to be a necessary consequence.

The terrorist's philosophy is aptly summarized in Ravachol's cry. There is blame—economic, social, and political injustice—that society shares and that should be punished and corrected through violence. Why through violence? Because this is the only instrument capable of pulverizing deceptive appearances created by the dominant class to make the exploited believe that social injustice can be solved through peaceful and legal means and forces them to remove the masks, in other words, to show their repressive and brutal nature.

In the face of the wave of terrorist attacks that have taken place in Peru, just a few months after having reestablished a democratic government—following twelve years of dictatorship—many were in disbelief; it seemed like they were living through a great misunderstanding. Terrorism in Peru, *now*? Just when there's a parliament in which all of the country's political leanings are represented, when there is again an independent press in which all ideologies have their own outlets for expression and when problems can be debated without restriction, the authorities criticized and even removed through the ballot box? Why use dynamite and the bullet just when Peruvians are going back, after such a long interval, to living freely in a democracy?

Because to the logic of terror, "living freely in a democracy" is a game of mirrors, a lie, a Machiavellian conspiracy by exploiters to keep the exploited resigned. Elections, a free press, the right to criticize, representative unions, elected representatives, and city government: traps, simulations, masks destined to hide society's "structural" violence, to blind the victims of the bourgeoisie regarding the numerous crimes committed against them. Are the hunger of the poor and the unemployed and the ignorance of the illiterate and the terrible and prospectless lives of those who receive miserly salaries not many acts of violence perpetrated by the owners of the means of production, a negligible minority, against the majority of the people?

This is the truth that the terrorist wants to highlight with the flame of his attacks. He prefers dictatorship to a liberal or social democratic democracy. Because a dictatorship, with its rigid control of information, its omnipresent police, its implacable persecution of all kinds of dissidence and criticism, its jails, torture, murders, and exiles, seems to honestly represent social reality as the genuine political expression of society's structural violence. In contrast, democracy and its "formal" freedoms are a dangerous fraud, capable of deactivating the rebellion of the masses against their condition, softening their will to free themselves and, as such, taking the revolution one step back. This is the reason terrorist attacks are more frequent in democratic countries than under dictatorships. ETA was less active during Franco's regime than after democracy was restored in Spain, which is when it entered a really homicidal frenzy. This is what has begun to happen in Peru.

Unless he is extremely short-sighted, the "social" terrorist knows quite well that blowing up electricity towers, banks, and embassies—or killing targeted people—in a democratic society is not going to bring about an egalitarian society or unleash a revolutionary process, enlisting the common people in acts of insurrection. No, the objective is to cause repression, forcing the regime to cast aside legal methods and respond to the violence with violence. Paradoxically, that man is convinced he is acting in the name of the victims; what he desires with such passion, through the bombs he plants, is for security organs to turn against those victims in their search for those responsible, and to crush and abuse them. And if jails fill up with innocents and workers, peasants, and students die and the army has to intervene and the famous "formal" freedoms are suspended and laws of exception are decreed, all the better: the people will no longer live deceived, they will learn how to overcome their enemies, they will have practically discovered the need for revolution. The fallacy of terrorist reasoning is in its conclusions, not in its premise. It is false that "structural" violence in a society cannot be corrected through laws and a regime of democratic coexistence: the countries that have reached the most civilized standards of living achieved it thus and not through violence. But it is true that a decided minority can, by resorting to attacks, create such insecurity that democracy can become debased and disappear. The tragic cases of Uruguay and Argentina are close enough to prove it. The spectacular operations of the Tupamaros, Montoneros, and the ERP effectively achieved the liquidation of regimes that, however limited they were, could be called democratic, and their replacement by authoritarian governments. It is false that a military dictatorship quickens the course to revolution, that it is the inevitable detonation for the masses to get mixed up in revolutionary actions. On the contrary, the first victims of a dictatorship are always leftist forces, who disappear or are left so wounded by repression that it takes them much time and effort to again rebuild what they had achieved, as an organization and audience, in a democracy.

But it is vain to attempt to reason thus with those who have made the logic of terror theirs. It is rigorous, coherent, and impervious to dialogue. The greatest danger to a democracy is not terrorist attacks, no matter how painful or onerous they end up being; it is accepting the rules of the game that the terrorist tries to impose. There are two risks to a democratic government in the face of terror: to become intimidated or to go too far. Passivity in the face of attacks is suicide. To allow instability, psychosis, and collective terror to spread is to contribute to creating a climate that favors a military coup d'état. A democratic government has the duty to defend itself, firmly and without any inferiority complexes, with the assurance that by defending itself, it is defending all of society from a greater misfortune than what ails it. At the same time, it cannot forget for a second that all of its power depends on its legitimacy, that in no case should it go beyond what laws and "ways"—which are also the essence of a democracy— allow. If it goes too far and commits abuses, jumps over laws like a bullfighter in pursuit of efficiency, relies on misdeeds, it could be that it defeats the terrorist. But the latter will have won, revealing a monstrosity: that injustice can lead to justice, that the path to freedom is dictatorship.

Lima, December 1980

Good Terrorists

I was reading Góngora's *Solitudes* when all of sunny Miami's news channels suddenly led with the news of the audacious surprise attack in Lima by the MRTA (Movimiento Revolucionario Túpac Amaru), which occupied the Japanese embassy with more than four hundred hostages inside, among them diplomats, ministers of state, businessmen, soldiers, high-ranking functionaries, and the usual bigwigs, gathered there to celebrate the Emperor's Name Day. The first thing that came to mind was a completely frivolous consideration: the extraordinary coincidence of having taken up again, just when this terrorist deed was occurring, a book that I read feverishly during all of my free time throughout the 1989–1990 Peruvian electoral campaign, when the MRTA perpetrated its noisiest operations. Since then, the cold and perfect beauty of Góngora's poetry was indelibly associated in my memory with the blood and turmoil of the terrorist violence marking that campaign. And, apparently, in the future, that mysterious relationship between the most skillful metaphor-maker in the Spanish language and political savagery in my country would continue, without the least hope that death (deaths) would part them.

I write these lines on the fourth day following the capture of the embassy, when no solution is yet hinted at, but with vows being made, of course, that this will be speedy and peaceful, with all hostages, among whom I have many acquaintances and some friends, being returned safely to their homes. But even making all due efforts not to seem imprudent or add fuel to the fire, I cannot help but comment on the way the large media outlets at my disposal have been covering the events.

I hear on the television in the United States, and read in its press, that there are two terrorist organizations in Peru: a radical and fanatical one, Sendero Luminoso, and another one, moderate and more political, the MRTA. The former are crueler and more inflexible because of their Maoist tendencies and hold the China of the Cultural Revolution and the Cambodia of the Khmer Rouge as the model societies to which they aspire, while the latter are more flexible and pragmatic because they follow Castro and, eventually, could become, like their Colombian brethren of the M-19 with whom they collaborated in the past in the so-called America Batallion of that nation's guerrillas with Peruvian volunteers, a legally operating political party. The good treatment of the hostages is held up as proof of the MRTA's moderation, as are the cordial controversies about economic politics that the leader of the operation has maintained with one of the kidnapped businessmen, and the talks that the kidnappers have offered to their victims so as to enlighten them about revolutionary ideals. In truth that nomenclature, "radical" and "moderate" terrorists, has always seemed a fallacy to me, and now more than ever. While it is true that there are marked ideological differences between Sendero Luminoso and the MRTA, as far as what really matters, because it is what defines a political movement—its methods—those differences are little less than invisible. It is true that the Senderistas have killed many more people, not because those from the MRTA are more benign, but rather because they were always fewer in number and had a more limited capacity for destruction. But its compendium from 1983, when the MRTA was founded, to the present day is covered with innocent blood and corpses, with attacks and kidnappings for ransom, with exactions of all kinds and an organic alliance with Huallaga's narco-traffickers, who, in exchange for millionaire-level compensation, have been providing armed protection for years. It's possible that my opinion commits the sin of subjectivity—an MRTA commando tried to annihilate me and my family in the Pucallpa airport during that electoral campaign, and since they didn't manage it, they resigned themselves to shooting a few peasants who discovered them— but what is true is that the use of the adjective *moderate* seems like a grotesque aberration for a movement that, in the name of a future socialist paradise, has killed countless people and made kidnapping for ransom its specialty. All of the great plagues that have taken place in Peru in the last ten years were at their behest and have earned them hefty millions, which have been invested, presumably, in weapons and munitions to facilitate new operations that swell their coffers and leave long-term suffering and horror.

One of my closest friends was one of their victims. For six months, they kept him buried in a tiny cave where he couldn't stand and where—in the sinister time of frequent blackouts—he would spend long periods of time submerged in the shadows, in the crunchy company of cockroaches, which he learned to kill at astronomic speed, guided only by their sound. His family, meanwhile, was subject to daily psychological torture, with phone calls and recordings conceived in a Machiavellian way to destroy their nerves. This person emerged successfully from this terrible test, but others did not survive or were psychologically destroyed. If these are the moderates of terror, what must the extremists be like? A compatriot of mine to whom I made this comment responded, "Sendero Luminoso blew up an apartment building on Tarata Street, in the neighborhood of Miraflores, for no other reason than that there were banks nearby. Compared with a collective crime of that caliber, aren't the MRTA's kidnappings and bombs just a harmless game?" My opinion is no, and that the number of terror attacks and the scale on which they are carried out in no way mitigates the ethical evil of the crime.

For that reason, from the start, I have fought Sendero Luminoso and the MRTA with the same conviction and severity, maintaining that, above their ideological divergences, there is a shared identity between them because of the vileness of their conduct since they both consider the extermination of adversaries and innocent people, as well as theft, attacks and kidnappings, or alliances with narco-trafficking, perfectly fair in achieving their political goals. And for that same reason, I have criticized the stupidity of all Peruvians who applauded Fujimori's regime when, to more "efficiently" combat terrorists, he borrowed their methods and spread the use of torture, disappearances, or open killings (such as those of La Cantuta's students and professors), or the very recent kidnapping, from the streets of Lima, by military commandos, of General Robles, who had the courage to publicly denounce the Grupo Colina of sinister fame and a branch of the army's intelligence services as the author of an attack against a television station, in Puno, in retaliation for its critical attitude toward the government and its denunciation of the collusion between narco-traffickers and the presidential adviser and regime's strongman, Vladimiro Montesinos.

Complacency in the face of state-sponsored terror is, unfortunately, widespread in countries where the insecurity and desperation caused in public opinion by extremist actions lead great sectors to approve of hardhanded policies, of counterterrorism, as the most efficient medicine for reestablishing order. It's pure illusion, a deceptive game of mirrors. What's true is that when the state uses terrorists' own methods to combat terrorism, the terrorists have won: they have managed to impose their logic and have deeply wounded institutions. How can one survive a legality worthy of its name in a society in which the one who is charged with looking out for it starts by violating it, exercising terror? The inevitable result is the generalization of violence, and along with it, corruption, which follows it like a shadow. Peru proves it in these bitter days, when it awakens from the slumber of authoritarian rule it embraced so enthusiastically: an authoritarian regime, not mediated by political parties, free press, independent judges, or parliamentary representatives, which would mercilessly beat terrorism and do away with the "politicking" of the supposed democracy. So it turns out that four years after the coup d'état that did away with democracy in Peru, terrorism was not struck down, as the government's propagandists said. The MRTA, at least, has given the most spectacular proof of its existence, occupying the front pages and prime TV hours around the world for the last four days. And regarding the rest, in the last few months, the so-called Peruvian model that made so many Latin American would-be coup leaders' eyes shine in recent years increasingly seems to be less like a peaceful and economically progressive regime, and more like a barely made-up version of the continent's traditional dictatorships, in other words, corrupt, with rank-and-file soldiers organically linked to the business of narco-trafficking, with the media on its knees through bribery or intimidation, an economy that leaks through all the holes, a growing social conflict aggravated by unemployment and poverty, and, consequently, progressive disenchantment with the authoritarian regime, and a public opinion that slowly seems to rediscover the benefits of their vanished liberty and legality.

I'd like to go back to where I began: making a vow for the hostages of the Japanese embassy to emerge safe and sound, although the price may be a trip to Cuba—where they would bronze themselves on the golden sands of Varadero, conscious of having met their duties and with their pockets lined with dollars—by Comrade Néstor Cerpa and his twenty-four moderate *compañeros*.

Miami, December 1996

Down with the Law of Gravity!

At the end of the nineteenth century in the red-hot northeastern states of Sergipe and Bahia (Brazil), there was a peasant uprising, led by a very charismatic preacher, the Apostle Ibiapina, against the metric system. The rebels, nicknamed the "kilo-breakers," attacked stores and warehouses and destroyed the new scales and measures adopted by the monarchy to bring the Brazilian system in line with the predominant one in the West and thus facilitate the country's commercial transactions with the rest of the world. This modernizing attempt seemed sacrilegious to Father Ibiapina, and many of his followers killed and died trying to impede it. The War of Canudos, which broke out a few years later in Bahia's backlands, against the establishment Brazilian Republic, was also a heroic, tragic, and absurd effort to detain the wheels of time, sowing corpses in its path.

The rebellions of the kilo-breakers and of the *yagunzos*, besides being picturesque and unusual, have powerful symbolic content. Both are part of a robust tradition that, from one end of the continent to the other, has accompanied the history of Latin America, and that, rather than disappearing, has become accentuated since emancipation: the rejection of what is real and possible in favor of what is imaginary and chimeric. No one has defined it better than the Peruvian poet Augusto Lunel, in the first lines of his *Manifesto*: "We are against all laws, starting with the law of gravity."

Rejecting reality, fixating on substituting it with fiction, denying what has actually been experienced in favor of something else that is invented, confirming the superiority of dreams over objective life, and behaving according to such a premise, is the oldest and most human of attitudes, that which has generated politicians, soldiers, scientists, artists, and the more attractive and admired saints and heroes, and, perhaps, the main engine of progress and civilization; literature and the arts were born of it and are its main nourishment, its best fuel. But at the same time, if the rejection of reality escapes the confines of the individual, the literary, the intellectual, and the artistic, and contaminates the collective and the political—the social—all idealism and generosity entailed in this position disappear, confusion replaces it, and the result is generally that catastrophe in which all attempts at utopia in the history of the world have ended.

Choosing the impossible—perfection, a masterwork, the absolute—has had extraordinary consequences in the creative sphere, from *Don Quixote* to *War and Peace*, from the Sistine Chapel to *Guernica*, from Mozart's *Don Giovanni* to Mahler's Second Symphony, but wanting to model society without concern for limits, contradictions, and variations in humanity, as if men and women were docile and easily manipulated clay capable of being adjusted to an abstract prototype, designed by philosophical reason or religious dogma with total disregard for the concrete circumstances of the here and now, has contributed, more than any other factor, to increasing suffering and violence. The 20 million victims who, in the Soviet Union alone, paid for the experience of the Communist utopia are the best example of the risks run by those who, in the social sphere, bet against reality.

The nonconformism of living in a battle with what is possible and what is real has made Latin American life intense, adventurous, unpredictable, full of color of creativity. What a difference from bovine and calm Switzerland, where I pen these lines. In these atrociously placid days, I have recalled that ferocious declaration by Orson Welles to Joseph Cotton in *The Third Man*, the Carol Reed film written by Graham Greene: "In a thousand years of history, the civilized Swiss have only produced the cuckoo clock" (or something like that). In reality, they have also produced fondue, a dish lacking in imagination, but decorous and probably nutritious. With the exception of William Tell, who, as far as everything else goes, never existed and must have been made up, I doubt that there has ever been another Swiss person who perpetrated that systematic rejection of reality which is the most widespread Latin American habit. A habit thanks to which we've had a Borges, a García Márquez, a Neruda, a Vallejo, an Octavio Paz, a Lezama-Lima, a Lam, a Matta, a Tamayo, and we've invented tango, mambo, boleros, salsa, and so many rhythms and songs that the whole world sings and dances. Nonetheless, despite having long ago left behind underdevelopment in the matter of artistic creativity—in that field, we are rather more imperialistic—Latin America is, after Africa, the region in the world with the most hunger, backwardness, unemployment, dependency, economic inequality, and violence. And small, sleepy Switzerland is the richest country in the world, with the highest quality of life any country can offer to its citizens (all of them, without exception) and to many thousands of immigrants. Although it is always bold to assume the existence of historic laws, I dare to propose that social and economic progress is in direct proportion to the vital boredom signified by complying with reality and inversely related to the spiritual effervescence that comes from rising up against it.

The kilo-breakers of our days are the thousands of young Latin Americans who, moved by noble ideals without a doubt, came to Porto Alegre to protest against globalization, a system as irreversible in our age as the metric system was when Apostle

Ibiapina's followers declared war on meters and kilograms. Globalization is not, by definition, good or bad: it is a reality of our time that has come out of a sum of factors, technological and scientific development, the growth of businesses, capital, and markets, and the interdependence that this has created among the world's different nations. Great harms and great benefits can be the result of this progressive dissolution of the frontiers that previously kept countries confined to their own territories and, many times, in open battle with everyone else. The good and the bad that globalization brings along depends, it's clear, not on itself, but on each country. Some, like Spain or Singapore, take splendid advantage of it, and the colossal economic development that both have experienced in the last twenty years has resulted in the greater part of those massive foreign investments that these two countries have been able to attract. I cite both of these because they are two exceptional examples of the extraordinary benefits that a society can obtain from internationalizing its economy. (Singapore, a city-state of Lilliputian size, has received in the last five years more foreign investment than the entire continent of Africa.)

In contrast, there is no doubt that for countries such as Nigeria under the now-deceased General Abacha, Zaire under the extinct Mobutu, and the Peru of the fugitive Fujimori, globalization brought more harm than benefits, because foreign investments, instead of contributing to the country's development, served above all to multiply corruption and increase both the wealth of the wealthy and the poverty of the poor. Nine billion dollars made its way into the Peruvian coffers thanks to the privatizations carried out during the dictatorial regime. Not one cent of that remains, and external debt has grown since the 1992 coup d'état to $5 billion. What magic, what miracles volatized those dizzying sums without their practically touching those 25 million Peruvians who are now living through the worst economic crisis in its entire history, with record rates of unemployment, hunger, and marginalization? Although a large percentage of it was squandered in populist operations, and another part in purchasing old weapons with bills for new ones, the truth is that the bulk of that income was purely and simply stolen by that crowd of gangsters led by Fujimori and Montesinos and the forty thieves around them, and today rests, safely, in the planet's abundant fiscal paradises. Worse still is the story of what was happening in Nigeria at the time of General Abacha, who, as is known, demanded that multinational oil companies pay the royalties they owed the country into private accounts in Switzerland, accounts that, like Mobutu's, reach the dizzying sum of $2 billion. In comparison with these titans, Vladimiro Montesinos, who is estimated to have stolen only $1 billion, is a midget.

The conclusion that can be made from these examples is fairly simple: the harms of globalization conspire with democracy. In countries where legality and freedom rule, in other words, with equitable and transparent rules of the game, respect for contracts, independent courts, and representative governments, subject to fiscal policies and the scrutiny of a free press, globalization is not a curse, rather, the opposite: a way of burning stages in the path to development. Thus, no solid democracy, in the first or third world, protests against the internationalization of the economy; rather, it celebrates it as an efficient instrument of progress. The opening of borders is harmful only to countries where authoritarian systems use these borders to multiply corruption, and where the lack of fair laws and freedom to criticize frequently allows these mafia-like alliances between corporations and political criminals, of whom Abacha, Mobutu, and Fujimori are typical examples.

The lesson we have to take from these precedents is the indispensable need to globalize democracy, not to end globalization. But democracy has great difficulty in adapting itself to countries that are inhospitable to it for traditional and cultural reasons; it struggles to accept the poor reality, the mediocre path of gradualism, of what is possible, of transactions and compromise, of the coexistence of diversity. This is fine for the dull Swiss, so pragmatic and realistic, but not for us absolutist dreamers, uncompromising revolutionaries, lovers of unreality and of social earthquakes. Thus, instead of demanding more globalization, of fighting, for example, for developed countries to lift those protectionary measures that close their markets to agricultural products from the third world—a flagrant injustice—we ask for less. In other words, like Father Ibiapina, we ask for the wheel of time to stop, to go backward and take us back to the isolation and nationalist fragmentation that has filled our countries with the hungry and miserable. But, it's true, with an abundance of risk, adventure, novelties, good music, and excellent artists.

Davos, January 2001

The Apogee of Horror

When Abimael Guzmán, the leader of Sendero Luminoso, unleashed the revolutionary war in 1980, did he imagine the horrors of his insurrection and that he would turn Peru into a fundamentalist Maoist society? Last year, the report by the Commission for Truth and Reconciliation, presided over by Dr. Salomón Lerner Febres, chillingly documented that war which, in a couple of decades, killed, tortured, and disappeared more than 69,000 Peruvians, the great majority of them poor and completely innocent people who saw themselves steamrolled under both Sendero Luminoso and the forces of order, and were sacrificed by both with a similar savagery. Despite its consideration and its efforts to adhere to the strict truth of the facts, this report was unfairly criticized and none of its conclusions and suggestions have been taken under consideration by the authorities, who have filed it away and forgotten it.

The same thing will probably happen to the materials to be added to this report by the journalist Ricardo Uceda, the former director of *Sí*, a left-wing weekly, that appear in his recently published book, *Muerte en el Pentagonito: Los cementerios secretos del Ejército Peruano* (Planeta), the result of eight years of research, which, thanks to firsthand testimonies, tracks the intelligence operations, tortures, and extrajudicial killings and disappearances that were carried out in the shadow of various police and military bodies, and a paramilitary organization under Alan García's APRA government, with the consent, complicity, or hypocritical Pontius Pilate–like attitude of the government. Although Uceda explores and rectifies some of the Truth Commission Report's statements, both works in essence agree on showing that during the years of the Sendero Luminoso revolution, Peru lived through what a verse by Miguel Hernández calls "the apogee of horror."

It was madness to initiate such an uprising, and to do so exactly when Peru was reestablishing democracy after twelve years of military dictatorship, since it is difficult to the point of impossibility for democratic institutions to revive and function at full speed. Sendero's terrorist actions, its killings and attacks on police, authorities, and supposed exploiters and "class enemies," forced Belaúnde Terry, shortly after assuming power, and unwillingly, to call on the armed forces to face the subversion that, in Ayacucho and nearby, seemed to be progressing like wildfire. The army was not prepared to face a subversive war, and Uceda writes in his book that when it received its mission, its intelligence services didn't have any idea what Sendero Luminoso was or how it operated. The soldier tasked with preparing a report to that effect did so based on the pamphlets and little books of propaganda purchased on the sidewalks of the Parque Universitario. This character, Julio Sosa's vice intelligence officer, Uceda's main informant, a real killing machine, seems like something taken from noir films or sadistic literature.

From the beginning, the counterrevolutionary strategy is basic: respond to terror with more terror, obtain information, and let the civilian population know what it risks if it collaborates with Sendero Luminoso. To brutality, in many cases, inefficiency was added. The first intelligence groups sent to Ayacucho submit all those detained to unspeakable violence, but they don't even know what to ask them, and, in many cases, one could say out of mere impotence, they simply kill them. The learning process is of quick dehumanization in which the defenders of legality, human rights, and the freedoms that democracy guarantees end up behaving as atrociously as those of Sendero Luminoso themselves.

Ricardo Uceda gives the full names, military ranks, as well as the companies and battalions to which they were assigned, of dozens of officers and lieutenants who, obeying command instructions, or convinced that acting as they did they were meeting the expectations of the army and the political powers, perpetrated the most execrable and abject violations of human rights, hanging their victims to the point of dislocating their joints, submerging them in tubs until their lungs burst, beating them, and subjecting them to all matter of insanities to later kill them and disappear their corpses, sometimes burning them or burying them in common graves in secret locations. Not even the most basic tenets and appearances of legality were followed; judges were not informed of detentions, and relatives who came to ask about their disappeared received absolute denials of any relevant knowledge.

The book is not easy to read, because many of its revelations are shocking and nauseating. The most terrible pages are surely the ones that describe, in great detail, the workings of the Toctos military base, where those suspected of collaborating with Sendero Luminoso were sent to be interrogated and later liquidated. Although the book does not give specific numbers, by internal evidence you can deduce that perhaps hundreds of men and women—students, peasants, union members, vagabonds—were taken there to be tortured for information and later exterminated. There is no doubt that not only those from Sendero Luminoso and their accomplices fell among them; a high percentage were absolutely innocent citizens whom luck or maliciousness or intrigue pushed into that grinding machinery from which no escape was possible. At the beginning, they killed to get information or to teach a lesson. Later—it became so easy to do it—so that there wouldn't be any inconvenient witnesses, and many times simply to steal from the victims. Before being killed, the tortured girls and women were handed over to the soldiers so they could rape them, right on the edges of the same tombs where they were to be buried. In addition to these testimonies, their treatment of the human body adds another hair-raising reality: some executioners collected the ears and noses of those killed and displayed them, proudly, in jars or on necklaces, like war trophies. A young sublieutenant, recently arrived to the Toctos base, was asked by his colleagues, while drunk, to prove his manhood by decapitating a terrorist. The young man went to the jail and came back with the bloody head in his hands.

The book makes it clear that these monstrosities were not outlandish exceptions, but in many cases behavior that was generalized because of the exasperation that Sendero Luminoso's killings and demands caused in the rank and file of the armed forces and in Peruvian society, and the complete incapability of the authorities, civil and military, to establish clear, unequivocal limits to the antisubversive action that would exclude them. The truth is that military leadership tolerated them, in many cases instigated them and covered for them, and that the political powers did not want to find out what was happening so that they would not have to act. That explains, without a doubt, why the recovery of democracy in Peru would last only through the governments of Belaúnde Terry and Alan García and why, in 1992, Fujimori would carry out a coup d'état in the face of the indifference of or with the support of so many Peruvians. What democracy were those citizens going to defend while living with the anxiety of terrorist bombs, crimes, and hold-ups, or the ones who, because they were in the middle of a battlefield, were brutalized by the terrorists as well as the ones who were supposed to protect them?

With Fujimori and Montesinos's dictatorship the exercise of

terror was not just an underhanded practice, but the official policy of the state, which, to make things worse, counted on the wide support of a civil society that had been made to believe out of fear and insecurity that an "iron fist" would reestablish citizens' security. The victims were no longer taken to the far-off mountains of Toctos, but to the basements of the Pentagonito, the very headquarters of the army in Lima, to be exterminated and dissolved in quicklime. And the letter bombs against human rights activists, opposition journalists, and supposed terrorist allies were devised in the offices of the Intelligence Services. Nonetheless, some of the abominable crimes that were committed in those years, such as the murder of fifteen attendees at a party in a house in the Lima neighborhood of Barrios Altos, among them an eight-year-old boy, in November 1991, and the killing of eight students and a professor at the University of La Cantuta—all of them supposed members of Sendero Luminoso or their allies—in July 1992, caused protests and inquiries that after some time would deeply undermine the foundations of the dictatorial regime and contribute to its downfall. Regarding both matters, Uceda's book contributes much previously unpublished information from which emerges the unequivocal responsibility in both crimes of the most important hierarchy of the regime.

Not all of the testimonies and information in *Muerte en el Pentagonito* have the same persuasive force. And some opinions, undocumented, are even disconcerting, such as the one by her former colleagues, who thought she was a press informant, that accuses Leonor La Rosa of lying—La Rosa, a member of the Intelligence Service who was tortured, raped, and turned into a human rag, and who now, a tetraplegic, lives in exile in Switzerland. Despite this, the book is not a diatribe or a sensationalist and demagogic pamphlet, but a serious and responsible effort to bring to light, going through all the existing contradictory and slippery material, and, without a doubt, taking a great personal risk, the most bitter aspect of a senseless ideological adventure that, rather than establishing the egalitarian paradise it sought, multiplied the tragedies of the poor in Peru and morally sullied the entire country.

Lima, December 2004

No More FARC

This is a story that could only have taken place in our times and that shows, better than any scientific attempt, the cultural and political revolution that the Internet has signified for the world.

Óscar Morales Guevara, a thirty-three-year-old Colombian engineer living in Baranquilla who was irritated by the Venezuelan president Hugo Chávez's request that the European Union remove the FARC (Fuerzas Armadas Revolucionarias de Colombia) from its list of terrorist organizations and promote them to that of guerrilla combatants, wanted to record his protest and sat down before his computer. As a member of Facebook, the most extensive social network on the Internet, he aimed to create, within that space, the virtual community "One million voices against the FARC." To this end, he designed a slogan, "No more kidnappings, no more deaths, no more lies, no more FARC," and a few lines of text directed "to Colombians and friends around the world," explaining the criminal nature of this organization, which has, for more than forty years, brought poverty and misery to Colombia with its kidnappings, narco-trafficking, murder, and indiscriminate attacks against the civilian population.

In just a few hours, hundreds of people had joined his project, and in a few days, the subscribers were in the thousands.

People joined at a rate of two thousand per hour. One of these enthusiasts, Carlos Andrés Santiago, a twenty-two-year-old man from Bucaramanga, then suggested the idea of a March for Peace on Monday, February 4. What happened that day in almost all of Colombia's cities and in dozens of other cities in the rest of the world, even in places as surprising as Baghdad, a village in the Sahara, Moscow, and in the capital of Ukraine, will remain a milestone of modern history. There are no precedents for this extraordinary mobilization of millions of people, on five continents, against terror and the political swindling embodied by the FARC. And less still that took place as a result of a call by independent citizens, without any political militancy or institutional support, guided only by an instinct for justice and a will for peace, which managed to hit a nerve and draw people out from their homes who have different creeds, languages, cultures, convictions, and who, in protesting against the FARC, were also protesting against the myriad fronts, parties, churches that in their own countries appropriate the right to kill, torture, and commit the worst violations against human rights under the cover of the struggle for social justice.

The most moving thing about these marches is that almost all of them were led by Colombian expatriates who, while peacefully marching with their flags and their posters and their catchphrases, showed the world their repudiation of the FARC's crimes, trying to dissipate the fantastic misunderstanding among those in certain "progressive" and liberal circles in Europe and the United States who, without going any further, still consider this organization a romantic and freedom-fighting movement that fights for the poor and society's victims and against their oppressors, and that, as such, warrants economic assistance and promotion in the media and politically. The 4 million or 5 million Colombians who, on February 4, inundated Colombia's cities and towns turned the March for Peace into one of the most important popular mobilizations in the country's entire history. Will it manage to open the eyes of the naïve Europeans and Americans who continue to insist on seeing Latin America as a continent where Robin Hood the warrior fights against the demons of the bourgeoisie and imperialism? Probably not all, because many of the FARC's admirers in advanced Western countries are the subjects of a guilty conscience that comes with being prosperous and living in boring democracies and because they need, albeit vicariously, to experience those great revolutionary adventures that in their countries are now merely history (and, above all, fantasy). These people will remain blind and deaf to reality. But let's hope that many others, less alienated by ideology or stupidity, give in to the evidence and understand, at last, that there is nothing admirable or respectable about the FARC, since they are, currently, nothing more than a pseudo-popular army at the service of narco-traffickers, who make a living on the basis of crime, who have enslaved hundreds of peasants and people from Colombia's humblest social strata—who, to their disgrace, live in the areas they rule—because of the brutal methods they employ, and who are the greatest obstacle in this country to advancing in its development and perfecting its democracy.

It is true that Colombian paramilitary organizations have perpetrated horrific crimes in their fight against the FARC. But those crimes do not counteract or make less offensive what this organization perpetrates daily, crimes that are infinitely more numerous and that are committed not out of any zeal for justice but rather purely and simply to make a profit, to fill the coffers of terror, to serve the operations of the large narco-trafficking cartels, to recruit, by force, peasant teenagers to feed their ranks, and, above all, to extort and intimidate civil society. Within those crimes, the most pervasive one is the kidnapping of politicians, businessmen, foreigners, professionals, and regular people, with the goal of receiving ransoms or using these victims in political and social blackmail operations. How many millions of dollars has the FARC obtained from the more than three thousand kidnappings in their compendium? It appears that the sum is over $300 million, which, as enormous as it is, is negligible compared with what it gets from the barons of narco-trafficking or from the very exercise of this industry, a good part of which has been under the command of the FARC for several years.

Was this movement something else at the beginning when it was led by the legendary "Tirofijo" ("Straight Shot")? Perhaps it was, before it was officially born, in 1966, when civil war bloodied Colombia after the assassination of Jorge Eliécer Gaitán, and the 1948 "Bogotazo," and the liberal and conservative guerrillas were killing each other in one of the worst bloodbaths of Latin American history. But if there was ever a strong dose of idealism and generosity among its leaders, and a genuine vocation for social altruism, it all started disappearing with the violent practices over decades in which, little by little, the means were imposed on the ends, and corrupted these until they disappeared them, as tends to happen to those who believe that "violence is the midwife of history."

The reality is that, because of the FARC and the other subversive movement, the ELN (National Liberation Army), Colombia is not a modern, developed democracy, such as Chile. What is notable is that despite the terrible challenge that terrorism presents to its institutions, Colombia has, for all these years, maintained civilian governments born from elections, a free press, an intense civilian political life, and an economy that has grown with high indices, although clearly without the benefits of this growth reaching all Colombians in an equitable way. What terrorism—and its consequence, counterterrorism—has represented in pain and sacrifice, in brutality and injustice, in abuses and trauma, has made Colombian society one of the most abused on the planet. But it has not resulted in breaking its love for life or its energy or creativity, as all who come from outside arrive there and are surprised by the happiness of their music and dances, the goodwill and cordiality of its people, the beautifully spoken and written Spanish of the Colombians, and the will not to allow themselves to be defeated by the agents of hate and fear among the people.

All of this came to the surface, in Colombia and at the hands of Colombian expatriates, this past Monday, February 4, with that mobilization for peace and truth, against lies and terror, made possible by a dark engineer from Barranquilla who, like the just in biblical stories, one day decided, in a burst of ethics, to do something against horror and deceit, and sat down in front of his computer and began to write. His example is extraordinary. Not only has he served his country and decency. He has shown us what a very powerful weapon modern communications technology can be if we know how to use it and place it at the service of truth and freedom.

Lima, February 5, 2008

For the History of Infamy

On Wednesday, July 16, tens of thousands of Nicaraguans protested on the streets of Managua to ask for the resignation of
President Daniel Ortega, whom they accuse of turning the fragile and imperfect democracy of their country into a dictatorship
as corrupt and authoritarian as the one Nicaragua experienced
under Somoza. The protest was called by the Civilian Coordinator, which brings together about six hundred civic organizations,
parties, and movements across the political spectrum, many of
them independent, feminist, and intellectual associations.

It's the first good news to reach us from that unfortunate
country—the second-poorest in Latin America, after Haiti—
since, in an act of true collective delirium, voters elected Daniel
Ortega last year to hold the place of the nation's first mandate,
forgetting his catastrophic first term (1985–1990) and legitimizing
his mafia-like pact with the former "liberal" president Arnoldo
Alemán, sentenced to twenty years in prison in 2003 for having
ransacked the state's coffers, squandering and stealing the dizzying sum of $250 million. The supposed thief is now serving his
sentence on a private farm, living like a king, receiving visitors at
will, and traveling to Managua when he feels like it to give instructions to his parliamentary legislators, who, in union with the

Sandinistas, unlawfully hold the majority in Congress. This mafia-like and unnatural alliance of a supposed left and a supposed right—in reality, two gangster-like groups dressed up like political parties—has allowed the alteration of justice, laid the groundwork for a new dictatorship, and opened the door for Daniel Ortega and Arnoldo Alemán to get their way and free themselves of paying for the crimes attributed to them. The electors who, naïvely, ignorantly, or out of fanaticism, consecrated this conspiracy already regret their mistake, since, according to the latest surveys, President Ortega's popularity has fallen drastically since he came to power in January 2007. Now, only 21 percent of the Nicaraguan population supports him.

That is still very high if you take into account "Commander" Ortega's criminal record. I'll summarize the story of his step-daughter Zoilamérica Narváez, as it appears in two publications that are worthy of absolute credibility (*El País*, in Madrid, dated June 29, 2008, and *Búsqueda*, in Montevideo, dated June 5, 2008), but those who can stomach it can read on the Internet the complete testimony of this episode, which seems like something taken out of a Marquis de Sade novel.

Zoilamérica is the daughter of Rosario Murillo, Ortega's wife, the Coordinator for the Council of Citizen Power, and, according to some, the real power behind the Nicaraguan throne. On May 22, 1998, Zoilamérica, a militant member of the Sandinista Front for National Liberation, made public her testimony against her adopted father, revealing that, since the age of eleven, "I was sexually harassed and abused by Daniel Ortega Saavedra, who continued these actions for nearly twenty years of my life." The specifics, details, and circumstances of Zoilamérica's tale are chilling and reveal a cynicism and cruelty just short of pathological in her persecutor, harasser, and rapist. The girl's stations of the cross began in 1979, when the revolutionary was working clandestinely in Costa Rica. Every time her mother went away, he took advantage to "put his hands all over me and touch my genitals. Until just recently, I also recall that he put his penis in my mouth."

The terror and shame made the girl withstand all of that without telling her mother, who, it seems, had handed herself over to politics body and soul and was on the moon regarding the bad behavior her husband carried out behind her back. The "Commander" would enter the bathroom when Zoilamérica was taking a shower and would masturbate while looking at her and caressing her clothing. At night, he would go into the room the girl shared with her brother Rafael, where "he proceeded to move part of the blanket away from my body, he put his hands all over me and later ended up masturbating. He told me not to make noise so as not to wake Rafael . . . and he would say, 'You'll see that in time, you're going to like this!' "

When the Sandinistas overthrew Anastasio Somoza in 1979, the Ortega Murillo family moved to Managua. There Zoilamérica was given her own bedroom. It was, she says, an even worse nightmare. At night, the "Commander" would slip into the twelve-year-old girl's bed and take pleasure as he wished. She began to suffer from "chills, nausea, and a trembling jaw." She lived with a sense of constant panic, due to the abuses she was subjected to, and out of the prospect that all of that would become known and turn into the focus of a great scandal. Stealing time away from his government responsibilities, the "Commander" would suddenly appear at the house at times when he knew Zoilamérica was alone and demand that she participate in his sexual games: "He would tell me to move, that it would feel good that way. 'You like it, right?' he would say to me, while I remained in absolute silence without the strength to yell or call my mother. The fear wouldn't leave me. I felt a dryness in my throat, I was choked and shaking. Contact with him left me intensely cold and feeling poorly, he caused me disgust and I thought myself dirty, very dirty, since I felt like a man whom I rejected dirtied all of me. I began to bathe many times per day, to wash myself of this dirtiness."

The "Commander's" boldness increased over time. He would force his stepdaughter to watch pornographic movies with him and would show her erotic magazines such as *Playboy*. One day he showed up at the house with a vibrator that he intended for Zoilamérica to use, but the device didn't work. In 1982, he threw her on the rug in her room and raped her. "I cried and felt nauseated. He ejaculated on my body so as not to run the risk of pregnancy and continued like that, doing it repeatedly: my mouth, my legs, my breasts were the areas where he most often spilled his semen, despite my disgust and repugnance. Since then, my life has had a painful meaning. Nights were much more feared, I could hear his steps in the hallway with his military uniform; I very clearly recall the olive green and the laurels embroidered on his uniform."

The testimony continues like this for many more pages, with countless instances of minutiae that make it difficult to determine whether the cowardice of the all-powerful "revolutionary" leader that kept his stepdaughter a sexual slave for twenty years of her life was worse than the villainy of the military and political apparatus at his service that aided those abuses by impeding the young girl from denouncing her persecutor.

When the scandal broke out, Madame Rosario Murillo came to her husband's defense and accused her daughter of conspiring with Sandinismo's enemies. A few years ago, in 2004—as a matter of political necessity—the "Commander's" wife appeared on a radio show to reconcile with her daughter, who, nonetheless, maintained all of her accusations against her adopted father. But the latter had already taken all due steps to mock justice. Managua's High Court for Crime, under the leadership of the guerrilla Juana Méndez, a loyal Sandinista militant, dismissed the case. Before the plaintiff's recusal, the principal of the Second District Court for Crime in Managua, Ileana Pérez, another proven Sandinista, needed just one day to reject the case. But the Interamerican Court of Human Rights has admitted the case against the state of Nicaragua for "denial of justice." Will the accusation against the rapist, the incestuous and pedophile "Commander," flourish there? Judging by the geological slowness with which the judges examine the case, you could say that the OAS's high court is more than reluctant to condemn a current head of state who is, besides, progressive and revolutionary.

This is also still Latin America, unfortunately. Not only that, happily. There is another Latin American reality, which is leaving behind those extremes of brutality and barbarism, where justice is already beginning to be worthy of its name and where a woman cannot be trampled and abused for two decades by a goon with guns and an olive-green uniform without judges acting to defend the victim. In Nicaragua itself, many decent Sandinistas, like the Mejía Godoy brothers—who have prohibited Ortega's use of their revolutionary songs—have come to fight against the new despot and his excesses, while many feminist groups have taken up the defense of Zoilamérica. But that someone capable of having committed such injustices could find himself in power again, anointed by the votes of his fellow citizens, instead of rotting in a jail cell, speaks volumes about how far the land of Rubén Darío and Sandino has yet to go to emerge from that cesspit of horror and shame which we call underdevelopment.

Madrid, July 22, 2008

Death of the Caudillo

Commander Hugo Chávez Frías belonged to the robust tradition of caudillos who, although more present in Latin America than in other parts, do not cease to pop up wherever, even in advanced democracies like France. It reveals the fear of freedom that is a legacy of the primitive world, prior to democracy and the individual, when man was still mass and preferred that a demigod, to whom he ceded his free will and capacity for initiative, make all the important decisions about his life. A cross between a superhuman and a jester, the caudillo makes and unmakes things at his will, inspired by God or by an ideology in which socialism and fascism—two forms of statism and collectivism—are nearly always confused, and communicates directly with his people through demagoguery, rhetoric, and multitudinous, passionate shows of a magical-religious nature.

His popularity tends to be enormous and irrational but also ephemeral, and the results of his acts unerringly catastrophic. You can't allow yourself to be too overcome by the crying masses holding a wake over Hugo Chávez's remains; they're the same ones who were shuddering with pain and abandonment over the death of Perón, Franco, Stalin, and Trujillo, and who will tomorrow accompany Fidel Castro to his burial. Caudillos do not leave heirs, and what will happen in Venezuela now is completely uncertain. No one among the people in his entourage, and naturally not in any case Nicolás Maduro, the discreet apparatchik he designated as his successor, is in a position to bring together and keep united that coalition of factions, individuals, and found interests that Chavism represents, nor of maintaining the enthusiasm and faith that the deceased commander awoke in Venezuela's masses with his torrential energy.

But one thing is certain: the ideological hybrid that Hugo Chávez engineered, called the Bolivarian revolution or Twenty-First-Century Socialism, had already begun to fall apart and will disappear sooner or later, defeated by the concrete reality of Venezuela, a country that has the potential to be the richest in the world but that has nonetheless been left impoverished, fractured, and embittered by the caudillo's policies, with the continent's highest inflation, criminality and corruption, a fiscal deficit that scrapes 18 percent of gross domestic product, and institutions—public companies, justice, the press, the electoral powers, the armed forces—semidestroyed by authoritarianism, intimidation, and obsequiousness.

Chávez's death brings into question that policy of interventionism in the rest of the Latin American continent, which, in a megalomaniac dream characteristic of caudillos, the deceased commander set out to turn socialist and Bolivarian through his checkbook. Will that fantastic lavishness of Venezuelan petrodollars continue, which has allowed Cuba's survival with one hundred thousand daily barrels that Chávez practically gifted his mentor and idol Fidel Castro? And what about the subsidies and/or debt purchases by nineteen countries, including his ideological vassals the Bolivian Evo Morales, the Nicaraguan Daniel Ortega, the Colombian FARC, and the countless parties, groups, and smaller groups that all across Latin America fight to impose Marxist revolution? The Venezuelan people seemed to accept this fantastic squandering, infected with their caudillo's optimism; but I doubt that even the most fanatic of Chavists now thinks that Nicolás Maduro could come to be the next Simón Bolívar. That dream and its subproducts, like the Bolivarian Alliance for the Peoples of Our America (ALBA), which included Bolivia, Cuba, Ecuador, the Dominican Republic, Nicaragua, Saint Vincent and the Grenadines, Antigua, and Barbados, under Venezuela's leadership, are already unburied corpses.

In the fourteen years that Chávez governed Venezuela, petroleum barrels multiplied in value by a factor of seven, which made that country, potentially, one of the most prosperous on the planet. Nonetheless, the reduction in poverty in that period has been less than, say, in Chile or Peru during the same period. Meanwhile, the expropriation and nationalization of more than a thousand private businesses, among them 3.5 million hectares of agricultural and stock-breeding estates, did not make the despised wealthy disappear, but rather created, through privilege and trafficking, a true legion of unproductive nouveaux riches who, instead of making the country progress, have contributed to sinking it in mercantilism, rentierism, and all the other degraded forms of state capitalism.

Chávez did not make the economy state-run in Cuba's manner, and never ended up closing off all spaces for dissidence and criticism, although his repressive policies against the independent press and opponents reduced them to a minimum. His compendium regarding abuses of human rights is enormous, as an organization as objective and respectable as Human Rights Watch has reminded us on the occasion of his death. It is true that he held many elections and that, in at least some of them, like the last one, he won fairly, if fairness is measured by respect for the votes cast and does not take into account the political and social context in which they take place, or that the disproportionate access to the media by the opposition compared with the government is such that it starts out with a colossal disadvantage.

In any event, that there is in Venezuela an opposition to
Chavism that in last year's election obtained 6.5 million votes is
something due, more than to Chávez's tolerance, to the bravery
and conviction of so many Venezuelans, who never allowed themselves to be intimidated by coercion and the regime's pressures,
and that, in these last fourteen years, maintained their lucidity
and democratic vocation, without allowing themselves to be run
over by the gregarious passion and abdication of a critical spirit
that foments caudillism.

That opposition, not without stumbling blocks, in which all
of the ideological variants from democratic right to left in Venezuela are represented, is united. And it now has an extraordinary
opportunity to convince the Venezuelan people that the true way
out of the enormous problems the country faces is not to persevere
in the populist and revolutionary mistake that Chávez embodies,
but rather in the democratic option, in other words, in the only
system that has been capable of reconciling freedom, legality, and
progress, creating opportunities for all under a regime of coexistence and peace.

Neither Chávez nor any other caudillo is possible in a climate
of skepticism and disgust with democracy like the one that Venezuela came to live through when, on February 4, 1992, Commander
Chávez attempted a coup d'état against the government of Carlos Andrés Pérez, a coup that was defeated by a constitutionalist
army and sent Chávez to jail, from which, two years later, in an
irresponsible move that would cost his people dearly, President
Rafael Caldera amnestied him. This imperfect democracy, spendthrift and rather corrupt as it was, had deeply frustrated Venezuelans, who, as a result, opened their hearts to the siren song of
the military coup organizer, something that has occurred, unfortunately, many times in Latin America.

When the emotional impact of his death lessens, the great
task of the opposing alliance presided over by Henrique Capriles
will be to persuade the people that Venezuela's future democracy

can shake off the imperfections holding it back and take advantage of the lesson to purge itself of mercantilist trade, rentierism, the privileges and wasteful spending that weakened it and made it so unpopular. And that the democracy of the future will put an end to abuses of power, reestablishing legality, restoring the independence of the judicial power that Chavism annihilated, ending that elephant-like bureaucratic policy that has led to the ruin of public companies, and creating a stimulating climate for the creation of wealth in which businessmen and companies can work and investors can invest such that the capital that fled returns to Venezuela and freedom goes back to being holy and a sign of the political, social, and cultural life of the country from which so many thousands of men left two centuries ago to spill their blood for the independence of Latin America.

Lima, March 2013

Part III

Elephant and Culture

I

The Chilean historian Claudio Véliz says that, when the Spanish arrived, the Mapuche Indians had a system of beliefs that ignored the concepts of aging and natural death. For them, man was young and immortal. Physical decline and death could only be the work of magic, black arts, or an adversary's weapons. This conviction, simple and comfortable, without a doubt helped the Mapuches to be the ferocious warriors they were. It helped us, in contrast, to forge an original civilization.

The attitude of the Mapuches is far from being an extravagant case. In reality, we're dealing with an extensive phenomenon. To attribute the cause of our misfortunes or defects to others— to "the other"—is a recourse that has allowed countless societies and individuals, if not to free themselves of evil, then at least to bear it and to live with a clean conscience. Masked behind subtle logic, hidden behind abundant reasoning, this attitude is the root, the secret basis, of a remote aberration that the twentieth century made respectable: nationalism. Two world wars and the prospect of a third and last, which would do away with humanity, have not freed us from it; rather, these appear to have made it more robust.

Let's briefly summarize what nationalism consists of in the realm of culture. Basically, it asks one to consider what is one's own absolute and unquestionable value and to devalue all that is foreign as something that threatens, undermines, impoverishes, or degenerates the spiritual personality of a country. Although such a thesis withstands the most shallow analysis with difficulty and it is easy to demonstrate how prejudiced and naïve its reasoning is, as well as how unrealistic its aims—cultural autocracy—are, history shows us that it takes root with ease and that even countries with an ancient and solid civilization are not immune to it. Without going too far afield, Hitler's Germany, Mussolini's Italy, Stalin's Soviet Union, Franco's Spain, Mao's China all practiced cultural nationalism, trying to create a culture that was pure, cut off from and protected from the hated corrupting agents—foreignism, cosmopolitanism—through dogma and censorship. But in our days, it is in the third world especially, in underdeveloped countries, where cultural nationalism is preached more stridently and has more followers. Its defenders start from a false assumption: that a country's culture is, like natural resources and the raw materials held by its soil, something that must be defended against the voracious greed of imperialism, and kept stable, intact, and unpolluted, since its contamination with anything from the outside would adulterate it and make it vile. To fight for "cultural independence" and to become emancipated from "foreign cultural dependence" with the goal of "developing our own culture" are habitual formulas in the mouths of so-called progressives in the third world. That such catchphrases are as hollow as they are cacophonous, true conceptual gibberish, is not an obstacle to the many people finding them seductive, due to the air of patriotism enveloping them. (And in the realm of patriotism, Borges has written, the people only tolerate affirmations.) They allow themselves to be persuaded by them, even the media who believe themselves to be invulnerable to the authoritarian ideologies promoting them. People who say they believe in political pluralism and in economic freedom and that they are hostile to the idea of only one truth and omnipotent, omniscient states subscribe nonetheless to the theses of cultural nationalism without examining what they mean. The reason is very simple: nationalism is the culture of the uneducated, and of these, there are legions.

We must resolutely combat these theses, ignorance on the one hand and demagoguery on the other, which have received their citizenship papers, since they are a major stumbling block for the cultural development of countries like ours. If they prosper, we will never have a rich, creative, modern spiritual life that speaks for us in all of our diversity and reveals to us what we are before ourselves and before the earth's other peoples. If the proponents of cultural nationalism win the game and their theories become the official policy of the "philanthropic ogre"—as Octavio Paz has called the state in our day—the result is foreseeable: our intellectual and scientific standstill and our artistic suffocation, to immortalize ourselves in a minority of cultural age and represent, within the concert of cultures of our time, the picturesque anachronism, the folkloric exception, which the civilized approach with contemptuous benevolence only out of thirst for exoticism or nostalgia for the barbaric age.

In reality, "dependent" and "emancipated" cultures do not exist, nor anything of the sort. There are rich and poor cultures, archaic and modern ones, weak and powerful ones. Inevitably, all are dependent. They always were, but are more so now, when the extraordinary advance in communications has made volatile the barriers between nations and made all peoples immediately and simultaneously coparticipants of current events. No culture has managed itself, developed and reached its full expression without feeding off of others and, in turn, nourishing others, in a continuous process of give-and-take, reciprocal influences and mixtures, in which it would be very difficult to ascertain what belongs to whom. Notions of what constitutes "one's own" and "the other's" are doubtful, without going as far as to say absurd, in the realm of culture. In the only area in which they have a foothold—that of language—they are undermined if we try to identify them with a country's geographic and political borders and turn them into something that sustains cultural nationalism. For example, for Peruvians, is the Spanish that we speak along with 300 million other people in the world "our own" or "the other's"? And, among the Quechua speakers of Peru, Bolivia, and Ecuador, who are the legitimate owners of the language and the Quechua tradition and who are the "colonized" and the "dependent" ones who should be emancipated from them? We would arrive at the very same perplexity if we wished to inquire which country can patent as native the interior monologue, that key resource of modern fiction. Is it France, because of Édouard Dujardin, the mediocre novelist who appears to have been the first to usurp it? Ireland, with Molly Bloom's famous monologue in Joyce's *Ulysses*, which cemented his status in the literary world? Or the United States, where, thanks to Faulkner's sorcery, it acquired unsuspected flexibility and sumptuousness? Via this path—that of nationalism—when it comes to the realm of culture, one arrives, sooner or later, at confusion and absurdity.

What is certain is that in this realm, although it appears strange, what is one's own and what is the other's get mixed up and originality is not at odds with influences or even with imitation and plagiarism, and the only way in which a culture can flourish is in close interdependence with others. Whoever tries to impede it does not save "national culture," but kills it.

I'd like to give two examples of what I am talking about, taken from the work that is most dear to me: the literary one. It is not difficult to demonstrate that the Latin American writers who have made a more personal mark on our letters were, in all cases, those who showed fewer inferiority complexes in the face of foreign cultural values and relied on them at their will and without the least scruples when it came time to create. If modern

Spanish-American poetry has a birth mother and father, these are modernism and its founder: Rubén Darío. Is it possible to conceive of a poet who is more "dependent" and more "colonized" by foreign models than this universal Nicaraguan? His excessive and nearly pathetic love for the French Symbolists and Parnassians, his vital cosmopolitanism, that endearing religiosity with which he read, admired, and devoted himself to acclimating his own poetry to the literary fashions of the time, did not make him a mere epigone, a creator of "underdeveloped and dependent poetry." Quite the contrary. Making use of magnificent freedom within the cultural arsenal of his time, everything seducing his imagination, his feelings, and his instinct, Rubén Darío combined with formidable irreverence those disparate sources in which the Greece of philosophers and tragedy is mixed with the France of licentiousness and eighteenth-century courtesans, with Golden Age Spain, and with his American experience, thereby carrying out the deepest revolution experienced by Spanish poetry since the time of Góngora and Quevedo, rescuing it from the traditional academicism in which it was languishing and placing it once again, like in the time of sixteenth- and seventeenth-century Spanish poets, in the vanguard of modernity.

Darío's case is that of almost all great artists and writers; it is that of Machado de Assis, in Brazil, who never would have written his beautiful human comedy without having first read Balzac; that of Vallejo in Peru, whose poetry took advantage of all the isms shaking up literary life in Latin America and Europe between the two world wars and is, in our time, the case of an Octavio Paz in Mexico and a Borges in Argentina. Let's pause for a moment regarding the latter. His stories, essays, and poems are, surely, the ones that have had the greatest impact on other languages of any contemporary author of our language, and his influence is noticeable in writers from a range of countries. No one like him has contributed as much to our literature as a respected creator of original ideas and forms. So: would Borges's work have been possible through the varied and fantastic cultural geography by way of continents, languages, and historical periods? Borges is a clear example of the best way to enrich with original work the culture of the nation where he has been born and the language in which he writes by being, culturally, a citizen of the world.

II

The way in which a country strengthens and develops its culture is by opening its doors and windows, widely, to all intellectual, scientific, and artistic currents, stimulating the free circulation of ideas wherever they come from, in such a way that its own tradition and experience is constantly put to the test, and corrected, completed, and enriched by those who, in other territories and with other languages and in different circumstances, share with us the misery and greatness of the human adventure. Only thus, subject to this continuous challenge and encouragement, will our authentic, contemporary, and creative culture be the best tool of our own economic and social progress.

To condemn "cultural nationalism" as atrophy for the spiritual life of a country does not, of course, signify disdain in the least for national or regional traditions and behaviors, nor an objection to their serving, even in a primordial way, the thinkers, artists, technicians, and researchers in a country for their own work. It only signifies reclaiming, in the realm of culture, the same freedom and the same pluralism that should reign in politics and economics in a democratic society. Cultural life is richer the more diverse it is and the more free and intense the exchange and rivalry is of ideas in its bosom.

We Peruvians are in a privileged situation to know this since our country is a cultural mosaic in which "all bloods," as Arguedas wrote, coexist or mix; pre-Hispanic cultures and Spain and all of the West that came to us with the Spanish language and history; the African presence, so alive in our music; Asian immigration and that collection of communities in the Amazon with their languages, legends, and traditions. That multitude of voices equally express Peru, a plural country, and neither has more of a right than any other to be more representative. In our literature, we notice this abundance. Martín Adán, whose poetry does not seem to have any other home or ambition than language, is as Peruvian as José María Eguren, who believed in fairies and revived, in his little house in Barranco, characters from Norse mythology, or as José María Arguedas, who transfigured the world of the Andes in his novels, or as César Moro, who wrote his most beautiful poems in French. Foreignizing at times and at times folkloric, traditional for some and in the vanguard for others, from the coast, the mountains, or the jungle, realistic or fantastic, Spanish-influenced or French-influenced, indigenous or North Americanized, in its contradictory personality, it expresses that complex and varied truth that we are. And it expresses it because our literature has been fortunate to develop with a freedom that we real, live Peruvians have not always enjoyed. Our dictators were so uncultured that they deprived men of freedom, but rarely books. This belongs to the past. Dictatorships today are ideological and also want to control ideas and spirits. That is why they rely on pretexts, such as that national culture should be protected against foreign infiltration. This is not acceptable. It is not acceptable that, for the purpose of defending culture against the danger of "denationalization," governments establish systems to control thoughts and words that, in reality, have no other objective than to impede criticism. It is not acceptable that, for the goal of preserving the purity of or ideological health of culture, the state assigns itself as the governing body or warden of a country's intellectual and artistic work. When this happens, cultural life becomes trapped in a straitjacket of bureaucracy and atrophies, plunging society into spiritual lethargy.

To ensure freedom and cultural pluralism, we must clearly define the state's role in this area. This role can only be that of creating the most propitious conditions for cultural life and meddling as little as possible in it. The state should guarantee freedom of expression and the free flow of ideas, foment research and the arts, guarantee access to education and to information for all, and rather than impose or favor doctrines, theories, or ideologies, to allow these to flourish and freely compete. I know that it is difficult and nearly utopian to achieve this neutrality in the face of the state's cultural life in our time, that big, unwieldy elephant whose very movement causes damage. But if we don't manage to control its trajectory, it will step all over and devour us.

Let's not repeat, in this day, the mistake of the Mapuche Indians, combating supposed foreign enemies without noticing that the main obstacles we have to conquer are within ourselves. The challenges we should face in the area of culture are too real and large to invent additional imaginary difficulties like those of foreign powers insistent on culturally attacking us and debasing our culture. Let's not succumb to the delirium of persecution nor to the demagoguery of uncultured carpetbaggers, convinced that everything goes in their fight for power and that, if they came to occupy that seat, they wouldn't hesitate to surround culture with censorship and suffocate it with dogmas so that, like Albert Camus's Caligula, they would do away with contradicters and contradictions. Those who propose these theses call themselves, through one of those dizzying magical substitutions of semantics of our time, progressives. In reality, they are modern retrogrades and obscurantists, the successors of that somber dynasty of jailers of the spirit, as Nietzsche called them, whose origin is lost in the night of human intolerance, and in which they stand out, identical and disastrous throughout the ages, the medieval inquisitors, the bearers of religious orthodoxy, the political censors, and the fascist and Stalinist cultural commissaries.

Besides dogmatism and the lack of freedom, the bureaucratic intrusions and ideological prejudices, another danger threatens the development of culture in any modern society: the substitution of the genuine cultural product by a pseudo-cultural product that is imposed on the market en masse by communications media. This is a certain and very serious threat and it would be foolish to downplay its importance. The truth is that these pseudo-cultural products are avidly consumed and offer an enormous swath of men and women the simulation of intellectual life, weakening their sensitivity, removing their sense of artistic values, and nullifying them to true culture. It is impossible for a reader whose literary tastes have been established reading Corín Tellado to appreciate Cervantes or Cortázar, or for another, who has learned everything he knows from *Reader's Digest*, to make the necessary effort to deepen his knowledge in whatever area, and for minds conditioned by publicity to think for themselves. The vulgarity and conformism, the intellectual drabness and artistic poverty, the formal and moral misery of these pseudo-cultural products profoundly affect the spiritual life of a country. But it is false that this is a problem inflicted upon underdeveloped countries by the developed countries. It is a problem that we all share, that results from the technological advance in communications and from the development of the cultural industry, and to which no country in the world, rich or poor, has yet to provide a solution. In cultured England, the most widely read author is not Anthony Burgess or Graham Greene but Barbara Cartland, and the soap operas that are the delight of the French public are as awful as the Mexican or North American ones. The solution to this problem does not consist, naturally, in establishing censorship that prohibits pseudo-cultural products and gives the green light to cultural ones. Censorship is never a solution, or, in other words, it is the worst solution, the one that always leads to worse ills than what it seeks to resolve. "Protected" cultures dressed up as officialism adopt more caricature-like and degraded forms than those that arise, along with the authentic cultural products, in free societies.

It happens that freedom, which in this area is also always the best option, has a price one has to be resigned to pay. The extraordinary development of the means of communication have meant that, in our era, the culture that was in the past, at least in its richest and most elevated forms, the patrimony of a minority has been democratized and is in a position to reach, for the first time in history, the immense majority. This is a possibility that should excite us. For the first time, the technical conditions exist for culture to be truly popular. It is, paradoxically, this marvelous possibility that has favored the appearance and success of the massive industry of semicultural products. But let's not confuse the effect with the cause. The means of mass communication are not to blame for the mediocre or mistaken use that is made of them. Our obligation is to conquer them for true culture, elevating, via education and information, the public, making them more and more rigorous, more restless, and more critical, and ceaselessly demanding of those who control the media—the state and private companies—greater responsibility and more ethical criteria in their use. But it is, above all, the intellectuals, technicians, artists, and scientists, the cultural producers of all kinds, to whom falls the audacious and formidable task of taking charge of our age, understanding that cultural life cannot today be, as it was yesterday, an activity for catacombs, for clerics locked away in convents or academies, but rather something to which the greatest number should recur and have access. This demands a reconversion of the entire cultural system, spanning from a change in psychology in the individual maker, and in his work mode, to a radical reform of the channels of distribution and means of promotion of cultural products; a revolution, in sum, of consequences that are difficult to foresee. The battle will be long and difficult, without a doubt, but the prospect of what victory would signify should give us moral strength and courage to undertake it. In other words, the possibility of a world in which, as Lautréamont wanted for poetry, culture will be at last for all, made by all and for all.

Lima, November 1981

Why? How?

Five presidents in just two weeks is a real record, even for the underdeveloped world. Argentina just patented it, in the midst of the uproar and fury of a popular uprising against a political class dangerously reminiscent of the one that preceded the meteoric political career of Commander Hugo Chávez in Venezuela and began the erosion of the democratic system.

Will Eduardo Duhalde, who has assumed the presidency of Argentina thanks to an agreement between the radicals and the Peronists, succeed in putting an end to the mandate of Fernando de la Rúa, which lasts until 2003, and stabilize political life in this period, reestablishing order and beginning to solve a very serious economic and institutional crisis that has led the country to the doors of anarchy and disintegration? You have to wish for that, certainly, but the brand-new leader's doctrinal background and statements do not justify optimism, but rather the opposite.

When you have read the analysis and explanations by technicians and economists—which have proliferated in these days—about the dreadful situation in Argentina, a country crushed by the dizzying external debt of $130 billion, the interest on which consumes a third of national assets, and the victim of the even more dreadful financial crisis of Latin America, you are left thwarted, unsatisfied. And with the same questions hammering away in your head: Why? How?

Why does this terminal crisis seem to have come to one of the earth's most privileged countries? How to explain that Argentina, which had one of the highest standards of living in the world just a few decades ago and seemed destined, in a few more generations, to compete with Switzerland or Sweden in development and modernity, should go backward like this until it is on a par with certain African countries in terms of poverty, disorder, and ineffectiveness in political and economic matters?

This is not a rhetorical question, but justified perplexity in the face of what seems to be the irresponsible, criminal waste of unique conditions for reaching development and well-being. If Argentina is not the most fortunate country in the world in natural resources, it must rank among the top three or four. It has everything from oil, minerals, and maritime wealth to fertile and abundant soil that would be enough to act, simultaneously, as the world's breadbasket and as the provider to all meat markets.

Given how large its territory is, its population is small and culturally homogeneous. Although, without a doubt, with repeated crises, its schools and universities must have gone down in quality; its educational system was, in the past, the envy of all of Latin America, and with reason, since it was one of the most efficient and elevated in the whole West. When I was a boy, it was still the dream of thousands of young South Americans to go study engineering, medicine, or any liberal profession in that great country that produced the movies we saw, the good books we read, and the magazines that entertained us. (In my case, I read *Billiken*, my grandmother and my mother, *Para ti*, and my grandfather, *Leoplan*.)

What cataclysm, plague, or divine curse fell on Argentina so that, in just half a century, it traded its outstanding and promising fate for the current imbroglio? No economist or political scientist is in a position to provide a comprehensive response to this question, perhaps because the explanation would not be statistically quantifiable or reducible to avatars or political formulas. The real reason is behind all of this, a distant, diffuse motivation, and has more to do with a certain mental and psychological predisposition than economic doctrines or the struggle for power by individuals or parties.

I beg you, my readers, not to think that I am mocking you, or that I am an insolent writer-jester, if I tell you that the best way to understand the chaos in Argentina, rather than consulting any economists' or social scientists' reflections, would be to read the book by a philologist, Ana María Barrenechea, who, in 1957, published an essay that, for me, continues to be the most solid and lucid one about Borges: "The Expression of Unreality in the Work of Jorge Luis Borges." It is a rigorous and subtle research paper about the techniques that the author of "The Aleph" relied upon to construct his amazing fictitious universe, that world of situations, characters, and matters that convey a vast literary culture, a singular and incredible imagination, and a richness and expressive originality comparable only with those of the greatest prose writers that have existed in this world.

Borges's universe has many unmistakable traits, but the main and supreme one is that of being unreal, of being outside of this concrete world in which we, his bewitched readers, are born, live, and die, in existing only as a miraculous mirage thanks to the literary witchcraft of its author, who rightly said of himself, "I've read many things and lived through few." The world created by Borges exists only in dreams, in words, although its beauty, its elegance, and its perfection conceal its essential unreality.

It is no coincidence that the most notable of creators of modern literature who evaded the real world were born and wrote in Argentina, a country that, for many lustrums already, not only in its literary life (a culture exempt from the genre of fantasy), but also socially, economically, and politically, manifests, like Borges, a notorious preference for unreality and a contemptuous rejection of the sordidness and pettiness of the real world, of feasible life. This vocation for fleeing from what is concrete toward the dream-like or the ideal thanks to fantasy could, in the realm of literature, yield products as splendid as those that came from the pen of Borges or Bioy Casares. But, to carry it over to social life and the common territory of the practical, to succumb to the temptation of unreality—of utopia, voluntarism, or populism—has the tragic consequences now endured by one of the richest countries on earth, which, because its ruling class insisted on living in a bubble of fantasies instead of accepting poor reality, one day awoke "broken and shattered," as was just recognized by the brand-new president, Duhalde.

To allow itself to accumulate an external debt of $130 billion was to live a suicidal fiction. It is, also, to prolong and aggravate a fiscal crisis indefinitely, as if by burying your head in the sand like an ostrich you could remain protected against the hurricane. To maintain, out of cowardice or political demagoguery, parity between the dollar and the peso, which no longer corresponds in any way to the real state of currency and only serves to suffocate exports, and to delay the financial catastrophe that the inevitable devaluation of the peso will bring, is likewise to wager for illusions and phantasmagoria against the mediocre pragmatism of the realists.

But this has all been coming for a long time, and began, no doubt, with the nationalist madness of the forties and fifties that led Perón and Peronism to nationalize the main and until then flourishing Argentine industries and to increase the size of the bureaucratic and interventionist state until it turned into a true Moloch, an unmanageable, suffocating monster, a tenacious obstacle for the system of creating wealth and a source of infinite corruption. Thus began the systematic dismantling of that country whose inhabitants, privileged citizens of a modern, prosperous, and educated society, came to believe themselves European at one point, exonerated from South American imbroglios and miseries, closer to Paris and London than Asunción or La Paz.

Will they at last open their eyes or, rattled by this terrible crisis that has filled the streets with dead and wounded and has shaken institutions to their core, will they rediscover the path of reality? In his first statements, President Duhalde is not giving any indication, but perhaps, when it comes time to act, he will be more realistic than when he speaks from a podium.

The reality for Argentina at this time is that it should reach some agreement with its creditors to restructure in a sensible way the payment of that insane debt, without implying, clearly, the immolation of the Argentine people on the altar of theoretical financial health. Because that agreement is the only thing that can bring the country the investments it needs and avoid the desperate flight of capital that this crisis has already set off and that will accelerate if Argentina is put in financial quarantine on the international stage. And to take energetic measures to drastically reduce the fiscal crisis, via a severe adjustment, because neither Argentina nor any other country can live in eternity spending (wasting) more than it produces. This implies a high cost, certainly, but it is preferable to admitting that there is no alternative and paying it as soon as possible, because later it will be even more onerous, especially for the poor. Society will better withstand the sacrifice if it is told the truth than if it continues to be lied to, as if aspirin could efficiently cure a brain tumor. The cancer must be excised as soon as possible or we run the risk of the person who is affected dying.

The first time I went to Buenos Aires, in the mid-sixties, I discovered that in that very beautiful city there were more theaters than in Paris, and that its bookstores were the most desirable and stimulating that I had ever seen. Ever since then, I have felt a special affection for Buenos Aires, for Argentina. To read, these days, about what is happening there has revived images for me of that first encounter with that ruined country. I ardently hope that it soon emerges from the abyss and that it one day comes to "deserve" (the verb and the image come from Borges, of course) the democracy that it *still* has not lost.

Lima, January 2002

The "Hispanics"

Myths, stereotypes, clichés, platitudes, prejudice, and ignorance have frequently made enemies of the United States and Latin American countries and thwarted what should, for reasons of geography and common sense, be a mutually advantageous relationship. But, as the saying goes, nothing bad can last one hundred years. This has lasted too long and today there are more possibilities than yesterday to correct it. Why? Because there are now two unprecedented factors that should work decisively in favor of a strategic closeness between the two halves of the continent.

The first is the proliferation in Latin America of civilian and democratic regimes inspired by legality and freedom, like the one in effect in North American society. There has been much talk in the world, with reason, of the fall of totalitarianism in Eastern Europe and the extinction of the Soviet Union. Less has been said about the fall, one after another, of the dictatorships—save for Cuba and Haiti—in Latin American countries. This is the most important phenomenon of the history of our republics and signifies a unique opportunity, one that recognizes that the vicious cycle of revolutions and military uprisings is forever over and that our countries are battling poverty and backwardness by tying their fate to that which they have been a part of since Columbus's arrival: the democratic West.

Naturally, the game is far from being won. Political democracy does not guarantee economic development—this demands a genuine market economy, a true opening to global markets, legal stability for businesses and property, and a minimum level of efficiency and honesty by the state, something that the majority of Latin American societies are still far from achieving—and the reality is that, with exceptions like that of Chile and, lately, of Mexico, the difficult economic situation is a sword of Damocles in the democratization process for many countries to the south of the Rio Grande.

Nevertheless, there are encouraging signs. The utopian model of violent revolution finds itself abandoned, even in countries such as Peru, El Salvador, Colombia, and Guatemala, where insurgent groups are active but are resigned to opening negotiations with their governments and are experiencing a notorious decrease in popularity. All over the continent, the widespread support of the majority for democracy, and its open rejection of the options of a Marxist revolution and a military dictatorship, are unequivocal. This can be confirmed in each new electoral process or when, as in Argentina, there have been attempts at a coup. Even in Cuba, despite the very tough repressive system and the regime's latest ferocious punishment of dissidents to freeze any protest, the signs of resistance against tyranny are ever greater. (Such as the manifesto, led by María Elena Cruz Varela and signed in June of last year by seventeen Cuban intellectuals residing on the island, many of them members of UNEAC—the National Union of Writers and Artists—asking for political amnesty and free elections.)

On the other hand, the idea that economic freedom is completely indispensable to political freedom to achieve development is making inroads, although still very slowly. Patricio Aylwin's Chilean democratic regime has maintained the previous liberal economic model, thus ensuring growth for Chile that is the highest in Latin America. And in Mexico, Salinas de Gortari's government is carrying out a noteworthy effort to privatize and open the economy that is starting to bear fruit. And in Argentina, Bolivia, Venezuela, and Peru, they likewise, although tentatively and at times with backward steps and stumbles, are moving in that direction. The philosophy of "internal development" and of economic nationalism, which Doctor Raúl Prebisch and CEPAL (the Economic Commission for Latin America) so successfully advocated and which was practiced by all governments—democratic or authoritarian—in the sixties and seventies with such catastrophic consequences, has almost no defenders anymore, and over its corpse, on the Latin American horizon, a modern consciousness emerges of the need for a competitive market and economic freedom so that the new democracies do not fail.

This fact is extraordinarily important, and if the United States understands it as such, and acts accordingly, a new era could begin that overcomes the mistrust and confrontations that have done so much damage to the continent. It is indispensable, politically, for Latin Americans who have opted for freedom to confirm that the United States is on their side and not on that of their enemies—the minority who are nostalgic for military uprisings—since they have understood that those adversaries are also theirs.

And in the economic area, collaboration is essential. This cannot mean gifts. There are many Latin Americans who, in the old mentality, now wait for Washington to resolve the crisis, canceling their debts and granting them all the credit they ask for. It would be a real blow to the democracies of the South if that were to happen. It is their responsibility to make the effort and impose order on the labyrinths of their economies, clean up their budgets and their administrative apparatuses, and impose stable rules that will promote and attract investment. The role of the United States cannot be any other—loyal to its Constitution—than that of opening its markets and stimulating exchange with its neighbors instead of obstructing it. While this is a lot to ask, if it comes to pass, the benefits for gringos and Hispanics will be enormous.

The incorporation of Mexico into the free-trade treaty that the United States and Canada have signed could be the starting point of that continental economic revolution. Despite the tremendous resistance that the initiative awakens in protectionist and nationalist groups, in the United States and in Mexico it is overcoming obstacles and all signs indicate that it will happen. Other Latin American countries should not fear being marginalized because of it. Rather, it should serve as an incentive to accelerate the modernization of their economies such that they can be incorporated into that treaty, something that should be understood as a starting point or a first stage of something that will perhaps one day be the common market of the Americas.

Many in South America, despite the new democratic leaning of their countries, do not understand that this option also means taking the side, without subterfuge, of the open societies of the free world whose leadership the United States exercises, in the face of totalitarianism and third-world dictatorships. There should be no mistakes made about this. Although their policies frequently reveal a lack of knowledge or an arrogance regarding our reality, if we've opted for democracy, our natural allies, for reasons of principle and pragmatism, will also be free countries. There is no room for neutrality here, since, as Arthur Koestler wrote, you can't be neutral toward the bubonic plague. Those who, for example, dealt with Castro's tyranny or the despotism of Saddam Hussein by defending a "neutral" position in the name of an obligation to "third-world" ethics are fooling themselves and their people. For anyone who declares himself to be a democrat, there is no neutrality possible between freedom and dictatorship, whatever its nature and wherever it may be located: each option excludes the other like oil and water.

But the United States and other countries in the West should understand that solidarity and friendship do not signify vassal-age or servitude, but respect and mutual understanding, and this demands a constant effort to understand reciprocal reasons and problems.

This will be achieved only when knowledge replaces the web of prejudices and myths that still greatly distort the images forged in the mind of the South about the North and vice versa. But now, besides the great wave of democracy in Latin America, there is another powerful instrument to achieve this difficult deed of communication and understanding. It is the other factor that can contribute to radically renewing relations between the Anglo and Latin American cultures. I am referring to that world that is so present and that has had such an important role in the modern history of the United States: that of the "Hispanics."

The Latin American community in the United States is, in many states, a presence as alive as it is in Miami. And it is increasingly conscious of its historic tradition, its language and culture, which affects all of North American society. As in Florida, California, Texas, Arizona, New Mexico, or New York, the Hispanic influence can be seen in culinary habits and ways of dress, in music and religion, and in the way Spanish-language usage has slipped into businesses, shows, services, schools, and street life. It is possible that, long-term, given the traditional ability of metabolism and freedom that it has forged, the United States will integrate this community, as it did with Italians and Poles. But the process will be long and it can be expected that when it peaks, integration will have achieved the feat of opening the minds and spirits of many North Americans to the realities—instead of the myths—of Latin America. Or, at least, to have incited the curiosity and interest of the United States in getting to know them, such that instead of the hate that seems like love, or that hateful love that is still the norm, an equitable and productive relationship can finally emerge between the people of the continent.

This is a task that the "Hispanics" of the United States are already carrying out, although they are not even aware of it. In contrast to politicians, prisoners of rhetoric and of calculations, and diplomats whose life is played out rather removed from the average citizen, they do know the hustle and bustle of men and women on the street. Those in their new homeland and in the homeland they left behind, because of political persecution, know how hard life is, or, simply, the legitimate desire for an improvement. And in contrast to expatriate intellectuals, who have to perform acrobatics to justify their ideological positions, the average immigrant can act with authenticity and dignity.

He knows both cultures in that intimate way born of direct experience, what is lived, and this has taught him—counter to what they say about stereotypes—that despite the different languages (and that in the North there is abundance while in the South there is poverty), the differences are not that big. That beneath the customs, beliefs, and prejudices that make groups distinct, there are basic similarities. Because men and women from both places are interested in the same thing: living peacefully, freely, without fear of the future, with work and the opportunity to succeed. The "Hispanics" of the United States—20 million strong—can be the bridge that gringos and Latinos cross to recognize each other and be reconciled.

Lima, January 4, 1992

Nostalgia for the Sea

My first four years of school took place in Cochabamba, Bolivia, and I can still recall how several times per month, almost every week, the La Salle students would line up in the courtyard and sing a patriotic song demanding the return of the Bolivian sea, which Chile seized as a result of the War of the Pacific in 1879. In that conflict, Peru and Bolivia lost important territories, but for the latter, to lose 480 kilometers of coast meant turning into a landlocked country, enclosed within the peaks of the Andes, cut off from the Pacific, a mutilation that Bolivia never accepted and that has continued to weigh upon Bolivian society like a psychic trauma.

The lost sea has been a perennial nostalgia that impregnates the country's literature and political life to the extent that until recently Bolivia had a symbolic navy (it might still) in the hope that, on the longed-for day when it would once again have access to the sea, it would already have at its disposal a body of officers and sailors prepared to take immediate possession of the recovered waters. It has also been the historic reason held up to explain Bolivia's economic backwardness and poverty and the matter to which presidents and dictators recur every time they need to conjure up internal divisions or create a distraction from their lack of popularity. Because, in fact, reclaiming the sea is, in Bolivian history, one of the few matters that consolidates national unity, an aspiration that always prevails over ethnic, regional, and ideological divisions among Bolivians.

The Bolivian aspiration to have a seaport deserves everyone's sympathy and solidarity—in fact, it has it—and, of course, that of this scribe, who recalls the ten years of his childhood in Bolivia like a Golden Age. But the matter should not be put forward as an inalienable right that Chile should recognize, admitting the plunder it committed and returning to Bolivia the territory that it took over through an act of force. Because if it proposed thus, Bolivia does not have the least possibility of making its maritime dreams a reality and the result would most likely be to light the bonfire of revanchism across Latin America, from Mexico, who could demand that the United States return California and Texas, to Paraguay, whom the Triple Alliance—Brazil, Uruguay, and Argentina—shrank like a sharkskin. Without going too far, Peru could demand not just Arica but all of Bolivia and Ecuador, which in the eighteenth century were as much a part of Peru as Cuzco and Arequipa.

All wars are unjust, they always favor brute force, and naturally this was so in the War of the Pacific and in all of the armed conflicts that bloodied the history of Latin America. As a result, the political geography of the continent has been taken apart and put back together thousands of ways. To try to correct the damages, brutalities, abuses, and undue territorial appropriations of the past at this point is not just a chimera; it is also the best way to incite nationalism, the extreme form of political irrationality that has certainly been one of the main factors in Latin American underdevelopment, since it has prevented bodies of regional integration from working, unleashing clashes and tensions between countries that served to waste massive quantities of resources on the purchase of weapons and to turn armies into arbiters of public life and all of their generals into potential dictators. This is a sinister past that Latin America should turn its back to, disregarding the nationalist demagoguery that, at this time, on the basis of the Bolivian demand for the sea that has been carried out by the government of Carlos Mesa, begins to be heard here and there, along with an interested anti-Chileism (lead by Fidel Castro and Commander Chávez) that, rather than finding solidarity with Bolivia, expresses a condemnation of the liberal economic model that has made Chile the most dynamic economy on the continent and of the Chilean left represented by Ricardo Lagos, the only one among us who seems to have taken a definitive step toward modernization, in the manner of Spanish and British socialists.

Throughout the twentieth century, the Bolivian desire for access to the sea had almost no occasion to be made reality. Bolivia was living with chronic instability in which governments and revolutions followed each other at a dizzying pace, impoverishing the country until it had reduced its ability to make itself heard by the international public to almost nothing. In 1975 the dialogue about this matter was broached when the dictators of both countries, Hugo Banzer and Augusto Pinochet, gave each other the so-called Charaña hug. The Chilean dictator then proposed ceding a five-kilometer-wide corridor and a maritime port, contiguous to the Peruvian-Chilean border, in return for equivalent territorial compensations. Since according to the 1929 treaty between Chile and Peru, any territory that Chile cedes that used to belong to Peru has to be approved by the latter, the Chilean government made the relevant consultations with the Peruvians. The military dictatorship of Morales Bermúdez responded with a counterproposal in which the territory ceded by Chile to Bolivia would have shared sovereignty among the three countries, which implied a revision of the 1929 treaty that fixed the limits between Chile and Peru. Santiago did not accept the proposal and the project went nowhere. Shortly after, Bolivia would break diplomatic relations with Chile.

Does Bolivia currently have more possibilities than in the

past to realize its maritime dream? Yes, it does, thanks to that globalization that is so reviled by obscurantist and obtuse demagogues, a reality that, despite governments and armies and the narrow lens of national interests, has been weakening borders and extending bridges, common denominators, and economic ties between the countries, one of the best things to happen to Latin America in the last twenty years and thanks to which, among other progress, there are fewer dictators on the continent today than in the past and better democratic habits. Only antediluvian politicians are incapable of understanding that, in our day, a country that does not open its borders and try to insert itself into the world market is condemned to poverty and barbarism. To open borders means many things, and the first of these is to harmonize their own economic policies with those of their neighbors, the only way to be better equipped to conquer world markets for national products and to accelerate the modernization of internal infrastructure. In contrast to what used to happen in the past, today Chile needs Bolivia as much as Bolivia needs Chile. And as for Peru, it also needs both of its neighbors.

An agreement is possible as long as it is negotiated with diplomatic discretion and looking exclusively at the future, without turning to the past. This should be, without saying that it must be, a bilateral negotiation between the two countries, in which Peru should only intervene once there is an agreement and it affects territories that were Peruvian in the past. It is inevitable that it should occur this way because Chile would never accept the division of its territory—no country would—as the basis of a solution. Bolivia is a very poor country but with a subsoil containing copious gas reserves and with enough hydrological resources to spare, and Chile needs these to develop the desert region of its northern border. Peru, rather that obstructing it, should facilitate this friendly Chilean-Bolivian agreement, which can only bring it benefits, since the entire Peruvian region on that southern border requires urgent investment to develop an industrial, commercial, and port infrastructure to bring it out of the abandon in which it finds itself.

The three countries currently have democratic governments (although Bolivian democracy has been left somewhat battered by the way in which Sánchez de Lozada was replaced by the current president, Mesa), which should be an incentive for rapprochement and the opening of negotiations. But for this to happen the tense climate created around the matter must soften, which certainly will not occur quickly. Because in Chile there is already a preelectoral atmosphere in which nationalism and chauvinism are in vogue, and the candidate or party that dares to even mention the possibility of giving Bolivia a path to the sea would be accused of treason and likened to Benedict Arnold by his adversaries. And in Bolivia, President Mesa, the consolidated statesman at the head of a great national movement espousing the Bolivian people's dearest desire, has been brought to his knees by an international scandal: he was, just barely a month ago, a precarious leader, without his own strength, checkmated by Evo Morales and Felipe Quispe, who rule the streets and could oust him as easily as Sánchez de Lozada was ousted.

May patriotic verses be eclipsed and the matter of Bolivia's landlocked plight come off the streets and the headlines move into the more tranquil atmosphere of the chanceries, where there is less yelling and more reasoning (sometimes), the interests at play are considered, and negotiation is set into motion out of which agreements are born. For the first time since the fateful War of the Pacific, there are circumstances that could give Bolivia the maritime port it dreams of. May short-term vision, pettiness, and stupidity not impede it. It will be not only Commander Chávez, but I, too, who will go take a dip in those freezing waters of the Bolivian sea for which I sang so many hymns in my Cochabamba childhood.

Lima, January 22, 2004

Repugnant Laudatory Farce

One of the most beautiful poems that Luis Cernuda wrote is called "Birds in the Night," and it is dedicated to Verlaine and Rimbaud. Or, rather, to the "repugnant laudatory farce" of which poets tend to be the victims after their death, while cursed and marginalized in life because of their bad habits, excesses, violence, and provocations, only to be turned into national glories later. Celebrated as "ambassadors and mayors," they deserve busts and plaques like the one the French government ("or was it the British?") placed at number 8 Great College Street, Camden Town, London, the very humble little house where, for a few weeks, the drunk, fifty-something-year-old poet and the insolent, brilliant teenager "lived, worked, fornicated," enjoying a freedom for which they would pay dearly later.

Cernuda's poem distills a frozen anger that is translated into self-contained imprecations, desperation, contempt, and, like a parenthesis of sun within the storm, delicate images of commiseration for the fate of that pair of provocateurs whom posterity—politicians, cultural dignitaries, snobs, and the establishment in general—recovers out of patriotism and national pride, castrating them thus of all that, when they lived, earned revulsion, and rejection of moral, religious, and enthroned values.

This poem came to mind because of the news that the Argentine government plans to repatriate the remains of Jorge Luis Borges from the cemetery of Plainpalais, in Geneva, where they rest—a pretty and inviting little plaza that looks like anything but hallowed ground—to Buenos Aires and bury them in the pretentious cemetery of La Recoleta.

The idea, apparently, has the support of the Argentine president herself, Cristina Fernández de Kirchner, and of her husband, the former President Kirchner, who—understandably and, in a way, inevitably—didn't want to miss the opportunity to bathe in culture and popularity by presiding over this pageantry in which, let there be no doubt, there would be speeches, flags, maybe even bugles, and adjectives such as "illustrious poet," "magical storyteller," and "transcendental essayist." The project was presented in Congress by the Peronist deputy María Beatriz Lenz, and since her party has the majority in parliament, it would surely be approved: How could those legislators, they too, miss the opportunity to shower themselves in culture as well? Thus, everything seemed well on its way to the grand grotesque: Borges's corpse elevated to the altars of the unfading nation that gave him his being by a government that emblematically embodies everything that Borges's life and work rejects and mocks: demagoguery, populism, poor taste, and vulgarity.

María Kodama, the writer's widow, was opposed to the repatriation, alleging that Borges decided at the end of his life, in full possession of his faculties, to leave Argentina, to die in Switzerland, a country where he had lived and studied as a teenager and that he always held quite dear. "In [a] democracy," she declared, "no person of any party can make use of, or try to make use of the body of another person, which is the most sacred thing, in the face of another who has given and continues to give his life for his love." María Kodama is utterly right, of course, but she may have shown too much optimism by calling a "democracy" that sui generis system in which, in each election, a few factions and Peronist gangs end up in disputes over power to then distribute it among themselves before the woeful impotence of the dwarfed opposition. In any event, there are enough educated and decent Argentines left in Borges's homeland who supported María Kodama and prevented this posthumous outrage against the most illustrious intellectual figure born in Argentina. Indeed, Deputy María Beatriz Lenz withdrew her project, at least for now, but it is not impossible that someone else might revive it in the future. (In Peru, from time to time, some deputy also proposes the repatriation of the remains of César Vallejo.)

It is true that circumstances have made Borges a "national glory" because this is the fate that awaits human beings who, because of their talent, virtues, and brilliance, offer humanity a great service in the fields of science, arts, or letters: to be immediately nationalized and transfigured for reasons of patriotic exaltation.

In reality, great talents are not "produced" by their countries, and, as such, Borges is not an Argentine "product." He came out of an almost indiscernible alliance of ideas, images, poems, novels, essays, philosophic and theological systems, coming from many languages and cultures, from the stimulating atmosphere of a family, a group of friends and acquaintances, but, mainly, from a disposition or personal gift, a unique and exclusive one, for dreaming, fantasizing, assimilating great literary creations and ordering Spanish words into phrases, pages, and books of extraordinary precision and unusual beauty. And for this reason, like Shakespeare, Goethe, Cervantes, and so many other eminent creators, Borges belongs not to Argentina but rather to all who read him and are dazzled by his imagination, his literary culture, his elegance, his irony, and his magnificent way of using our language, imposing on it the exactitude of English and the intelligence of French without losing the wild vigor of the Castilian.

Borges left his country because, as occurs with many writers, he was disgusted by what was happening there, or simply sick of being a "national glory" (after having been an unknown illustrious man until France, the rest of Europe, and the United States made it known that the Argentines had a genius in the house) or because, in his old age, as they say elephants do when they feel they are about to die, he wanted to spend the last stage of his life in a place where the kind of life that mattered to him—intellectual life—had begun: in that Switzerland where he was, or thought he was, happy, reading voraciously, learning languages, and infected by Swiss austerity and frugality, contracting the correctness and modesty that were permanent characteristics of his private life.

It was a perfectly legitimate decision, and those who truly admire Borges—who are not ignorant carpetbaggers, nor the semiliterate gossip columnists who also bathe themselves in culture as they traffic in genius—should honor it. It was unbecoming to invoke as a reason, to justify the repatriation, a citation of Borges's that was made in a random interview, according to which he wanted to be buried in La Recoleta just like his ancestors. Haven't those poor people realized that human beings, as opposed to rocks and animals, sometimes change their minds? If they had read Borges, they would know that he changed his mind countless times about several things (although never out of convenience or opportunism).

The decision that counts is the last one he took. The one that led him, when he was already a well-known and feted (but ravaged by illness) old man to leave it all and, as he would have done when he was an adolescent bookworm, begin again in a country where he would always be an unknown, in that dull, repressed, polyglot city of Calvin where, among libraries, classrooms, books, and foreign languages, he began to be Borges. It is a good resting place for the most international and cosmopolitan of writers, who was, in a way, also, paradoxically, viscerally provincial, that hallucinatory and erudite fantasist who was irreverent toward erudition, that shy old man-boy, at times moody, who never matured and as such was never corrupted.

Take heed, writer friends: no one can safeguard what he wrote against future manipulations, distortions, and misuse. But, in contrast, it is possible to take precautions against posthumous attacks like the one that was launched against poor Borges's bones and happily failed. Have yourself cremated and spread your ashes out over unreachable places, like the forest or the sea. It is preferable a thousand times over to feed fish or birds than those unscrupulous cannibals who fatten themselves on the vestiges of good writers!

Lima, February 2009

The Other State

A while back, I heard the president of Mexico, Felipe Calderón, explain to a small group of people that it took him three years to declare total war on narco-trafficking and to involve the army in it. This ferocious war has left more than 15,000 dead, countless injured, and enormous material damages.

The panorama that President Calderón outlined is hair-raising. The cartels had infiltrated state bodies like a hydra and were suffocating them, corrupting them, paralyzing them, or putting them at their service. They had formidable economic machinery at hand for this, which allowed them to pay functionaries, policemen, and politicians better salaries than public administration, and infrastructure of terror capable of liquidating anyone, no matter how protected. He gave some examples of cases in which it was proven that the final candidates of competitions to provide candidates for important official positions relating to security had been previously selected by the mafias.

The conclusion is simple: if the government didn't act immediately and with utmost energy, Mexico would run the risk of soon turning into a narco-state. The decision to incorporate the army, he explained, was not easy, but there was no alternative: it was a body prepared to fight and relatively untouched by the long, corrupting reach of the cartels.

Did President Calderón expect such a brutal reaction from the mafias? Did he suspect that narco-traffickers would be equipped with weaponry so lethal and a communications system so advanced that it allowed them to counterattack the armed forces so efficiently? He responded that no one could have foreseen such a development in the narcos' capacity for war. They were being beaten, but, they had to accept it, the war would last and, unfortunately, there would be many victims along the way.

This policy of Felipe Calderón's, which was, at the beginning, popular, has been losing support as Mexican cities fill with dead and wounded, and violence reaches indescribable manifestations of horror. Criticism has increased and opinion surveys indicate that now the majority of Mexicans are pessimistic about the dénouement and condemn this war.

The reasons critics cite are mainly the following: You should not enter a war you cannot win. The result is to mobilize the army into a type of battle for which it has not been prepared and will have the perverse effect of contaminating the armed forces with corruption and will give the cartels the possibility of also using soldiers for their ends. Narco-trafficking should not be confronted openly and in the light of day, like an enemy country: it must be combated the same way it acts, in the shadows, with stealthy and specialized security bodies, which is a police task.

Many of these critics do not say what they really think, because we're dealing with something *beyond words*: that it is absurd to enter a war that the drug cartels have already won. That they are here to stay. That no matter how many bosses and fugitives are struck dead or taken prisoner, or how many shipments of cocaine are captured, the situation will only get worse. The fallen narcos will be replaced by other, younger ones, more powerful ones, better-armed ones, greater in number, who will keep an industry running that has done nothing more than extend itself across the world for decades, without being significantly wounded by the hits it receives.

This truth is applicable not only to Mexico but also to a fair part of Latin American countries. In some, such as Colombia, Bolivia, and Peru, it is already evident, while in others, like Chile and Uruguay, it is happening more slowly. But we are dealing with an irresistible process that, despite the dizzying sums of resources and effort, is still there, vigorous, adapting itself to new circumstances, overcoming the obstacles placed in its way with notable quickness, and making use of new technologies and of globalization like the most developed transnational companies of the world do.

The problem is not one of policing, but an economic one. There is a market for drugs that is growing in an unstoppable way, as much in developed countries as underdeveloped countries, and the narco-trafficking industries feed it because it yields abundant wealth. The victories that the war against drugs can show are insignificant compared with the number of consumers on the five continents. And it affects all social classes. The effects are as damaging to health as they are to institutions. And in the democracies of the third world, like cancer, it is eating away at them.

So, then, is there no solution? Are we condemned to living, sooner or later, in narco-states like the one President Felipe Calderón wanted to prevent? A solution does exist. It consists of decriminalizing drug consumption through an agreement between consuming countries and producing countries, as *The Economist* and a fair number of lawyers, professors, sociologists, and scientists in many countries have been saying without being heard. In February 2009, the Commission on Drugs and Democracy, created by three former presidents, Fernando Henrique Cardoso, César Gaviria, and Ernesto Zedillo, proposed the decriminalization of marijuana and a policy that prioritizes prevention over repression. These are encouraging signs.

Legalization entails dangers, naturally. And as such it should be accompanied by a redirection of the enormous sums that are

today invested in repression toward education campaigns and rehabilitation and information policies like the ones that had such
good results when applied to tobacco. The argument according
to which legalization would incite consumption like a fire, especially among young people and children, is, without a doubt,
valid. But it is probably a passing and containable phenomenon
if countered with effective prevention campaigns. In fact, in countries like Holland where permissive steps have been taken in the
consumption of drugs, the increase was fleeting and after a certain
time has stabilized. In Portugal, according to a study by the Cato
Institute, consumption decreased after the decriminalization of
drug possession for personal use.

Why do governments, who confirm daily how costly and
useless political repression is, refuse to consider decriminalization and carrying out studies with the participation of scientists,
social workers, judges, and agencies who specialize in the gains
and consequences it would bring? Because, as explained twenty
years ago by Milton Friedman, who foresaw the magnitude the
problem would reach if not resolved in time and suggested legalization, powerful interests prevent it. Not only those who oppose
it for reasons of principle. The greatest obstacles are the bodies
and people who benefit from the repression of drugs and, naturally, defend the source of their labor tooth and nail. Their reasons are not ethical, religious, or political; rather, crude interest is
the greatest obstacle to ending the overwhelming criminality associated with narco-trafficking, the greatest threat to democracy
in Latin America, more so than the authoritarian populism of
Hugo Chávez and his satellites.

What is happening in Mexico is tragic and is a harbinger of
what, sooner or later, will be lived in countries that insist on unleashing a war that has already been lost against the other state that
has risen up right under our noses without our wanting to see it.

Lima, January 2010

The Defeat of Fascism

The victory of Ollanta Humala in the second round of the presidential elections this past June has saved Peru from installing a dictatorship that, with the protection of an electoral majority, would have exonerated the regime of Fujimori and Montesinos (1990–2000) of the crimes and theft it committed, as well as the trampling of laws and the Constitution that marked that decade. And it would have given power back to the seventy-seven civilians and soldiers who, for crimes committed in those years, are in prison or on trial. In the most peaceful and civilized of ways—an electoral process—fascism would have been revived in Peru.

Fascism is a word that has been used so lightly by the left, more as an incantation or an insult against an adversary than as a precise political concept, that to many it will seem like a label without greater significance to designate a typical third-world dictatorship. It isn't, rather, something deeper, more complex, and all-consuming than those traditional coups d'état in which a caudillo mobilizes the barracks, climbs to power, fills his pockets and those of his buddies, until, repelled by a country that has been overexploited to the point of ruin, he goes on the run.

The regime of Fujimori and Montesinos—it shames me to say it—was popular. It was backed by the solidarity of the business class because of their free-market policy and the bonanza brought by the increase in prices of raw materials, and by wide sectors of the middle class due to the blows delivered by Sendero Luminoso and the Movimiento Revolucionario Túpac Amaru, whose terrorist actions—blackouts, kidnappings, protection fees, bombs, murders—had them in a state of insecurity and panic. Rural and working-class sectors were won via paternalistic policies of distributions and handouts. Those who decried the abuses of human rights, torture, disappearances, and massive annihilation of peasants, workers, and students accused (falsely in the majority of cases) of collaborating with terrorism were persecuted and intimidated, and suffered all kinds of reprisals. Montesinos adopted the flowering of a foul tabloid press, whose raison d'être was drowning the opposition in opprobrium through invented scandals.

Communications media were bribed, extorted, and neutralized, such that the regime had only to contend with a minimal and muffled opposition, the sufficient amount to boast of respecting the freedom to criticize. Journalists and the owners of communications media were called by Montesinos to his dark cave in the Intelligence Services, where not only was their complicity paid for with bags of money, they were also secretly filmed so that there would be graphic evidence of their vileness. Businessmen, judges, politicians, soldiers, journalists, and representatives of the entire professional and social spectrum passed through there. They all came out with their gift under their arms, happy and despicable.

The Constitution and the laws were modified for the dictator's needs, so that he and his accomplices in parliament could comfortably reelect themselves. There was no limit to the cunning, and they ended up breaking all records in Peru's history of corruption. Illicit sales of weapons, businesses with narco-traffickers to whom the dictatorship opened wide the doors of the jungle so they could come with their small planes to take coca paste, elevated commissions for all major commercial and industrial operations, until they accumulated in ten years of impunity the amazing sum of about $6 billion, according to estimates by the general prosecutor who, with the restoration of democracy, investigated the illicit activities of that decade.

This is, to summarize, what would return to Peru with Peruvians' votes if Madame Keiko Fujimori won the elections. In other words, fascism in the twenty-first century. This is no longer embodied by swastikas, an imperial salute, goose steps, and a hysterical commander in chief vomiting out racist insults from up on a platform. But rather, precisely, what it represented in Peru, from 1990 to 2000, with Fujimori's government. A gang of the soulless and voracious who, allied with immoral businessmen, despicable journalists, gunmen, paid assassins, and the ignorance of wide sectors of society, established a regime of intimidation, brutality, demagoguery, bribery, and corruption that, under the guise of guaranteeing social peace, perpetuates itself in power.

The victory of Ollanta Humala has shown that there is still in Peru a majority that was not damaged by so many years of injustice and perverse civic values. That this was only the majority by three points is hair-raising, since it indicates that the underlying foundations of democracy are very weak and that almost half of voters in the country prefer to live under despotism than freedom. It is one of the great tasks now in the hands of Humala's government. The moral and political regeneration of a nation that, through terrorism on the one hand and, on the other, through a comprehensive dictatorship, have led to such an ideological deviation that a good part of it now longs for the authoritarian regime it suffered under for ten years.

A particularly sad characteristic of this electoral campaign has been how aligned with the option of dictatorship the so-called A-listers—the most prosperous and best-educated people in Peru, who went through excellent schools where one learns English, who send their children to study in the United States, that "elite" which is convinced that culture comes down to two words: whiskey and Miami—have been. Terrified by the lies invented by their own newspapers, radio programs, and TV stations that Ollanta Humala would replicate in Peru the policy of nationalizations and economic interventionism that has ruined Venezuela, they unleashed a campaign of indescribable poisoning, slander, and infamy to block the path for the Gana Perú candidate that included, of course, dismissals of and threats to the most independent and capable journalists. That the latter, without allowing themselves to feel intimidated, resisted the threats and fought, putting their professional survival on the line, to make spaces in the media where the opponent could have a voice, has been one of the most dignified occurrences in this campaign. (For example, the work carried out by the digital publication *La Mula* stands out.) That is how one of the most indignant of roles was carried out by the archbishop of Lima, Cardinal Cipriani of Opus Dei, one of the pillars of the Fujimori-Montesinos dictatorship, who honored me by reading in the pulpits of Lima's churches during the Sunday mass a pamphlet attacking me for having accused him of remaining silent when Fujimori forced the sterilization, under false pretenses, of almost three hundred thousand peasant women, many of whom died of hemorrhages from that villainous operation.

And now, what will happen? I am reading an editorial in *El Comercio*, the daily belonging to the group that overcame all manner of infamy in the campaign against Ollanta Humala, that is written with great moderation and, I would say, with enthusiasm, for the economic policy that the new president plans to apply, which has also been celebrated in a television program by board members of the Confederation of Business Leaders, one of whom stated, "In Peru, what we need is social policy." What has happened for all of them to suddenly turn in favor of Humala? The new president has only repeated in these recent days what he said throughout his whole campaign: that he would respect businesses and market policies, that his model was not Venezuela, but rather Brazil, since he knew very well that development had to continue so that the fight against poverty and exclusion would be efficient. Naturally it is preferable for those nostalgic for the dictatorship to now hide their fangs and purr, affectionately, at the doors of the new government. But you don't have to take them seriously. Their vision is small, petty, and self-interested, as they showed in these last few months. And above all, you don't have to believe them when they talk about freedom and democracy, words to which they resort only when they feel threatened. The system of free-market business is worth more than they are, and that is why the new government should maintain it and perfect it, opening it to new business leaders who finally understand that economic freedom cannot be separated from political freedom and from social freedom, and that equality of opportunity is an inalienable principle in all genuinely democratic systems. If Ollanta Humala's government understands it thus and proceeds accordingly, we will at last have, as in Chile, Uruguay, and Brazil, a left that is genuinely democratic and liberal, and Peru will not again run the risk it has run in these last few months, of going back to being mired in the backwardness and barbarism of a dictatorship.

Madrid, June 2011

A Call for Harmony

Soon the hearings will begin regarding the dispute over maritime borders between Chile and Peru that is taking place before the International Court of Justice in The Hague. Many of us would have preferred that this discrepancy be resolved through bilateral negotiations, with the discretion of chanceries, but since no agreement was possible, litigation is where reason and common sense indicate it should be: before an international legal body that both countries recognize and whose verdict the Peruvian and Chilean governments have committed to accepting.

With this motive, on July 25 of this year, in Lima, Santiago, and Madrid simultaneously, we made public "A Call for Harmony," signed by fifteen Chileans and fifteen Peruvians, of different professions, vocations, and political positions, but all of us firmly committed to democratic culture. This is the initiative of two writers, Jorge Edwards and myself, who, thirty-three years ago, in June 1979, upon the occasion of the centennial of the War of the Pacific, also led a declaration of ten Chileans and ten Peruvians, proclaiming our will to work for our two countries to live "always in peace and friendship." We recall on this occasion that the main enemy of Peru and Chile was not our group of neighbors, but rather underdevelopment, and that the battle against hunger, ignorance, unemployment, the lack of democracy and freedom, "can only be won together, fighting in solidarity against those who seek to make us enemies and obstruct our progress."

When that first manifesto appeared, Chile and Peru were suffering under military dictatorships (presided over by General Pinochet and by General Morales Bermúdez, respectively) that censored the press, persecuted dissidents, and committed barbarous violations against human rights. Today, fortunately, both countries enjoy freedom and legality, have governments born out of free elections that respect the right to criticize, practice market policies, and encourage investment such that they have given great momentum to their economic policies. Although, of course, there is still much to do and the inequalities in income and opportunities are still very large, the lessening of poverty, the growth of the middle class, the influx of foreign investment, the control of inflation and public spending, and the strengthening of institutions in both societies are notable, the fastest on record in their history.

Within this framework of sustained progress, the economic exchange between Chile and Peru also denotes an unprecedented dynamism. Chilean businesses operate all over Peru and have created many thousands of job positions, and, for a few years now, several Peruvian companies have also started to invest in and work in Chile. The number of Peruvians who, since the Chilean economy began to take off, have emigrated to their neighboring country and put down roots there is in the tens of thousands.

All of this is good and beneficial to both countries and should be encouraged because, besides contributing to the material progress of Chile and Peru, it will increasingly cause the disappearance of the susceptibilities, resistances, animosity, and prejudices that nationalist sectors (as exalted as they are irresponsible) are determined to maintain and are inciting on the basis of the border dispute that is being settled in The Hague. These manifestations of cheap patriotism with which certain press bodies and extremist political groups try to sow discord between both countries are not disinterested. Their secret intention is to justify the buildup of weapons, in other words, the dizzying investments signified by the purchase in our day of those lethal toys with which armies play, taking resources that would be better invested in areas of health, education, and infrastructure, indispensable for economic development not to remain confined to the level of high and medium income and to reach where it is most needed, the disadvantaged and marginal sectors. Although it is true that in recent years these sectors have shrunk, they continue to be intolerably extensive today. And there is no development worthy of that name if a democracy is not capable of creating, in the economic realm, equal opportunities for all of its citizens.

This is the raison d'être of our "Call for Harmony." Whatever the verdict of the International Court may be, it should serve to definitively fix those borders and annihilate forever that focus of periodic discord between both countries. And at the same time show the rest of Latin America the civilized and peaceful way in which it should settle border conflicts. It is necessary to remember, in this context, that the dispute of limits has been, for two centuries, one of the most fecund sources of Latin American underdevelopment. It has caused senseless wars in which the majority of corpses are always provided by the poor and that have served as a pretext for a buildup of weapons that, without a single exception, allowed corrupt big shots and politicians to fill their pockets with illegal commissions. Another consequence has been the elephantine growth of the military forces and their role in political life, one of the reasons for which democratic culture has been, until quite recently, an exotic plant that acclimated with such difficulty in the majority of Latin American countries.

But, without a doubt, the most disastrous legacy of these quarrels, artificially provoked in many cases, has been the planting of nationalism, an obtuse ideology that separates and makes countries enemies of each other. This explains why, although they speak the same language and share a tradition, history, and social issues, Latin American countries have not been capable of uniting, as, for example, Europe has done, in a great political confederation, and cannot even make the regional free-trade treaties that they sign from time to time work efficiently, and so, sooner or later, these end up stuck or annulled by the spirit of pettiness with which they are carried out in practice. Many of these conflicts are only put off and are still lurking, like sinister threats that can come to pass under any pretext, unleashing wars or coups d'état that would ruin in days the economic achievements made over many years.

It is true that Latin America, with the exceptions of the Cuban dictatorship of the Castro brothers—the longest in its history—and the semidictatorship of Commander Chávez (which, if there are free elections, could end this October), has started to leave behind this terrible period of military dictatorships, opting for democracy. Today the immense majority of the continent's countries have civilian governments, elections, and a more or less free press, and institutions are beginning to work, despite the high indices of criminality, generally associated with narco-trafficking and the gigantic differences in income between the ruling class and its base. But even taking into account these negative factors, there is unequivocal progress, especially in the economic realm, thanks to some pragmatic policies and an opening that has been replacing the catastrophic policies of yesteryear, when economic nationalism advocated for closing borders, nationalizing "strategic industries," and practicing inward development. Only a small handful of countries, such as Bolivia and Ecuador, still cling to those anachronisms, and so it goes for them. But the rest are growing, and some countries, among them Chile and Peru, at a very good pace. Inarguable proof is how little Latin America has suffered during the financial crisis shaking Europe and the United States. It still has not affected too much a region that, until very recently, would get pneumonia when the United States and the rest of the West had a mere cold.

So that this progress can be perfected and accelerated, the old quarrels over borders that have kept Latin American countries distanced from one another or as enemies must vanish and follow the fine example of Europe, growing closer and closer to one another so that their borders, thanks to the exchanges of all kinds that foster cooperation and friendship, start disappearing and allow for a lasting union under the sign of freedom.

Madrid, July 2012

Empty the Shelves!

Since shortages and scarcity are affecting Venezuela and increasing popular discontent, President Nicolás Maduro, who may not know much about economics but is a real man of bravado, decided to deal with the problem immediately. He explained to his people that the high inflation the country is suffering (the highest in Latin America by 57 percent) is the product of a plot devised by the United States, the hoarding businessmen, retailers, and opposition parties set on destroying the Bolivarian revolution, or "Twenty-First-Century Socialism." And, in one stroke of the pen, he ordered that the prices of food and appliances be cut by 50 and even 70 percent, while he simultaneously sent soldiers and combat corps to occupy retail establishments and sent a good number of "conspirators"—in other words, the owners of stores and warehouses—to prison.

The campaign was launched by President Maduro with the slogan "Empty the Shelves!" The order was understood by a good number of the confused as carte blanche for looting, and, especially in Valencia but also in Caracas and other cities, there were attacks and robberies in the midst of extreme chaos. It was pathetic to listen to long-suffering Venezuelan housewives explaining to reporters from official TV how happy they were about those spectacular sales that would, going forward, refresh their refrigerators and kitchens and ensure their families two meals per day.

At the same time that he defeated inflation with a fist to the table, auctioning and confiscating food-product and appliance chains, President Maduro, through the approval of the Enabling Law, ensured for himself the absolute power that for one year would allow him to govern without laws, in the comfortable and efficient manner of dictator. To obtain this attribute, the Venezuelan National Assembly proceeded to withdraw immunity from an opposition deputy, María Mercedes Aranguren, and to replace her with her substitute, Deputy Carlos Flores, who, from day to night (and through generous sinecures) became a Chavist and voted in favor of the aforementioned law. In sum, once the hope these operations created for a public desperate to end corruption had passed, the growing poverty and anarchy in Venezuela will be the very high price the country will have to pay for the irresponsible demagoguery of this time. Without a doubt, contrary to the government's calculations, it will be translated into a new and more crushing defeat of the government in the next elections, on December 9, which will force it, as occurred with the presidential elections, to undertake a new act of monumental fraud in order to stay in power despite being discredited and despite the ruin into which its wretched country plunges further every day.

Venezuela never had a flourishing agricultural industry commensurate with the enormous agricultural possibilities available to it, but with Chavism its expropriations and invasions, the arbitrary taking of farms, and the suffocating prevailing bureaucratization, agrarian production in certain regions was reduced to a minimum and simply disappeared in others. The result of all of this is that the country must import almost 95 percent of what it consumes, something that in the time of oil's apogee was barely noticed. But the revolutionary control instituted by

Chávez and Maduro in the industry has radically reduced Venezuelan oil production, while, at the same time, the policy of currency control, one of the most prosperous sources of corruption, has turned from providing dollars to the retailers and businessmen for the import of raw materials and products from abroad into a real nightmare. Only the most government-connected can get dollars, or those who are willing to pay very expensive commissions for them. Others must obtain dollars on the black market, where the dollar is worth ten times the official price. This is the explanation for the out-of-control increase in prices and for generalized scarcity. The brave sales imposed *manu militari* by Maduro will only serve to accelerate the generalized scarcity—the shelves will, in fact, end up empty—and the black market, which will grow enormously, will only be within reach of the privileged, in other words, those favored by the regime or by the dizzying corruption generated by interventionist policies in the economy. In other words, the policies of Chavist socialism will have contributed to aggravating the economic and social differences it set out to abolish.

At the same time that these things were happening in Venezuela, in Beijing the Central Committee of the Chinese Communist Party was announcing a new economic policy, widening already-existent free markets to ensure a better distribution of resources and allow the participation of private companies, Chinese as well as foreign, in the state's industries. (It also warned, however, that this economic opening would not have a corresponding political one, since the Communist Party would continue being the supreme arbiter of social life.) It is improbable that the Chinese Communist Party will happily adopt these measures of unequivocal capitalist orientation through ideological conversion. No, it is resigned to them because, loyal to the traditional pragmatism of China's culture, it has understood that collectivism and economic statism lead to the ruin of countries, and, besides impoverishing them and setting them backward, they multiply social injustices, creating a growing distance between privileged functionaries of the nomenclatura and the average citizens who, besides suffering insecurity and fear, spend their lives waiting in lines and earning miserable salaries without the least equality of opportunities. These elemental truths, which already reached the Soviet Union before its collapse and are beginning to appear, although very shyly, in Cuba, seem out of the intellectual reach and political senses of President Maduro and his economic advisers.

It's not difficult to foresee, as such, what the immediate future holds for Venezuela, a country that given its copious abundance of resources should have the highest standard of living in Latin America. In light of the worsening shortage and scarcity—which obey the laws of economics and not political ukase—the regime's next step will be to proceed to the progressive nationalization of stores and businesses that "conspire" against the revolution, speculating and starving its people. The small spaces for private economy will start closing until they disappear and fall into the hands of an inept and corrupt bureaucracy, such that the rationing of products from the family basket, which already exists to a large degree, will start extending like a hydra through all the gaps in the economy until it makes Venezuela a country as state-dominated as Cuba or North Korea. The inevitable corollary of this state hegemony will be the disappearance of the scarce independent communications media that, through enormous sacrifices and courage, still resists governmental harassment.

Will everything that the Chavist revolution has signified in hopes, efforts, and violence be worth it? It is true that the democracy it brought down was inefficient, spendthrift, demagogic, and rather insensitive to great social problems and had thus generated the great discontent of a people who naïvely saw—once again in Latin America's wretched history—a savior in a charismatic and foul-mouthed caudillo. The result is in plain view: an impoverished, damaged Venezuela, devastated by demagoguery and corruption, full of nouveaux riches with ill-gotten wealth, which, once freedom and good judgment are recovered, will spend many years recovering everything it lost with the collapse of its democracy.

Madrid, November 2013

Part IV

Between Namesakes

Although it is with certain delay, now that I have some time, I'd like to comment on the article by my friend Mario Benedetti accusing me of political frivolity and of resorting to a low blow ("protected perhaps in the warehouses of fame") and illicit games in an ideological debate that appeared in *El País* (April 9, 1984) and which has been reprinted all over the world, from Holland to Brazil.

Although it has been a few years since I last saw Benedetti, and although our political ideas have grown apart, my affection for the good companion with whom I shared political and literary anxieties in the 1960s and 1970s has not changed, and less still my admiration for his good poetry and excellent stories. I am, even, an avid reader of his articles, which, despite often differing with them, I take as a model of well-written journalism. It pains me, as such, that he thought me capable of insulting him in the interview that appeared in Italy in the magazine *Panorama* that Valerio Riva titled, dramatically, "The Corrupt and the Content." One thing that's clear is that intellectual controversy is possible only by excluding from it insults, and I challenge anyone to look, even with a magnifying glass, for any in a text with my signature. Of interviews, I am less sure. Benedetti knows as well as I the subtle or brutal alterations of which one is victim when agreeing to an interview, especially if they touch on politics, something that is always white-hot when it comes to Latin America.

The interview with *Panorama* is faithful in essence to what I said, but not in the emphasis given to certain phrases. Some of the matters I touched upon in it, it's true, demanded to be developed more carefully and with more nuance to not come across as mere ukases. Since they are currently outstanding, it is worth revisiting them in this—cordial—controversy with my namesake.

The first is the intellectual as a factor in the *political* underdevelopment of our countries. I highlight *political* because this is at the root of the matter. It is an extraordinary paradox that the same person who, in poetry or novels, has demonstrated audacity and freedom, an aptitude for breaking with tradition and conventions, and for renewing forms, myths, and languages from the root, should also be capable of a disconcerting conformism in the ideological realm that he unhesitatingly adopts with prudence, shyness, and docility, while supporting with his prestige the most doubtful dogmas and, even, the mere slogans of propaganda.

Let's examine the case of the two great creators Benedetti mentions—Neruda and Carpentier—asking me mockingly if they are more to blame for our miseries "than the United Fruit Company or Anaconda Copper Mining." I consider Neruda's poetry to be the richest and most liberating written in Castilian Spanish in this century, a poetry as vast as a painting by Picasso, a firmament in which there is mystery, wonder, extreme simplicity and complexity, realism and surrealism, lyric and epic, intuition and reason, and an artisanal knowledge as vast as the capacity for invention. How could it be that the same person who revolutionized the poetry of language thus was the disciplined militant who wrote poems in praise of Stalin and for whom none of the crimes of Stalinism—the purges, the camps, the rigged trials, the murders, the sclerosis of Marxism—caused the slightest ethical disturbance, none of those conflicts and dilemmas that many artists experienced? The entire political dimension of Neruda's oeuvre is affected by the same conformist schematic of his militancy. There was no moral duplicity in him: his view of the world, as a politician and as a writer (when he wrote about politics), was Manichaean and dogmatic. Thanks to Neruda, countless Latin Americans discovered poetry; thanks to him—his influence was gigantic—countless young people came to believe that the most dignified way to fight the injustices of imperialism and chain reactions was opposing them through Stalinist orthodoxy. The case of Alejo Carpentier is not that of Neruda's. His elegant fictions enclose a deeply skeptical and pessimistic concept of history; they are beautiful parables, of refined learning and cunning words, about the futility of human endeavors. When, in his final years, this aesthete tried to write optimistic novels, more in consonance with his political position, he had to attack some vital center of his creative forces and wound his unconscious vision, because his oeuvre became artistically impoverished. But what political moral lesson did this great writer impart to his Latin American readers? That of a respectful functionary of the revolution who, in his diplomatic post in Paris, completely abdicated the faculty of, let's not call it criticizing, but rather of thinking politically. Everything he said, did, or wrote in this realm, starting in 1959, was not opining—which would mean taking risks, inventing, running the risk of being right or being wrong—but rather, beatifically repeating the dictates of the government he served.

I will surely be reproached for being petty and obtuse: perhaps the literary contribution of a Neruda or a Carpentier is enough for us to forget about their political behavior? Are we going to turn into inquisitors demanding that writers be rigorous, honest, and audacious not only when they invent but also in politics and morality? I think that in this Mario Benedetti and I would agree.

In Latin America, a writer is not just a writer. Due to the nature of our problems, to a very deep-rooted tradition, to the fact that we have a platform and a way to make ourselves heard, this is, also, someone from whom an active contribution is expected in solving problems. This could be naïve and mistaken. It would be more comfortable for us, without a doubt, for the writer in Latin America to be viewed as someone whose exclusive function is to entertain or spellbind with his or her books. But Benedetti and I know that it is not like this; that it is also expected— rather, demanded—that we continuously make pronouncements about what is happening and that we help others take a position. It is a tremendous responsibility. Of course a writer can shun this and, despite it, write masterpieces. But those who do not shun it have the obligation, in that political arena where what they say and write reverberates in others' ways of acting and thinking, of being so honest, rigorous, and careful when it comes to dreaming.

Neither Neruda nor Carpentier seems to me to have carried out that civic role in the way they carried out the artistic one. My reproach, to them and to whoever believes, as they did, that the responsibility of a leftist intellectual consists of putting themselves at the unconditional service of a party or regime of this label, is not that they were Communists. It's that they were Communists in a way undignified for a writer: without independently reformulating their words or checking them against the facts, the ideas, anathemas, stereotypes, or slogans that they promote; that they were Communists without imagination or any spirit of criticism, abdicating an intellectual's highest duty: being free. Many Latin American intellectuals have renounced risky ideas and originality, and that is why, among us, political debate tends to be so poor: invective and cliché. That there might be, among Latin American writers, a majority with this attitude seems to comfort Mario Benedetti and give him a feeling of triumph. It causes me anguish, since it means that despite the very rich artistic flourishing that our continent has produced, we have still not come out of ideological obscurantism. There are, fortunately, some exceptions, within the intellectual poverty that characterizes our political literature, such as the authors I cited in the interview: Paz, Edwards, Sábato. They are not the only ones, of course. In recent years, to mention only the case of Mexico, writers such as Gabriel Zaid and Enrique Krauze have produced splendid essays about current politics and economics. But why are these exceptions so scarce? I think there are two reasons. The first one: the damages and horrors of military dictatorships lead the writer eager to combat them to choose what seems most efficient and expeditious, to avoid all nuances, ambiguities, or doubts that could be confused for weakness or that might "give the enemy ammunition." And the second reason: the fear of being "Satanized" if he/she exercises criticism against the left itself, which, just as it has been inept in Latin America at producing original thought, has demonstrated an unsurpassable mastery in the art of disfiguration and slander of its critics (I have a trunk full of clippings to prove it).

Benedetti cites a good number of poets and writers who were murdered, jailed, and tortured by Latin American dictatorships. (It is significant to what I am trying to say that he forgot to mention a single Cuban, as if writers had not been through the jails on the island and as if there were not dozens of intellectuals from that country in exile. On the other hand, out of carelessness, he places Roque Dalton among the martyrs of imperialism: in truth, he was a martyr of sectarianism, since he was murdered by his own comrades.) Have I ever placed the bloody and stupid character of those dictatorships in question? I feel the same disgust for them that Benedetti does. But in any event, those murders and abuses show the cruelty and blindness of those who committed them and not necessarily the political clairvoyance of their victims.

Which some of them had, naturally. Others were lacking. Heroism does not always come from lucidity; it is often the offspring of fanaticism. The problem is not in the brutality of our dictatorships, about which Benedetti and I agree, as well as the need to do away with them as soon as possible. The problem is, with what do we replace them? With democratic governments, as I would like? Or with other dictatorships, like the Cuban one, which he defends? Just like in long novels, which we two Marios like so much, this remains to be continued next week.

London, May 1984

Liberalism Across Two Millennia

Not long ago, the local government of a small town of a thousand inhabitants called El Borge, in the province of Málaga, called for a referendum. Neighbors had to choose one of these two options: humanity or neoliberalism. Many citizens took to the polls and the result was as follows: 515 votes for humanity and 4 votes for neoliberalism. Since then, I cannot stop thinking about those four musketeers, who, faced with such a dramatic dilemma, did not hesitate to attack in the name of that macabre scarecrow, neoliberalism. Are we dealing with four clowns or four lucid beings? With a "Borgesian" joke or the only manifestation of sense in that farcical plebiscite?

Soon after, in Chiapas, the last media hero of Western political frivolity, Subcomandante Marcos, called an International Congress Against Neoliberalism, which many Hollywood luminaries attended, some late Gaullist or other, like my friend Regis Débray, and Danielle Mitterand, the ever-present widow of President François Mitterand, who gave her socialist blessing to the event.

These are picturesque episodes, but it would be a serious mistake to underestimate them as the insignificant fluttering of human idiocy. In reality, they are just the climactic and extreme exasperation of a vast political and ideological movement, solidly implanted in left, center, and right sectors, united in their tenacious mistrust of freedom as an instrument for solving humanity's problems, that has found in this very new ghost built by fears and phobias—"neoliberalism," also called "the unique way of thinking" in the slang of sociologists and political scientists, a sacrificial goat on whom to offload past and present calamities of global history.

If wise professors from the University of Paris, from Harvard, or in Mexico bend over backward to show that free markets only serve to make the rich richer and the poor poorer, and that internationalization and globalization only benefit large transnational corporations, allowing them to squeeze underdeveloped countries to the point of asphyxiation and to destroy the planet's ecology at will, why wouldn't the uninformed citizens of El Borge or Chiapas believe that the true enemy of the human being, the one to blame for all evil, suffering, poverty, exploitation, discrimination, abuses, and crimes against human rights committed on five continents against millions of human beings is that destructive threatening chimera: neoliberalism? It's not the first time in history that that which Karl Marx called a "fetish"—an artificial construct, but at the service of very concrete interests—acquired consistency and started to cause great disturbances in life, like the genie unwisely catapulted into existence by Aladdin when he rubbed the marvelous lamp.

I consider myself a liberal and I know many people who are and many more who are not. But throughout a trajectory that is starting to become long, I still have not met a single *neo*liberal. In contrast to Marxism, or•to fascisms, liberalism doesn't really constitute any kind of dogmatism, a closed and self-sufficient ideology with predetermined responses for all social problems, but, rather, is a doctrine that, starting with a relatively small and clear number of basic principles structured around the defense of political and economic freedom—in other words, democracy and free markets—admits a great variety of tendencies and degrees. What it has not admitted until now, nor will it in the future, is that caricature made by its enemies with the tag of "neoliberalism." A "neo" is someone who is something without being so, someone who is simultaneously within and outside of something, a slippery hybrid, a factotum who settles in without ever coming to identify completely with a value, an idea, a regime, or a doctrine. To say "neoliberal" is akin to saying "semi" or "pseudo" liberal, in other words, the pure opposite. You are either for freedom or against it, but you can't be semi or pseudo in favor of freedom, just like you can't be "semipregnant," "semialive," or "semidead." The formula was invented not to express a conceptual reality, but rather to semantically devalue, with the corrosive weapon of derision, the doctrine that symbolizes, better than any other, the extraordinary advances that, as we approach the end of the millennium, freedom has made over the long course of human civilization.

This is something that we liberals should celebrate with serenity and happiness, not triumphalism, and with the clear conscience that, although what has been achieved is notable, what still remains to be done is more important. And also that, since nothing is definitive or fateful in human history, the progress obtained in recent decades for a culture of freedom is not irreversible, and, unless we know how to defend it, it could come to a standstill, and the free world could lose ground, due to a push by the two new masks of authoritarian collectivism and the spirit of tribalism that have come to substitute communism with the most hardened adversaries of democracy: nationalism and religious fundamentalism.

To a liberal, the most important thing that has happened in this century of great totalitarian offensives against the culture of freedom is that fascism as well as communism, which came, each at its own moment, to threaten the survival of democracy, now belong to the past, to a dark history of violence and unspeakable crimes against human rights and rationality. And nothing indicates that their ashes can be resuscitated in the near future. Of course, there are still remnants of fascism in the world that, at times, embodied by ultranationalist and xenophobic parties such as Le Pen's National Front, in France, or Jorg Haider's Liberal Party, in Austria, attract dangerously high electoral support. But neither these sprouts of fascism, nor the anachronistic vestiges of the vast Marxist archipelago represented today by the withering specters of Cuba and North Korea, constitute a serious alternative, or even a considerable threat, to the democratic option. Dictatorships still abound, of course, but in contrast to the great totalitarian empires, they lack a messianic aura and ecumenical aspirations; a good deal of them, such as China, now try to reconcile the political monolithism of one party with market economies and private business. In vast regions of Africa and Asia, especially in Islamic societies, fundamentalist dictatorships have emerged that, regarding women, education, information, and the most basic civil and moral rights, have made their countries go backward to a state of primitive barbarism. But with all the horror they represent, countries such as Libya, Afghanistan, Sudan, and Iran are not challenges that should make us seriously doubt the culture of freedom: the anachronism of the ideology they profess condemns those regimes to be quickly left behind in the race in which free countries already have a decisive advantage—that of modernity.

Now, along with this somber geography of the persistence of dictatorships in recent decades, we also have to celebrate an overwhelming advance in the culture of freedom in vast swaths of Central and Eastern Europe, in countries in Southeast Asia and Latin America where, with the exception of Cuba, an explicit dictatorship, and Peru, a veiled dictatorship, all the other countries—for the first time in history—have civilian governments, born of more or less free elections, and, even more novel, they all apply—some with more reluctance than enthusiasm, at times with more clumsiness than skill—market policies, or at least policies that are closer to a free economy than one that is interventionist, populist, and state-run, which traditionally characterized the continent's governments. But, perhaps, what is most significant about this change in Latin America is not the quantity but the quality. Because despite the fact that it is still common to hear howling against "neoliberalism" (like wolves at the moon), to some intellectuals who've been sent to the unemployment lines by the fall of collectivist ideology, what is certain is that, at least for now, from one corner to another of Latin America there is a dominant, solid consensus in favor of democratic systems against dictatorial regimes and collectivist utopias. Although this consensus is more restricted in economic policies, all governments, although it may shame them to admit, and some even, with real hypocrisy, allow themselves to also unleash rhetorical harangues (to cover their own backs) against "neoliberalism," do not have any recourse save for to privatize businesses, liberalize prices, open markets, try to control inflation, and seek to insert their economies in international markets. Because after many mishaps, they have ended up understanding that in our day it is suicidal for a country not to follow those guidelines. Or in clearer terms, they would condemn themselves to poverty, backwardness, and even disintegration. Even a good part of the Latin American left has evolved from being the fiercest enemy of economic freedom to adopting as their own Václav Havel's known confession: "Although my heart is on the left, I've always known that the only economic system that works is the market. This is the only natural economy; the only one that really makes sense, the only one that can lead to prosperity; because it is the only one that reflects the very nature of life."

This progress is important and gives liberal theses historic validation. But it in no way justifies complacency, since one of the most untarnished (and rare) liberal certainties is that historical determinism does not exist, that history is not written in advance, that it is the work of humans and that, just as they can get measures right to move it in the direction of progress and civilization, they can also be wrong, and out of conviction, apathy, or cowardice can direct it toward anarchy, poverty, obscurantism, and barbarism. The consolidation of the advances achieved for democratic culture will fundamentally depend on us, that is, on our ideas, our votes, and on the decisions of those we bring to power, as will the ability of these to expand, or have the spaces they control shrink, like Balzac's sharkskin.

For liberals, the struggle for the development of freedom in history is, above all, an intellectual struggle, a battle of ideas. The Allies won the war against the Axis, but that military victory only confirmed the superiority of a view of man and a wide, horizontal, pluralist, tolerant, and democratic society over one that was narrow-minded, limited, racist, discriminatory, and vertical. And the disintegration of the Soviet Empire in the face of a democratic West (with its arms crossed and even, let's recall, full of inferiority complexes because of the scarce sex appeal of the pedestrian democracy as it compared with the artificial fireworks of the supposed classless society) demonstrated the validity of the theses of Adam Smith, Tocqueville, Popper, or Isaiah Berlin about open societies and a free economy against the fatal arrogance of ideologues such as Marx, Lenin, or Mao, convinced of having gotten to the bottom of history's inflexible rules and having correctly interpreted them with their policies of a proletarian dictatorship and economic centralism.

The actual battle is perhaps less arduous for liberals than the one our teachers fought, when central planning, police states, a one-party regime, and state-controlled economies had on their side an empire armed to the teeth and a formidable publicity campaign, in the heart of democracies, of an intellectual fifth column seduced by socialist theses. Today the battle we should fight is not against great totalitarian thinkers, like Marx, or very intelligent social democrats, of the John Maynard Keynes variety, but against the stereotypes and caricatures that, like a multi-pronged offensive launched from distant trenches against the offspring called neoliberalism, try to sow doubt and confusion in the democratic camp, or against the apocalyptic ones, a new kind of skeptical thinker who, instead of opposing democratic culture, as Lukács, Gramsci, or Sartre did, a resolute contradiction, are happy to deny it, assuring us that, in reality, it doesn't exist, we're dealing with a fiction, behind which the ominous shadow of despotism crouches.

Of this kind I'd like to point out an emblematic case: that of Robert D. Kaplan. In a provocative essay,* he maintains that, contrary to the optimistic expectations about the future of democracy prompted by the death of Marxism in Eastern Europe, humanity is on the path toward a world dominated by authoritarianism, revealed in some cases and, in others, hidden by institutions of civilian and liberal appearance that, in fact, are mere decorations, since true power is, or soon will be, in the hands of large international corporations, owners of technology and capital that, thanks to their ubiquity and extraterritoriality, enjoy almost complete impunity for their actions. "I submit that the democracy we are encouraging in many poor parts of the world is an integral part of a transformation toward new forms of authoritarianism; that democracy in the United States is at greater risk than ever before, and from obscure sources; and that many future regimes, ours especially, could resemble the oligarchies of ancient Athens and Sparta more than they do the current government in Washington." His analysis is particularly negative regarding the possibilities of democracy managing to take root in the third world.

All Western attempts to impose democracy in countries lacking in democratic traditions, according to Mr. Kaplan, have turned out to be terrible failures, at times very costly ones, like

* "Was Democracy Just a Moment?," *The Atlantic Monthly*, December 1997, pp. 55–80.

in Cambodia, where the $2 million invested by the international community has not managed to advance legality and freedom an inch in the former kingdom of Angkor. The results of these efforts, in cases such as Sudan, Algeria, Afghanistan, Bosnia, Sierra Leone, Congo-Brazzaville, Mali, Russia, Albania, and Haiti, have generated chaos, civil war, terrorism, and the reestablishment of ferocious tyrannies that carry out ethnic cleansing or commit the genocide of ethnic minorities.

Mr. Kaplan views with apparent contempt the Latin American process of democratization, with the exceptions of Chile and Peru, countries where, he believes, the fact that the former went through Pinochet's explicit dictatorship, and that the latter is going through the slanted dictatorship of Fujimori and the armed forces, guarantees these nations a stability that, in contrast, the supposed Rule of Law is incapable of preserving in Colombia, Venezuela, Argentina, or Brazil, where, in his opinion, the weakness of civil institutions, the high incidence of corruption, and the astronomical inequalities can revolt against democracy: "millions of poorly educated and recently urbanized inhabitants of marginal neighborhoods, who see very few palpable benefits in the western systems of parliamentary democracy."

Mr. Kaplan doesn't waste his time in circumlocution. He says what he thinks clearly, and what he thinks about democracy is that it and the third world are incompatible: "Social stability comes from the establishment of a middle class. And it is not democracies but rather authoritarian systems, including monarchic ones, that create middle classes." These, when they have reached a certain level and certain confidence, rebel against the dictators responsible for their prosperity. He cites the examples of the Pacific Rim in Asia (his best case is Singapore under Lee Kuan Yew), Chile under Pinochet, and, although he does not mention it, he could have also cited the Spain of Francisco Franco. Currently the authoritarian regimes like these that are creating middle classes that will one day make democracy possible are, in

Asia, the People's Republic of China of "market socialism," and, in Latin America, Fujimori's regime—a military dictatorship with a civilian puppet as a figurehead—which he perceives as models for the third world that wishes to "forge prosperity from abject poverty." For Mr. Kaplan, the choice in the third world is not "between dictators and democrats," but rather between "bad dictators and some that are slightly better." In his opinion, "Russia is failing in part because it is a democracy and China is experiencing success in part because it is not."

I've taken the time to summarize these theses because Mr. Kaplan has the courage to say out loud what others—many others—think but either do not dare to say or say in hushed voices. Mr. Kaplan's pessimism regarding the third world is great; but it is not more than the first world inspires in him. In fact, when efficient dictatorships come to develop those poor countries and provide them with a middle class, according to his framework, and these want to gain access to a Western-style democracy, it will only be a ghost. It will have been replaced by a system (like those of Athens and Sparta) in which some oligarchies—multinational corporations, operating on five continents—will secretly snatch away from governments the power to make transcendental decisions for society and the individual, since power, for large corporations, comes not from an electoral mandate, but from economic-technological forces. In case anyone is unaware, Mr. Kaplan recalls that of the top one hundred economies, fifty-one are not countries, but rather companies. And the five hundred most powerful companies alone represent 70 percent of world commerce.

These theses are a good starting point to contrast them against the liberal vision of the state of things in the world, since, if they are true, the end of the millennium will also find that that human construct, freedom—while having caused an abundance of disruptions and having been the source of the most extraordinary advances in the fields of science, human rights, technological

progress, and the struggle against despotism and exploitation—
is taking its last breaths.

Mr. Kaplan's most widely disseminated thesis is, naturally, that
only dictatorships create middle classes and stabilize countries. If
this were so, with the zoological collections of tyrants, caudillos,
and Maximum Leaders in Latin American history, the paradise of
the middle class would not be the United States, Western Europe,
Canada, Australia, and New Zealand, but Mexico, Bolivia, and
Paraguay. On the contrary, a dictator such as Perón—to give just
one example—managed to nearly disappear the Argentine middle
class, which, until he came to power, was vast, prosperous, and
had developed in their country at a faster pace than their equivalent in a great part of European countries. Forty years of dictatorship have not brought Cuba the least prosperity but have taken
the country back in time, making it an international beggar and
forcing Cubans to eat grass and flowers and prostitute themselves
to the tourists of capitalism so as not to die of hunger.

It is true, Mr. Kaplan can say he's not talking about just any
dictatorship, only the efficient ones, such as in Pacific Rim Asia
and those of Pinochet and Fujimori. I read his essays—what a
coincidence—precisely when the supposed efficient autocracy of
Indonesia was collapsing, General Suharto was forced to renounce,
and the country's economy was in pieces. Shortly before, the former autocracies of Korea and Thailand had collapsed and the
famous Asian miracle was going up in smoke, like in a Hollywood horror movie. Those market dictatorships were not, apparently, as successful as he believes, since they have gone on their
knees before the IMF, the World Bank, the United States, Japan,
and Western Europe to avoid complete ruin.

From an economic standpoint, General Pinochet's does fit
Mr. Kaplan's model, and to a certain point—if efficiency is measured solely in terms of inflation, fiscal deficit, reserves, and growth
of gross national product—so does Fujimori's. Now, we're referring to an efficiency that is very relative, if not counterproductive,

when those efficient dictatorships are examined, not as the es-
teemed Mr. Kaplan does from the comfortable security of an open
society—the United States in his case—but rather from the condition of one who suffers firsthand the excesses and crimes committed in these dictatorships that can wring the neck of inflation.
In contrast to Mr. Kaplan, we liberals do not think that doing
away with economic populism constitutes the least progress for a
society if, at the same time that prices are liberated, expenses are
cut and the public sector is privatized, a government causes citizens to live in fear of imminent trampling, deprives them of freedom of the press and an independent judicial power to which they
can recur when they are harassed or swindled, violates their rights,
and allows that anyone may be tortured, disappeared, murdered,
or have his goods confiscated according to the caprices of the
governing gangsters. Progress, from a liberal doctrine, is simultaneously economic, political, and cultural, or, simply, it is not
liberal. For moral reasons and also practical ones: open societies,
where information flows unimpeded and in which there is rule
of law, are better protected against crises than satrapies, as proven
by the Mexican regime of the PRI a few years ago and recently
by General Suharto in Indonesia. The role that a lack of genuine
legality plays in the crisis of authoritarian countries of the Pacific
Rim has not been sufficiently emphasized.

How many efficient dictatorships have there been? And how
many inefficient ones, which have sunk their countries at times in
a prerational savagery, as has happened in our time to Algeria and
Afghanistan? The immense majority are like the latter, with the
former being an exception. Is it not reckless to choose the recipe of
dictatorship in the hope that it will be efficient, honorable, and
transitory, instead of the opposite, in order to obtain development?
Are there not less risky and less cruel methods to obtain it? Yes,
there are, but people like Mr. Kaplan don't want to see them.

It is not true that the "culture of freedom" is a long-standing
tradition in countries where democracy flourishes. It was not in

any of the current democracies until, with stumbles and setbacks, these societies chose that culture and went about perfecting the path, until they made it theirs and arrived at the levels they currently enjoy. Pressure and international assistance can be a primary factor for a society to adopt a democratic culture, as the examples of Germany and Japan demonstrate. They were two countries that had a very minor or nonexistent tradition of democracy, like any country in Latin America, and that, since the end of World War II, have gone on to be a part of the world's most advanced democracies. Why wouldn't third-world countries (or Russia) be capable of emancipating themselves, like the Japanese and the Germans, from the authoritarian tradition and making the culture of freedom their own?

Globalization, in contrast to the pessimistic conclusions that Mr. Kaplan extracts from it, opens a first-rate opportunity for the world's democratic countries, and especially the advanced democracies of the Americas and Europe, to contribute to expanding the culture that is now synonymous with tolerance, pluralism, legality, and freedom, to countries that are still—and I know there are many—slaves to the authoritarian tradition, a tradition that has hung, let's recall, over all of humanity. It is possible, as long as we:

(a) Clearly believe in the superiority of this culture over those that legitimize fanaticism, intolerance, racism, and religious, ethnic, political, or sexual discrimination; and

(b) Act coherently in economic and foreign policies, orienting them such that they, while encouraging democratic tendencies in the third world, penalize and discriminate without hesitation the regimes that, like the People's Republic of China or the civilian-military clique in Peru, push liberal policies in the economic realm but are dictatorial in their politics.

Unfortunately, in contrast to what Mr. Kaplan maintains in his essay, this positive discrimination in favor of democracy, which brought so much benefit to countries like Germany, Italy, and Japan half a century ago, is not applied by democratic countries today to the rest of the world, or it is practiced in a partial and hypocritical way (as in the case of Cuba).

But perhaps now they have a greater incentive to act in a firmer and more principled way in favor of democracy in a world of authoritarian shadows. And the reason is, precisely, that which Mr. Kaplan mentions when he prophesies, in apocalyptic terms, a future nondemocratic world government of powerful multinational companies operating, unrestrained, in all corners of the earth. This catastrophic vision points at a real danger, of which it is necessary to be conscious. The disappearance of economic borders and the multiplication of world markets stimulates the fusions and alliances of companies, to compete more efficiently in all areas of production. The formation of gigantic corporations does not constitute, in and of itself, a danger to democracy, while the latter is a reality, in other words, while there are fair laws and strong governments (which to a liberal does not mean large ones, but rather small and efficient ones) that make them obey. In a market economy open to competition, a large corporation benefits the consumer because its scale allows it to reduce prices and multiply services. It is not in the size of the company where danger lies: it is in the monopoly, which is always a source of inefficiency and corruption. While there are democratic governments that make large companies respect the law, bring a Bill Gates to trial if they suspect he has made a transgression, keep markets open to competition, and institute firm antimonopoly policies, these large corporations, which have proven in many cases to be the starting point of scientific and technological progress, will be welcome.

Now it is true that with this chameleon-like nature that characterizes the capitalist company that Adam Smith described so well, an institution that benefits development and progress in a democratic country can be the source of rage and catastrophe in countries where there is no rule of law, no market freedom, and where everything is solved through the absolute will of a clique or leader. The corporation is immoral and easily adapts itself to the rules of the game of the medium in which it operates. If in many third-world countries the efforts of multinationals are reproachable, ultimate responsibility falls on those who set the rules of the game of economic, social, and political life, not on those who do nothing but apply these rules in search of benefits.

From this reality Mr. Kaplan extracts this pessimistic conclusion: the future of democracy is somber because in the next millennium the large corporations will act in the United States and Western Europe with the same impunity that they do in, say, the Nigeria of the deceased Colonel Abacha. In reality there is no historical or conceptual reason for such an extrapolation. The conclusion it begs, rather, is the following: the imperative need that Nigeria and the countries subject to dictatorships today evolve as soon as possible toward democracy and also move to have a legality and a freedom that forces corporations operating within them to act according to the rules of the game, fairly and cleanly as they are forced to in an advanced democracy. Economic globalization could become, in fact, a serious danger for the future of civilization—and, especially, for the environment—if it does not have as a correlative legality and freedom. The great powers have the obligation to promote democratic processes in the third world not only for reasons of principle and morality but also because, owing to the evaporation of borders, in order to best guarantee that economic life will flow within the limits of freedom and competence that benefit citizens, it must have, across the whole wide world, the same incentives, rights, and restraints that democratic society imposes on it.

None of this is easy, nor will it be achieved in short order. But for liberals, it is a great incentive to know that it is a possible goal and that the idea of a world united around a culture of freedom is not a utopia, but a beautiful and obtainable reality that justifies our efforts. Karl Popper, one of our best teachers, put it this way: "Optimism is a duty. The future is open. It is not predetermined. No one can predict it, except by chance. We all contribute to determining it by what we do. We are all equally responsible for its success."

Berlin, May 12, 1998

Dreams and Reality
in Latin America

In the middle of the seventeenth century, the lawyer Antonio
León Pinelo, a native of Valladolid who had spent his formative
years in Lima, where he studied with the Jesuits, and who later
achieved a distinguished position in Spain—he was Royal Adviser
of Castille and Chronicler of the Indies—wrote a book titled
Paradise in the New World, in which he demonstrated, in two volumes stuffed with biblical quotes and historical, mythological, and
linguistic references, that the heavenly territory where human life
began was in the Peruvian Amazon, and, more specifically, close
to what is now the city of Iquitos. The historian Raúl Porras
Barrenechea rescued the voluminous folio that was sleeping
the slumber of unborn books in the Royal Library of Madrid
and published it in 1943, with a study in which, with erudition
and elegance, he reviews the tenacious predilection of chroniclers and historians of the Indies to perceive the vast dominion
discovered by Columbus as a land of wonders, in which fantastic
kingdoms and cities of Greco-Roman and medieval mythology
and the most extravagant characters and riches appeared.

"The artificial love for the rare and exotic takes precedence
over what is real or common," Porras Barrenechea says of those
first historians of the Americas. "Legend is preferable to history.

It is the tendency of Montesinos, attempting to prove that Ophir was in Peru; of Dávalos and Figueroa, collecting rare and curious cases; of Calancha, narrating miracles and marvels; of Garcilaso, idealizing the Incan Empire; of Morúa, dressing the court of Cuzco's Incas in Oriental splendors; of Pinelo, moving Paradise to the Amazon. Pinelo agrees mainly with Dávalos and Figueroa in a love of curiosities, and with Montesinos in the Hebrewism and the fondness for treasures and mines." He himself confesses his propensity for the wondrous, although he boasts of a certain true caution: "While I do seek news of the extraordinary, I do not follow the most extraordinary ones, but rather the ones that I can take to be most proper and truthful."* We doubt, nonetheless, the sensibility and historical equanimity of someone who wanted to prove to us that the Tigris was the Magdalena and that South America was the old biblical Ethiopia.

The European tendency to project on the Americas the dreams of fiction, religion, and mythology was born with the discovery of a continent on which, let us not forget, Christopher Columbus insisted on seeing not what was in front of his eyes and beneath his feet, but rather India and China, the Asia of silks and spices that he brought in his desires and imagination. The admiral, besides, recorded in the journal of his first voyage that in the lands he had recently discovered "there were one-eyed men and others with dogs' snouts that ate men, and that they slit the throats of men when taking them and drank their blood and cut off their manhood."† This inclination to idealize the Americas, projecting on its jungles, high plateaus, and seas the oldest fables and legends, was not something exclusive to educated people. The humblest of Europeans, those peasants and common people who in Portugal and Spain enlisted as soldiers and sailors, came to this

* Antonio de León Pinelo, *El Paraíso en el Nuevo Mundo*. Prologue by Raúl Porras Barrenechea. Lima, 1943, p. ix.
† See *La conquista de América. Antología del pensamiento de Indias*. Edición de Ricardo Céspedes Piqueras. Barcelona, Ediciones Península, 2002, p. 37.

side of the Atlantic drawn by the prospect of fabulous riches and extraordinary adventures in those far-off lands where, according to what people on the streets were saying and the dignitaries' treatises, what was unreal in Europe became a daily reality.

Irving A. Leonard bore a revealing testimony to this systematic idealization of Spanish and Portuguese America in his research for *The Books of the Conquistador*.* In its pages, he outlines how the conquest and colonization of the New World was also an imaginary labor incited by literature, an adventure in which, along with greed and a missionary spirit, conquistadors and explorers were guided by the will to find on American soil those cities and places with which romances of chivalry and fantastic stories in popular narratives had filled their heads. The hope of finding the creations of literary fantasy and European mythology in the Americas often pushed them to put together impossible expeditions and to repeat the "entrances" in unknown jungles, to go down into ravines or to scale the heights of a mountain range and cross the plains and high plateaus in search of mirages that faded away just when those hunters of enchantment thought they were about to reach them.

That many of these men did not know how to read or write was not a hindrance to their chivalrous fantasies since these, besides being read, were also conveyed by troubadours and wandering storytellers in Europe's plazas and taverns.

According to Leonard, the myth that most perturbed the conquistador was the legend of the Amazons, "the women warriors," to such an extent that in the contracts to finance the conquest's expeditions there were clauses "requiring the search for these mythological women."† Many chroniclers, from Columbus to Pedro Martín de Anglería, Oviedo, Herrera, and, incidentally,

---

* Irving A. Leonard, *Los libros del conquistador*. Fondo de Cultura Económica, 1953. The first edition, in English, was published in 1949. All citations refer to this edition.
† Ibid.

Fray Gaspar de Carvajal, who accompanied Orellana on his Amazon adventure, claim to have seen the mythological women who cut off a breast in order to better shoot arrows, kidnapped men to make themselves pregnant, and later sent them off with the male children they bore, keeping only the females to perpetuate the tribe's exclusively feminine character. Fray Gaspar de Carvajal confirms that Orellana not only "saw" the Amazons but was personally attacked by those who gave their name to the great river of the South American jungle. The myth of the Amazons, one of the most persistent during the colonial years, is mentioned by Cortés in one of his letters to Carlos V, relaying the rumors of the existence of tribes of female warriors in New Spain. According to Leonard, the legend of the Amazons had become popularized on the peninsula thanks to a novel in a series of the Amadises, the *Sergas de Esplandián*, in which Calafia, the queen of the Amazons, lives on an island called California. Like the land with this name, many cities and places in the Americas would be christened with names taken from the literature of chivalry and classical mythology. Leonard gives many examples of this generalized proclivity by the Europeans in the early colonial years to associate the Americas with fictional mirages.

The chronicler Bernal Díaz del Castillo, in his *Verdadera historia de la conquista de la Nueva España*, said that the first impression the Aztec capital made on Cortés and his companions was "that it seemed like one of the wonders told of in Amadis's book."

A brother of Saint Theresa's, Agustín de Ahumada, from Quito on October 25, 1582, asks the Peruvian viceroy to organize an expedition in search of El Dorado, whose tracks he says he has found. To arrive at El Dorado, the city of gold and dizzying riches, is another of the plans pursued by the first wave of Europeans who arrive in the Americas and one of the greatest incitements to expeditions and searches that frequently end in tragedy, like that of Lope de Aguirre, who went mad.

Other fatuous flames that dazzle the conquistadors and launch them on reckless adventures are the Fountain of Youth and the Seven Cities of Cibola. The first viceroy of Mexico, Antonio de Mendoza, received a report from Fray Marcos de Niza, gathered by him among the "Indians of Puebla," about the nearby existence of the seven legendary cities. Because of this information, Vázquez de Coronado's expedition was organized and, Leonard says, for two years searched in vain for "the famous cities paved in emeralds." They did not find them, but they did discover the Grand Canyon.

The discovery of the Americas by the Europeans was carried out under the empire of myth and fiction. This would come to nearly sketch a destiny for Latin America: to be often seen or understood with the same fantasizing eyes with which the first navigators who set foot on its soil saw it. Since then, and throughout its history, Europe has frequently transferred to the Americas its utopias and artistic and ideological frustrations (also religious ones), born in its bosom and condemned, over there, to live confined in the kingdoms of illusion. Let's recall that at the end of Victor Hugo's *Les Misérables*, the villain in the story, the tavern owner Thénardier, leaves for South America via Panama, an exotic place where the natives tend to live crowded together in narrow homes and that even today, in France, has left the eighteenth-century exclamation *c'est n'est pas le Pérou!* (This is not Peru!) to say that something is not as opulent as the Thousand-and-One-Nights-esque riches of that continent across the seas.

This contribution by the Americas to the history and culture of the West—having served as the receptacle of its desires and utopias, relieving Europeans of the limits they had already imposed on themselves—is hardly ever mentioned among the Americas' contribution to the life, customs, ideas, and beliefs of Western civilization. The most earthly ones are recognized, corn, potatoes, chocolate, and the many foods without which the diets of countries such as France, Germany, Ireland, Switzerland,

Belgium, and Austria would be considerably weaker; and medicinal plants, for example, the cinchona tree, whose pharmaceutical product, quinine, drastically contained the damages of malaria; even a vital cultural and geopolitical event: the idea of a truly universal history. The articulation of the Americas in the rest of the world inaugurates an irreversible process of encounters and exchanges—violent and peaceful—that would make up what had until then been the particular histories of countries, regions, and communities, in a global process in which all regional histories are pieces of a single crossword puzzle in motion, perpetually undoing and remaking itself. From the arrival of three fragile caravels on the island of Guanahaní to the so-called globalization of our days, there are ties that were never broken, that, quite the opposite, were fortified and grew, mostly for good, but, at times, also for bad, until they absorbed all the world's peoples in one sole vertiginous and protoplasmic history, irrevocably tangled together.

But just as European languages, knowledge, uses, customs, gastronomies, artistic ways, and ideas about humanity were enriched with the incorporation of the Americas into the rest of the world after 1492, it is also advisable to highlight the subtle service we have been providing for five centuries to the imagination and frustrations of Europeans (to whom, in the modern era, we should add many North Americans): bringing to life their religious and ideological fantasies, embodying the paradises of their longing or the infernos that terrified them.

The paradise that the lawyer Antonio León Pinelo situated in the Amazon in the seventeenth century was religious and passé. The paradise seen in Latin America in the 1960s by a young and brilliant French *normalien*, a disciple of the Marxist philosopher Louis Althusser, was revolutionary, Communist, and belonged to the future that, according to him, had begun to develop with the Cuban Revolution. Since so much water had run under the bridge since then, many had already forgotten the repercussions around the world of a small book by Régis Debray, *Revolution in the Revolution?*, published in 1967, with Fidel Castro's blessing, released in a massive printing by Casa de las Américas in Havana, and the theoretical and practical catechism, for a long time, for young people who, in different parts of the world, but especially in Latin America, tried during the 1960s and 1970s to reproduce the revolutionary efforts of the bearded Cubans.

It has made some smile to hear me compare Debray's little book with León Pinelo's mammoth one. But the comparison is not arbitrary. Both books, one in the religious sphere and the other in the political and ideological one, move a Western utopia to Latin America and give it form there. To Debray, the Cuban Revolution has brought to light a truth that had been wandering lost in the labyrinth of mistakes, concessions, compromises, disillusions, prejudices, and betrayals that had blocked progress on the global stage: what a revolution is and how it is made. Fidel, Che, and their companions have not only reminded with their example that the first duty of a revolutionary is "to make the revolution," something that the bourgeois Communists or those subtly reclaimed by the system tended to forget, but also the correct method of turning that ideal into living history. The book goes over all the erroneous conceptions that thwarted revolutionary attempts until that point, the "economicism" of militants who, like in the Bolivia of Paz Estenssoro and de Lechín's MNR (Movimiento Nacionalista Revolucionario), focused the struggle in the union sphere, and Trotskyites' spontaneity and "double power" tactics and general strikes, who have always come together in the face of so many other popular defeats by bourgeois armies. There is also the corrupting and bourgeoisizing function of cities for revolutionaries, compared with the stimulating and purifying environment of the countryside for revolutionary morale and the will to act, and the superiority of armed action over exclusively political work.

Revolutionary truth, Debray explains, was discovered by Fidel and his cohorts through instinct, transparency, and pragmatic spirit, starting with the Moncada attack and the two years in the Sierra Maestra. The focalism theory of guerrilla warfare, an always mobile military vanguard that uses hit-and-run tactics and with its "propaganda armada" operations goes about wearing down the enemy and politically educating and incorporating peasants and workers into the struggle, allows what in principle seemed like a chimera—the victory by a small number of poorly armed combatants over a powerful army, equipped to the teeth and supported by the United States—to become reality. This reality is already a fact, it exists as historical proof of how the theoretical model represented by Cuba is the only one in which, at last, the "attack on the heavens" that, according to Marx, the Parisians tried during the days of the Commune is finally consummated. Reading that essay by Debray, you get the impression that beginning with the Cuban Revolution, history has been divided into a before and an after, and that now the advance of communism will be irreversible for the entire world.

It would have been difficult for the Cuban myth, the first society in which supposedly freedom and socialism are combined like two sides of the same coin, to proliferate and last for so long without the utopian legend, so at odds with the historical truth of what was happening on the island, that so many Europeans, in the manner of Régis Debray, wove around it, insistent, according to a tradition that goes back to conquistadors and colonizers, on seeing paradise in it. Debray was not alone. Sartre, let's recall, following an official visit of only a few days to Cuba, wrote *Hurricane over Sugar*, where he described an island on which "a democracy in action" was practiced for the first time. It is true that, almost half a century later, that revolution has lost its aura for many Europeans, including Régis Debray himself, but there are still those on the old continent who are resistant to seeing reality, and in the manner of Ignacio Ramonet, director of *Le Monde Diplomatique* and courtesan of Fidel Castro and Commander Hugo

Chávez, continue embellishing and promoting as exemplary a dictatorship that has earned the dubious honor of being the longest that Latin America has known and that none of them would likely accept in their own country. Let's recall, regarding everything else, that Debray himself was one of the most enthusiastic promoters of Subcomandante Marcos and his Zapatistas when the masked revolutionary appeared in the jungles of Chiapas, whom he put on a pedestal not just as the new social redeemer of Latin America but also, due to his proclamations and communiqués—he said so—as the best prose writer in the Castilian language. Would his enthusiasm have been similar if Subcomandante Marcos had tried to carry out his "postmodern revolution"—as Carlos Fuentes called it—not in Chiapas, but in Brittany or the Auvergne?

I debated this paradox a few years ago with Günther Grass, the author of at least one excellent novel, *The Tin Drum*, but who is rather less lucid regarding his political recipes for Latin America. Why did someone like him, who in Germany campaigned for social democracy and criticized Communists, ask that we Latin Americans follow the "example of Cuba"? Why is it that what is bad for Europeans is good for Latin Americans? For a very simple reason: because for Günther Grass, Ignacio Ramonet, and that Régis Debray of *Revolution in the Revolution?*, as for Antonio León Pinelo in the seventeenth century, Latin America, more than a concrete reality, is a fictitious reality in which they spill their failed utopias and with which they make up for their political disappointments. Those who proceed that way continue to treat us with the mentality of the old colonizers, for whom Latin America was not a reality, but rather a fiction.

Fortunately, not all Europeans or North Americans who have an interest in Latin America idealize it to fit within their political illusions. The list would be very long of scientists, archaeologists, anthropologists, historians, sociologists, and political scientists, not to mention the numerous artists, poets, and writers from Europe and the United States, who have studied Latin American reality with devotion and objectivity, contributing decisively to revealing it as it really is or who, inspired by it, have produced literary and artistic creations as beautiful as Conrad's *Nostromo* or Malcolm Lowry's *Under the Volcano*. But curiously, those who have most influenced the cultural, political, and, let's call it thus, mythified image of Latin America, abroad and on the American continent itself, have been those who idealized it, beautifying it or making it ugly in an example of what Freud called the phenomenon of transference. This is the most widespread image of Latin America by the media, promoted especially by progressive intellectuals in the West.

Nonetheless, it would be a mistake to believe that the religious or ideological mythification of the Americas has always had a revolutionary and leftist tendency. Among the various attempts by libertarian Europeans who came to Latin America at the end of the nineteenth century and beginning of the twentieth to build those small utopian paradises were those of reactionary and racist fanatics. Among them, the one led by Elizabeth Nietzsche, the philosopher's sister, and her husband, Bernhard Förster, vehement anti-Semites who traveled with forty German families to Paraguay to found the colony of "Nueva Germania" in San Bernardino, where they hoped to revive the vitality of the German people impoverished by mixing and create a society of pure Aryans. Their sinister adventure ended in disaster. Worse still was the tragedy of Jonestown: an evangelist sect from Indiana led by the Reverend Jim Jones with hundreds of followers who moved to the jungles of Guyana in the middle of the twentieth century to found Paradise. What they built in reality was an inferno of slave work and endless violence until the small sacrifice of the entire community, in which more than nine hundred members of the sect perished by poisoning or murder. To confuse reality and fiction has always generated tragedy.

To embody fiction for "the other" has had a curious derivation in Latin America: many Latin Americans have adopted these re-touched and deeply unrealistic images of themselves due to fan-tasy or religious alienation or Western ideology and, instead of facing their own reality, have re-created it according to those imported models and myths. The result has been enormously beneficial for Latin American arts and letters, for whom this fictionalization of life and history has served as inspiration, firing the imagination and creative flight of poets, writers, and artists in works that very soon broke the provincial conditioning and reached a universal horizon. From Inca Garcilaso de la Vega and Sor Juana Inés de la Cruz to the poems of Vallejo, Neruda, and Octavio Paz, our literature, like other creative genres, has built a fictional Latin America that is on a par with the paradigm that the first Europeans who disembarked here saw in it. In the political field, however, in which, in contrast to what is happen-ing in the artistic and literary fields, it is advisable to clearly discern what separates reality from fiction, that tendency has turned out to be dangerous and, on occasion, catastrophic.

I would like to examine in this respect a text that is as beau-tiful as it is false by one of the greatest novelists of our language, the Cuban Alejo Carpentier. I am referring to the prologue he wrote to his first masterpiece, the tight, astute, and perfect nar-rative transfiguration of Haiti's early years of independence and the life of miracles of the Haitian government of Henri Chris-tophe, *The Kingdom of This World* (1949). In this brief and fasci-nating text, Carpentier describes how, on a trip he made in 1943 to Haiti, passing by the ruins of Sans-Souci, the Citadel of La Ferrière, and Cap-Haitien (formerly Cap-Français), he had discov-ered that the "marvelous real" which European poets and paint-ers, especially surrealists, insisted on fabricating with so much tenacity was, in Haiti and in all of our America, a daily reality, a living history. "The marvelous real is found at each step." Here the marvelous real was neither "a literary ruse" nor "magic tricks" with which Europeans tried to "revive the marvelous" thirty years prior. In contrast, the marvels and miracles were "the patrimony of all the Americas," a land where myth had not frozen in libraries, but was tangible, in its plazas and hamlets, in its magic-impregnated dances and music, and, above all, in its human beings and its social happenings. The beautiful text ends with a dramatic exclamation: "What, after all, is the history of all the Americas but a chronicle of the marvelous real?"

This marvelous real Latin America is, in fact, the one shown by many works of our greatest literature, such as novels and stories by Juan Rulfo and by García Márquez, by Jorge Luis Borges, Julio Cortázar, and Alejo Carpentier himself, and by painters no less notable than Wilfredo Lam, Rufino Tamayo, Matta, Frida Kahlo, Cuevas, Szyszlo, Fernando Botero, and the one that prowls, leaving showy marks and an aura of hasty fantasy, through popular arts, folklore, handicrafts, and, of course, music. But it goes without saying that a similarly seductive reading of our reality loses all its persuasive power when it is separated from fiction and the arts and runs into the historical, social, economic, and cultural reality of the continent, which, as in Europe and any other part of the world, can only be truly understood, for what it really is, not with poetic metaphors or allegories but rather with rational observation and objective and scientific analysis. Observed in this way, without the deforming goggles of mythology and utopia, Latin America is neither paradise nor inferno, although for millions of its poor and marginalized it is closer to the latter than the former. It is, pure and simple, a continent that has still not overcome basic obstacles that impede development or deform it and that, in contrast to what is already luckily happening in all of North America, nearly all of Europe, and a good part of Asia and Oceania, has not yet accepted itself for what it is, preferring, in the manner of those who would still like to find in it the Seven Cities of Cibola, the Fountain of Youth, or the

Paradise of León Pinelo, the visions of the marvelous real over simple reality.

Let's try to approach the reality of Latin America that lies beneath the phosphorescence of images, witches, or horrendousness with which ideology, religion, and literature have dressed Latin America, making an effort to be rational—and knowing that this is difficult, since we Latin Americans, whether we like it or not, are infected with mythology and utopianism.

Let's start with a very simple question that throughout our history has received contradictory answers. What does it mean to feel Latin American? Above all, it means feeling beyond national borders, like an active member of a transnational community. To be conscious that the territorial demarcations dividing our countries are artificial, arbitrarily imposed during the colonial years and that, instead of repairing them, the leaders of the emancipation and republican governments legitimized and sometimes aggravated them, dividing and isolating societies in which the common denominator went deeper than particular differences. The Balkanization of Latin America, as opposed to what happened in North America, where the thirteen colonies united and their union set the United States on its way, has been one of the conspicuous factors of our underdevelopment, since it stimulated nationalisms, wars, and conflicts in which Latin American countries have bled, wasting huge resources that could have served for their modernization and progress. Only in the field of culture has Latin American integration come to be something real, a product of experience and necessity—everyone who writes, composes, paints, or carries out any other creative task discovers that what unites them with other Latin Americans is more important than what separates them from other Latin Americans— while in other realms, politics, economics, and especially attempts to unify governing and market actions have always been restrained by nationalist reflexes, very deep-rooted in the continent: this is the reason for which all of the organisms conceived to unite the region have never prospered.

National borders do not signal true differences existing in Latin America. They happen in the heart of every country in a transversal way, engulfing regions and groups of countries. There is a Westernized Latin America that speaks in Spanish, Portuguese, and English (in the Caribbean and in Central America), and is Catholic, Protestant, atheist, or agnostic, and an indigenous Latin America that, in countries such as Mexico, Guatemala, Ecuador, Peru, and Bolivia, is made up of millions of people and maintains pre-Hispanic institutions, practices, and beliefs. But contrary to what other stereotypes would have us believe, the indigenous Americas are not homogeneous, but rather an archipelago that experiences different levels of modernization. As much as languages and traditions are the shared heritages of great social conglomerates, such as Quechua and Aymara, others, such as the Amazon cultures, survive in small communities of only a handful of families at times. The latter are the ones in danger of being annihilated.

Mestizaje, fortunately, is extensive and creates bridges, bringing closer and blending these two worlds together. In some countries, like in Mexico, they have culturally and racially integrated the majority of society—the best achievement of the Mexican Revolution—leaving the two ethnic extremes turned into minorities. This integration is less dynamic in other countries, but continues occurring and, in the long run, will end up giving Latin America the distinct profile of a mestizo continent. Although, we hope, without making it totally uniform and depriving it of nuances. What is indispensable is that, sooner rather than later, thanks to democracy—freedom and legality conjugated—all Latin Americans without regard to race, language, religion, or culture will be equal before the law, enjoy the same rights and opportunities, and coexist in diversity without suffering discrimination or exclusion. Latin America cannot renounce the cultural diversity that makes it a prototype of the world.

Mestizaje should not be exclusively understood as an alliance between what is Indian and what is Spanish or Portuguese, although, naturally, these are the most important ethnic and cultural components of Latin American reality. But also significant, and, in countries of the Caribbean basin and certain regions of Brazil, essential, is the African contribution, which came to the Americas at the same time as the conquistadors and has left in all manifestations of art and culture—especially in music—a substantial impression. Likewise, Asia has been present in the continent's life since the colonial era, and a recent exhibit has documented with magnificent examples the way that the techniques and use of visual and decorative arts from the Far East came to our lands and were assimilated by native artists and artisans. When you start to dig into Latin America's past without prejudice or preconceived views, you discover that our cultural roots extend through all corners of the world.

Despite this, one of the recurring fixations of Latin American culture has been that of defining its identity. In my opinion, it is a useless, dangerous, and impossible exercise, since identity is something that individuals have, not collectivities once they overcome tribal conditioning. Only in the most primitive cultures, where the individual exists only as part of the tribe, does the idea of a collective identity have a raison d'être. There it reigns because the isolated individual would not be able to survive in a world he knows nothing about and where he finds himself helpless, defenseless, facing the beasts, thunder, and the myriad of mysteries and enemies surrounding him. But that which we call civilization, precisely, is the long process that the majority of Latin Americans have already lived through in which, as they progress and start exercising control over nature and freeing themselves of the incubus and succubus of ignorance, prejudice, and mystical irrationality, the individual is born, separating himself from the tribal placenta and acquiring sovereignty, his own personality, choosing with greater and greater freedom, in other words, distinguishing himself from others, like a sovereign creature. To be part of a community is a fundamental fact in the fate of individuals, of course. But it is civilization itself that allows the individual to be so at the same time as being many at once, according to his own tradition, circumstances, vocation, and will: the nation is only one of them and, for many, less decisive than others such as language, religion, family, ethnic group, profession, political ideology, or sexual orientation. A modern society is composed of free citizens, who differ among themselves, who can show and be proud of their differences and singularities regarding others, without weakening or suppressing the group's solidarity. On the contrary, that spirit of solidarity is much more profound when it is born of free choice, of a rational evaluation of the privilege symbolized by being part of a community where, in contrast to a tribe, one can be different without being excluded or discriminated against, where each one can invent himself, creating his own identity, an identity freely decided through daily choices, not imposed like a straitjacket by the collective group. In Latin America there are still some tribal communities, submerged in flocks and that magic-religious reality dear to Carpentier, but the great majority have already left behind that primitive and archaic state. Despite this, the tribal mentality and the collectivist temptation to disappear the individual within a supposedly homogeneous and identical collectivity are far from disappeared. They return cyclically, like constant threats to our modernization and to Latin America accepting, with all of its consequences, the culture of freedom.

Just as in other parts of the world, this eagerness to determine the historical-social specificity or metaphysics of a group that inhabits a common place has made oceans of ink flow in Latin America and generated diatribes and controversies. The most famous and prolonged of all concerned Hispanists, for whom the

real history of Latin America began with the arrival of the Spanish and Portuguese and the coupling of the continent with the
Western world, and Indigenists, for whom the genuine reality of
the Americas is in pre-Hispanic civilizations and their descendants, not in the contemporary heirs of the conquistadors, who
still marginalize and exploit the indigenous peoples.

Although muted for long periods, this schizophrenic and
racist vision of what Latin America is has never completely
disappeared. From time to time it resurfaces in the political field,
because, like all Manichaean simplifications, it allows demagogues
to stir up collectivist passions and give superficial answers and
solutions to complex problems. We have seen it recently with the
rise to power, in Bolivia, of President Evo Morales, whom the
myth-seeking European and North American press have been
quick to present as the first Indian to serve in such a high political office in that country of the high plateau. It's a flagrant in-
exactitude that can be confirmed by taking a cursory look at the
admirable essay by the essayist and historian Alcides Arguedas
about *Los caudillos bárbaros*, a considerable collection of big shots and
strongmen and tyrants, among which there were several Aymara
and Quechua Indians who held the position—by fire and
blood—of head of the Bolivian state. But in contrast to Evo
Morales, they were clearly not revolutionaries, nor did they use
the rhetoric of class warfare and the still more dangerous one of
race warfare that, currently, certain irresponsible progressives use
to agitate and propagandize. To lay out Bolivia's problem, or that
of any Latin American country, in racial terms is to propitiate
confusion and falsify reality. It is true that among us there exist
stupid prejudices that discriminate against Indians, those of mixed
race, black people, Asian people, and vice versa, equivalent prejudices in the opposite direction as, unfortunately, almost everywhere on the planet. These prejudices will start languishing with
education and culture and with the solution of basic problems—
economic and social—that pit the privileged of all races against

the discriminated and exploited, also of all races, due to the existence of an unfair system, without equal opportunities, and where certain influential minorities with political power monopolize the creation of wealth and keep the majority of society facing discrimination and marginalization. This is not a racial problem, but an economic and political one and, in the end, a cultural one. Latin America is simultaneously Spanish, Portuguese, Indian, African, Asian, and several more realities. Any effort to fix a single identity on Latin America is to carry out a discriminatory surgery that excludes and abolishes millions of Latin Americans and many forms and manifestations of its lush cultural and ethnic variety.

The richness of Latin America lies in being many things at once, so many that they make of it a microcosm in which almost all the races and cultures of the world coexist. Five centuries after the arrival of the Europeans on its shores and mountain ranges and in its jungles, Latin Americans of Spanish, Portuguese, Italian, German, African, Chinese, or Japanese origins are as much natives of the continent as those who have ancestors in the ancient Aztecs, Toltecs, Mayas, Quechuas, Aymaras, or Caribs. And the mark that Africans have left on the continent where they have also been for five centuries is present everywhere: in human beings, in ways of speaking, in music, in food, and even in certain ways of practicing religion. It is not an exaggeration to say that there is no tradition, culture, language, or race that has not contributed something to that vortex of mixtures and alliances that can be seen in all aspects of life in Latin America. This amalgam is our best patrimony. To be a continent that lacks one identity because it has them all. And because, thanks to its creators, it keeps transforming, every day.

The qualifier of "colonial" art is only exact in a historical and political sense, but inappropriate to define its achievements, forms, and content. From the dawn of the incorporation of the new continent to Western culture, this art denotes a certain singularity, distancing itself from European models and motives that, on the surface at least, inspired it. It could not have been otherwise. The discoverers and conquistadors did not arrive on virgin territory, but rather to a continent of cultures and civilizations that had reached, through the course of many centuries, an elevated level of refinement in their uses and beliefs and in their systems of social organization. Those who painted, sculpted, carved, and worked with feathers and metals, or wove cloaks and erected temples, altars, and pulpits, were, in the majority, descendants of those civilizations and cultures that, with the arrival of the Europeans, were destroyed and subjugated but not disappeared. From the shadows, they persisted and continued operating in the spirit of the creators and artisans. The colonial system imposed new beliefs and ways of behavior, changed appearances, but not souls, that intimate space that is the refuge where the old gods, habits, devotions, and mythologies that, even despite the artists themselves, started to surreptitiously impregnate the manifestations of American "colonial" art, imprinting nuances on it that, without breaking with the prototypes brought by the colonizer, would renew with additions or alterations attuned to the native idiosyncrasy. The facades of churches, their altars, pulpits, altarpieces, frescos, and sculptures, would start becoming subtly Americanized, with an uncontainable eruption of native fruits and flowers; the Virgins and angels would become more Creole or Indian, in their skin, in their facial and corporeal features, in their dress, in the colors and landscapes, the disorder of the perspective, and the syncretism between Christianity and abolished religions.

It would be a mistake to attribute that fusion exclusively to indigenous artists and sculptors of religious images. The Europeans transplanted to the American colonies became creolized very quickly. The Americanization of European art begins to occur in Hispano and Luso-America in the seventeenth century, until it flagrantly asserts itself in the eighteenth century. Although the

Americans would still take another century or so to extrapolate it from the political ambience and dream of emancipation, when they painted, composed, sculpted, or wrote, the Europeans of the Americas had ceased to be European and were already in more than one sense creoles; in other words, Hispano- or Luso-Americans, although the notion still did not exist or was rather cloudy. From a cultural and artistic point of view, the process of the emancipation of Latin America begins discreetly at first but grows increasingly more obvious as time goes on.

Although it is not usually explicitly addressed, one matter lurks around all of the twists and turns of Latin American culture: the abysmal contradiction that exists between its social and political reality and its literary and artistic production. The same continent that, because of its income differences between rich and poor, its dictatorial and populist governments, the levels of illiteracy, its indices of criminality and narco-trafficking, and the exodus of its inhabitants is the very embodiment of underdevelopment also carries, since before the colonial age, a high coefficient of literary and artistic originality. In the field of culture, you can only talk about underdevelopment in Latin America in its sociological aspect: the smallness of the cultural market, how little people read, the stifled atmosphere for artistic activities. But regarding production, its writers, filmmakers, painters, or musicians (who make the whole world dance) could not be called underdeveloped. Neither were those who, in their day, built the citadel of Machu Picchu, the Mayan pyramids, or the lake city of Anáhuac. They could be compared with the most original creators of the West. In its best examples, the art and literature of the Americas left the picturesque and the folkloric centuries ago and reached universal levels of production and originality.

How to explain this paradox? By the great contrasts in the reality of Latin America, which sees not only the coexistence of all geographies, ethnicities, religions, and customs but also all historical eras, as Alejo Carpentier fantasized about in *The Lost*

Steps, a novelesque journey through space from the most modern industrial city to the most primitive rural life, which is simultaneously a journey through time. While the cultural elite became modernized and opened the world and were renewed thanks to a constant encounter with great centers of thinking and cultural creation in contemporary life, political life, with few exceptions, remained anchored in a past of caudillos and cliques who exercised despotism, sacked public resources, and maintained economic life frozen in feudalism and mercantilism. A divorce occurred: while the bastions of cultural life—spaces of freedom left unencumbered to their fate by a political power that was generally contemptuous of culture—found themselves in contact with modernity, and while high-quality writers and artists evolved from this, the rest of society remained practically immobilized in a self-destructing anachronism.

You cannot understand Latin America without observing it with your eyes and engaging the myths and stereotypes that have been developed about it abroad. This mythical dimension is inseparable from the historical reality of a community and, likewise, because many of those myths and stereotypes have been metabolized by a Latin America dead set on being what, for ideological and folkloric reasons, many Europeans and North Americans said it was and wanted it to be. One of those myths attributes to Latin America a unity it does not have—that of cultural homogeneity—and ignores the diversity or variety on which, precisely, its common denominator is situated: that different historical eras and cultures coexist in Latin America. Arturo Uslar Pietri explained, several years ago already, that it was in this sense that you had to understand Latin American literature as "mestiza": because it expressed a polyhedral world, of traditions, uses, beliefs, cultures, and levels of evolution that were different and, at times, radically antagonistic.

This interrogation has been the subject of impassioned arguments: Is Latin America part of the West, culturally speaking, or is it essentially different, like China, India, or Japan? I agree with Octavio Paz's opinion: Latin America is an overseas continuation of the West that, since the colonial era, has acquired its own contours, which, without splitting off from the common trunk, give it a differentiated personality. This is an opinion that is far from being shared by all Latin Americans. Often it is refuted with the argument that if this were so, Latin America would be in its culture and art only an ancillary derivation of Europe.

Those who believe this are, at times without being aware of it, nationalists convinced that each people or nation has a unique emotional and metaphysical configuration, of which its culture is an expression. It is not so. Latin America is so many dissimilar things that only by fragmenting it and excluding a good part of those fragments making up its reality would you be able to determine a specific trait valid for the entire continent. That which is diverse, compatible in its case with a subterranean unity, ends up being largely a consequence of the Western sources feeding it. That is why Latin Americans mostly express themselves in Spanish, English, Portuguese, and French. That is why they are Catholic, Protestant, atheist, or agnostic. And the ones who are atheist and agnostic are thus in the way they learned from the West, just like their reactionaries and revolutionaries, their democrats and their liberals, their traditional or vanguard artists, romantics, classicists, or postmodernists. Now, in their most creative moments, Latin Americans were never merely a "carbon copy" of what they took from Western culture. The phrase comes from José Carlos Mariátegui, one of the very few Latin American Marxists who did not limit himself to mouthing, like a ventriloquist, the European Marxists among whose pages he grew up, but used those readings to make an original analysis, although not always a correct one, of the social and economic problems of his country, Peru.

Another interesting example of this phenomenon is Euclides da Cunha, the Brazilian writer who in *Rebellion in the Backlands* scrutinized the War of Canudos in the Brazilian northeast at the end of the nineteenth century, relying on all of the reigning sociological and philosophical theories in Europe. The result was contrary to what he had foreseen: instead of figuring out the deep meaning of that war unleashed by a messianic movement, it became obvious that those European conceptual schemas were insufficient to explain the conflict, born precisely from a deep distortion of certain values and religious doctrines that, in the primitive world of Bahia, were transformed into their antithesis.

Mariátegui and da Cunha are two instances among many of the way that Latin America, starting from European sources, found its own music that distinguishes it without animosity from the voices of the old world. The artistic feats that the great Latin American creators have carried out would have been impossible without dominating some techniques that they learned to acclimate to their own circumstances. Is this not the most valuable characteristic of what we call Western culture? The perpetual renewal of forms and ideas as a product of criticism and self-criticism. The constant assimilation of imported values and principles that enrich its own. All of it within a coexistence of difference that makes freedom possible, a critical spirit and vocation for universality.

Those who have been most insistent on distancing Latin America from the West have been those Western writers, thinkers, or artists who, disappointed with their own culture, go out in search of others that can better satisfy their appetite for the exotic, the primitive, magical, irrational, and the innocence of the Rousseauist noble savage, and have made Latin America the location of their utopias. This has yielded excellent literary fruits, as we have seen. But it has inhibited our development, setting us back with regard to other regions of the world. We should reject those lovers of cataclysms for whom Latin America does not seem to have any other raison d'être than to serve as the stage for their romantic fantasies that European spaces, with their boring democracies, no longer tolerate in their confines. And above all we should stop forcing ourselves to represent those fictions that certain Europeans and North Americans invent for us, disenchanted with mediocre democracy and impatient to live those strong emotions of the revolutionary adventure that, they believe, Latin America can offer them. Let the utopia be confined to our literature and our arts and our private lives, where it is always stimulating and beneficial. The utopian vocation has impregnated American art and made of it an ambitious, audacious, and free art without blinders that has left an important mark on the culture of our time. But it should not leave that area and jump into the political and social realm where only realist visions, pragmatism about what is possible in the framework of coexistence, legality, and freedom bring progress and prosperity.

We now need Latin America to carry out in the political and social arena the same feats that its creators carried out in the realms of literature, visual arts, music, and film. For that, we need less delirium and more sense and rationality. To give up what is impossible and the siren songs of unreality, beneficial and succulent to the makers of fiction, but damaging to those who want to focus on the hard task of defeating ignorance, hunger, exploitation, and poverty, creating a world without despotism, a just and free world with equal opportunities for all, where happiness is reached not only by closing your eyes to the surrounding reality and taking refuge in dreams and fiction, but also, at times, in real life.

Mexico, April 2007

Hunting Gays

The night of last March 3, four Chilean neo-Nazis, led by a brute nicknamed "Pato Core," found lying, near Santiago's Parque Borja, Daniel Zamudio, a young homosexual activist who was twenty-four years old and worked as a sales clerk in a clothing store. For six hours, as they drank and joked, they devoted themselves to punching and kicking the "faggot," to throwing rocks at him and carving swastikas on his chest and back with a broken bottle. In the morning, Daniel Zamudio was taken to a hospital, where he agonized for twenty-five days, at the end of which he died due to multiple traumas caused by the ferocious beating.

This crime, the offspring of homophobia, has caused a vivid impression on public opinion, not only Chilean, but South American, and we are seeing more open condemnation of discrimination against and hate for sexual minorities, so deeply rooted in Latin America. The president of Chile, Sebastián Piñera, called for exemplary punishment and asked lawmakers to reconsider an antidiscrimination law that has been languishing for seven years in the Chilean parliament, stalled by the fear of certain legislators that, if approved, it would open the path for same-sex marriage.

We hope that the immolation of Daniel Zamudio serves to

bring to light the tragic condition of gays, lesbians, and trans-sexuals in Latin American countries, where without a single exception they are the object of ridicule, repression, marginaliza-tion, persecution, and campaigns to discredit them that, in gen-eral, have the open and massively enthusiastic support of the bulk of public opinion.

The easiest and most hypocritical thing to do in this matter is to attribute Daniel Zamudio's death only to four villainous poor devils who call themselves neo-Nazis probably without even knowing what Nazism is or was. They are no more than the crudest and most repulsive patrols of the time-honored tradition that presents gays and lesbians as sick or depraved creatures that should be kept at a preventive distance from normal people because they corrupt the healthy social body and induce it to sin and to moral and physical disintegration in perverse and abomi-nable practices.

This idea of homosexuality is taught in schools, is transmit-ted in the heart of families, is preached from pulpits, disseminated in every means of communication, appears in public discourse, in radio and television programs, and in plays where "faggots" and "dykes" are always grotesque characters, anomalous, ridicu-lous, and dangerous, altogether worthy of the disgust and discrim-ination of decent, ordinary people. The gay is always "the other," the one that negates and frightens us, but also fascinates, like the gaze of the cobra that freezes the innocent bird.

In such a context, what is surprising is not that abominations such as the sacrifice of Daniel Zamudio occur, but that they hap-pen so infrequently. Although, perhaps, it would be fairer to say that they are so little known, because homophobic crimes that are publicized are surely only a small part of those actually commit-ted. And in many cases, the families themselves of victims prefer to throw a veil of silence over them, to avoid dishonor and shame.

I have here before me, for example, a report prepared by the Homosexual Movement of Lima, sent to me by its president,

Giovanny Romero Infante. According to this investigation, between the years 2006 and 2010 in Peru, 249 people were killed for their "sexual orientation and gender identity." In other words, one per week. Among the appalling cases detailed in the report, that of Yefri Peña stands out. Her face and body were disfigured by five "machos" with the top of a bottle, and police refused to help her because she was a transvestite while the doctors of a hospital refused to treat her because they considered her a "ground zero of infection" who could infect those around her.

These extreme cases are atrocious, of course. But surely the most terrible aspect of being lesbian, gay, or transsexual in countries such as Peru or Chile is not these exceptional cases, but rather a daily life condemned to insecurity, fear, and a permanent awareness of being considered (and coming to feel so) a reprobate, abnormal, a monster. To have to live in hiding, with the permanent fear of being discovered and stigmatized, by parents, relatives, friends, and an entire prejudiced social environment that is cruel to gays as if they were a plague. How many young people tormented by this social censure have been pushed to suicide or suffer traumas that ruined their lives? In my social circle alone, I know of many cases of this monumental injustice that, in contrast to others, like economic exploitation or political trampling, does not tend to be denounced in the press or appear on the social programs of those who consider themselves to be reformists and progressives.

Because when it comes to homophobia, the left and the right are mixed up as one sole entity devastated by prejudice and stupidity. It is not only the Catholic Church and Evangelical sects that repudiate homosexuals and stubbornly oppose gay marriage. The two subversive movements that in the 1980s undertook armed rebellion to establish communism in Peru, Sendero Luminoso and the MRTA (Movimiento Revolucionario Túpac Amaru), systematically executed homosexuals in every town they captured (the Spanish Inquisition did no more or less throughout all of its sinister history).

To liberate Latin America from the inveterate defects of machismo and homophobia—two sides of the same coin—will be long and difficult, and the path to this liberation will have many other victims along the way like the unlucky Daniel Zamudio. The matter is not political, but rather religious and cultural. We have been brought up since time immemorial to believe that there is a sexual orthodoxy from which only perverts and the mentally ill stray, and we have seen this aberrational nonsense transmitted to our children, grandchildren, and great-grandchildren, helped by the dogmas of religion and entrenched moral customs and habits. We are afraid of sex and it is difficult for us to accept that in this uncertain domain there are differing and various options that should be accepted as manifestations of rich human diversity. And that in this aspect of the condition of men and women, freedom should also reign, allowing that, in sexual lives, each chooses his or her behavior and vocation without any limitations besides the respect and consent of their partner.

The minority of people who are beginning to accept that a lesbian or gay man is as normal as a heterosexual, and that, as such, she or he should be given the same rights as the latter— such as being able to marry and adopt children, for example—is still reticent to fight a battle in favor of sexual minorities, because they know that winning that battle will be like moving mountains, struggling against a deadweight born of this primitive rejection of "the other," he who is different, because of the color of his skin, his customs, his language, and his beliefs, and that is the fodder of wars, genocides, and holocausts that fill the history of humanity with blood and corpses.

We have made many advances in the struggle against racism, undoubtedly, although without eliminating it. Today, at least, we know we shouldn't discriminate against black, yellow, Jewish, mixed race, and Indian, and, in any case, it is viewed very negatively to proclaim oneself a racist. This is not the case when it comes to gays, lesbians, and transsexuals, who can be scorned and abused with impunity. They are the most eloquent demonstration of how far a good part of the world is from true civilization.

Lima, April 2012

Marijuana Comes Out of the Closet

Little by little, the battle for the legalization of drugs is making headway and pushing back those who, against all evidence, believe that the repression of production and consumption is the best way to combat the use of narcotics and the cataclysmic consequences of narco-trafficking in the lives of nations.

We should applaud the brave decision by the Uruguayan government and its president, José Mujica, to propose a law to parliament legalizing the cultivation and sale of cannabis. If it is approved—which seems likely since the Frente Amplio has the majority in both chambers and, besides, there are deputies and senators in the opposition parties, Blanco and Colorado, who approve of the measure—this will inflict a hard blow to the mafias who use the country not only as a market for drugs but also as a platform for exporting them to Europe and Asia. This law is part of a series of orders meant to combat "citizen insecurity," which has been aggravated for a while now in Uruguay, like in all of Latin America, by the criminality associated with narco-trafficking.

"Someone has to be the first," President Mujica stated to Brazil's *O Globo*. "Someone has to start in South America. Because we are losing the battle against drugs and crime on the continent." Uruguay's minister of defense, Eleuterio Fernández Huidobro, as the central reason for this audacious step, pointed out that "the prohibition of certain drugs is generating more problems for our country than the drugs themselves." This truth—of which we have proof every day throughout the world with the news of the murders, kidnappings, torture, terrorist attacks, and gang wars planting innocent corpses in cities, and in the systematic deterioration of countries' democratic institutions, more numerous by the day, where the powerful drug cartels corrupt functionaries, judges, police, journalists, and sometimes decide the results of electoral disputes—cannot be said any more lucidly and concisely. The prohibition of drugs has only served to turn narco-trafficking into a dizzying economic and criminal power that has multiplied violence and insecurity and that could very soon fill the third world with narco-states.

According to preliminary information, this legal project would put in the hands of the Uruguayan state control over the quality, quantity, and price of marijuana, and buyers would have to register and be at least eighteen years of age. Each buyer would be able to acquire a maximum of forty joints per month and the sales taxes would be used for rehabilitation treatment and prevention, and in the creation of a center to control product quality. A comment regarding the Uruguayan initiative that I just read in *Time* magazine, which is otherwise favorable to the measure, reminds us what a poor manager the public sector tends to be, and with good judgment, it deplores not allowing the private sector the freedom to carry out this task, although, of course, under strict regulation.

This same essay examines what happened in Portugal, where, over a decade ago, marijuana was partially legalized without bringing an increase in the consumption of stronger drugs, which is what those who are unyieldingly opposed to the legalization of the so-called soft drugs allege. *Time* also reminds us that, according to the latest polls, 50 percent of citizens in the United States declare themselves in favor of the legalization of marijuana. This is an extraordinary development when you recall the tempest of criticism, and even insults, that Milton Friedman received a few decades ago when he defended the legalization of drugs and predicted the absolute failure of repression policies on which the U.S. government had already spent billions of dollars.

The government of Uruguay, as it dares to legalize marijuana, is taking on many of the reasons and studies disseminated by the Latin American Commission for Drugs and Democracy, led by the former presidents Fernando Henrique Cardoso of Brazil, César Gaviria of Colombia, and Ernesto Zedillo of México, and of which I myself am part, along with eighteen other people from various professions and interests in the region. Initially received with reticence and concern, and at times hard criticism, this commission has won an audience and respectability due to the seriousness of its work, in which distinguished specialists have always participated in the spirit of dialogue and a clear democratic vocation.

The problem with drugs no longer only concerns public health, the way it destroys the lives of so many children and young people, and not even the terrible indices of increases in criminality that it causes, but the very survival of democracy. Repressive policies have not restricted consumption in any country. Rather, in all of them, developed or not, use continues to slowly grow, while on the other hand having the perverse consequence of increasing the price of drugs all the more. This has transformed the cartels that control drug production and commercialization into real economic empires, armed to the teeth with the most modern and lethal weapons, with resources that allow them to become infiltrated in all levels of the state and a capacity for intimidation and corruption that is practically unlimited.

What happened in Mexico is extremely instructive. President Calderón, conscious of the enormous risk narco-trafficking represented to the functioning of institutions, decided to combat it head-on, incorporating the army into this struggle. The fifty thousand dead that this war has already claimed do not seem to have made the least impact on the mafia's criminal activities, nor have they at all diminished the consumption of soft or hard drugs in Mexican society, while in contrast, it has unleashed a growing desperation and disappointment in the government, which is even reproached for "having declared a war it could not win." Fantastic conclusion! So, then, should they have lowered their weapons, surrendered, looked away, and let the gunmen and drug traffickers take control little by little of all of Mexico's institutions, until they came to be the country's real leaders?

Obviously this is not the solution. What then? The answer is what the Uruguayan government, with great merit, is undertaking. To change the tactic, since the purely repressive one is counterproductive. In the current circumstances, the first priority is not putting an end to the production and consumption of drugs, but doing away with the criminality that intimately depends on these activities. And for this, there is no other path but legalization.

Naturally, legalizing drugs implies risks. These should be taken into account and combated. Those of us who defend legalization always highlight that this measure should be accompanied by a parallel effort to inform, rehabilitate, and prevent the consumption of narcotics that are dangerous to one's health. It has been done fairly successfully in the case of tobacco, all over the world. The consumption of cigarettes has diminished, and today there are few places left where citizens are not aware of the risks to which they expose themselves by smoking. If they want to run them, knowing full well that they do so, isn't it their right? I think so, and that it is not within the bounds of the state to prevent a citizen who is of sound mind to fill his lungs with nicotine if he feels like it.

I have always had great affection for Uruguay, ever since 1966, when I went to Montevideo for the first time and discovered that Latin America was not just a land of guerrillas and terrorists, revolutionaries and fanatics, exploiters and exploited, that it could also be the land of tolerance, coexistence, democracy, culture, and freedom. It is true that Uruguay came to later live the atrocious experience of a military dictatorship. But the time-honored tradition of democracy has allowed it to recover more quickly than other countries, and today, who would have predicted it, under the government of a Frente Amplio that seemed so radical, and a seventy-seven-year-old president who was a guerrilla, it is again a paragon of legality, freedom, progress, and creativity, an example that the rest of the Latin American countries should follow.

Madrid, June 2012

Julian Assange on the Balcony

In a cubicle of the Ecuadorian embassy in London where Julian Assange, the founder of WikiLeaks, is taking refuge, he must now have more than enough time to reflect on the extraordinary story of his life, beginning as an obscure little thief of others' intimacies (this is what a computer hacker does, although the label tries to inject some dignity into this ignoble profession) in the land of kangaroos and eventually becoming a contemporary icon, as famous as soccer players or the latest rock star, to many, a free expression here at the center of an international diplomatic conflict.

There is such a web of confusions and lies about this character, created by him and his fans, and propelled by the avid journalism of the scandal, that there are millions of people in the world convinced that the awkward Australian with yellow-white hair who appeared on the balcony of the Ecuadorian embassy in the neighborhood favored by Arab sheiks in London—Knightsbridge—to give lessons about freedom of expression to President Obama, is a person politically persecuted by the United States, saved in extremis by no less than President Rafael Correa of Ecuador, in other words, the government that, after Cuba and Venezuela, has committed the worst offenses against the press in Latin America, closing radio stations, newspapers, taking to servile courts journalists and dailies that dared to denounce the traffic and corruption of his regime, and presenting a gag law that would practically seal the disappearance of independent journalism in the country. In this case, the old refrain is true: "Tell me who your friends are and I'll tell you who you are." Because President Correa and Julian Assange are made for each other.

In reality the founder of WikiLeaks is not even the object right now of a judicial investigation in the United States, nor has that country made any request asking anyone to take him to court. The supposed risk that, if he is handed over to the Swedish police, the government of Sweden could send him to the United States is, for now, a presumption devoid of any basis and has no other objective than to surround this character with an aura of a freedom martyr that he certainly does not deserve. Swedish justice is not asking for him for his hacking deeds—better said, his betrayals—but rather, because of accusations of rape and sexual harassment against him by citizens of that country. That is how the Supreme Court of Great Britain has understood it and thus decided to move him to Sweden, whose judicial system, in all respects, is equal to Britain's, one of the most independent and reliable in the world. So Mr. Assange is not actually a victim of freedom of expression, but rather a fugitive who uses that pretext not to respond to the accusations weighing on him like a presumed sexual criminal.

The popularity he enjoys is due to the hundreds of thousands of private and confidential documents of different divisions of the U.S. government—starting with the diplomatic corps and ending with the armed forces—obtained through theft and piracy, that WikiLeaks disseminated, presenting them as a great feat for freedom of expression that brought to light intrigues, conspiracies, and behavior at odds with legality. Was it really like that? Did WikiLeaks's denunciations contribute to airing the criminal depths of U.S. political life? So say those who hate the United States, "the enemy of humanity," and are still not happy that liberal democracy, of which this country is the prime defender, won the Cold War instead of Soviet communism or Maoism. But I think that any serene and objective evaluation of the oceans of information that WikiLeaks disseminated shows, besides petty, bureaucratic, and unsubstantial gossip, abundant material that justifiably should remain within a confidential preserve, such as that which affects diplomatic life and defense, through which a state can function and maintain due relations with its allies, with neutral countries, and, especially, with all of its manifest or potential adversaries.

We will never know how all of WikiLeaks's revelations served to undo the information networks laboriously and dangerously assembled by democratic countries in the satrapies that sheltered the international terrorism of Al Qaeda and its brethren, or how many agents and informants of the West's intelligence services were detected and possibly eliminated as an effect of those publications, but there is no doubt that this was one of the sinister consequences of that famous operation of information discharge. Isn't it curious that WikiLeaks made it such a priority to reveal the confidential documents of free countries where, in addition to freedom of the press, there exists a legality worthy of that name, instead of doing so with dictatorships and despotic governments that still proliferate around the world? It is easier to gain the credentials of a freedom fighter by practicing disloyalty, using contraband and information piracy in open societies, under the shelter of a legality that is always reticent to sanction the press's crimes in order to not give the impression of restricting or placing obstacles to the freedom of criticism that is effectively an essential mainstay of democracy, than in filtrating the secrets of totalitarian governments.

WikiLeaks's fans should remember that the other side of the coin of freedom is legality, without which the former disappears sooner or later. Freedom is not, nor can it be, anarchy and the right to information; it cannot mean that in one country what is private and confidential disappears and all of an administration's activities should be immediately public and transparent. This would signify pure and simple paralysis or anarchy, and no government would be able, in such a context, to meet its duties or survive. Freedom of expression is complemented by, in a free society, courts of justice, parliaments, and opposing political parties, and these are the adequate channels to which one can and should recur if there are indications that a government is hiding or criminally obscuring its initiatives and actions. But to bestow that right upon yourself and proceed to forcibly dynamite legality in the name of freedom is to alter that concept and irresponsibly degrade it, turning it into an abuse of liberty. This is what WikiLeaks has done, and even worse, I think, is that it was not in line with certain principles or ideological convictions, but pushed by frivolity and snobbishness, the dominant vectors of the reality-show-obsessed civilization we live in.

Mr. Assange has not practiced in the institution he founded the complete transparency and integrity that he demands of the open societies against which he has fought so fiercely. The defections WikiLeaks has experienced are due, fundamentally, to his resistance to account, to his collaborators, for the several millions of dollars he has received as donations, according to what I have read in an article signed by John F. Burns in the *International Herald Tribune*, dated August 18/19. It is a good indication of how complicated and subtle things can be when they are observed up close and not through the lens of commonplaces, stereotypes, and clichés.

In the current circumstances, there is no reason whatsoever to consider Julian Assange a crusader for freedom of expression; rather, he is an opportunistic freeloader who, thanks to his good instincts, sense of opportunity, and computer skills, assembled a scandalous operation that brought him international fame and the false sense that he was all-powerful, invulnerable, and could allow himself all excesses. He was mistaken and now is the victim of such. In truth, his journey seems to have brought him to a dead-end street, and it is not impossible that, once the storm that brought him fame has passed, he will be remembered for the involuntary help he gave, thinking he was acting in favor of freedom, to its staunchest enemies.

Salzburg, August 2012

Lost Identity

In the September 7 issue of *The New Yorker* this year, there is an "Open Letter to Wikipedia" by the American novelist Philip Roth that is extremely instructive. It narrates how Roth, when he discovered the erroneous description Wikipedia had of his novel *The Human Stain*, sent a letter to the administrator of this virtual encyclopedia, asking for a correction. The response he received was surprising: although the entity recognized that an author is "an indisputable authority regarding his own work," his word was not sufficient for Wikipedia to admit it was mistaken. They needed, in addition, "other secondary sources" to support the correction.

In his open letter, Philip Roth demonstrates, with accuracy and irrefutable facts, that his novel is not inspired, as Wikipedia affirms, by the life of the critic and essayist Anatole Broyard, whom he met only in passing and about whose private life he knows nothing at all, but rather by that of his friend Melvin Tumin, a sociologist and department chair at Princeton University who, because of having used a word considered derogatory to African Americans, saw himself embroiled in a real nightmare of attacks and punishment that nearly destroyed his life, despite many years spent fighting discrimination and racial prejudice as an intellectual and academic in the United States. Philip Roth published this open letter in *The New Yorker* to try to counteract in some way the falsehood concerning his work that the multitudinous Wikipedia has spilled all over the world already.

This is not the first time that the great American novelist has engaged in a Quixote-like battle in defense of the truth. Some years ago he discovered in *The New York Times* that a statement was attributed to him that he did not recall making. After more than a few gestures, he managed to get to the source that the daily had used to cite him: an interview with an Italian newspaper, signed by Tommaso Debenedetti, but which Roth had never given. That investigation led to the discovery of the fraudulent exploits of Debenedetti, who, for years, had been publishing in the Italian press and in other countries reports regarding people of various professions and backgrounds, all of them invented head to toe. (I earned the honor of being one of his victims, and another one of them was no less than Benedict XVI.) It goes without saying that the seventy-nine false profiles have not warranted any punishment and the story of his fraud has turned the likable Tommaso Debenedetti into a real hero of reality-TV-show civilization.

Now I would like to enter this article and relay two episodes from my recent life that demonstrate a disquieting similarity to what happened to Philip Roth. I was in Buenos Aires and a woman on the street stopped to congratulate me for my "In Praise of Women" (*Elogio a la mujer*), which she had just read on the Internet. I thought she was confusing me with someone else, but, a few days later, once I was back in Peru, two more people claimed they had read this text, signed by me. Finally a charitable, or perverse, soul sent it to me. In short, it was stupid and annoyingly vulgar ("True beauty is in the wrinkles of happiness," "All the beautiful women I have seen are the ones who walk on the streets with long coats and miniskirts, who smell clean and smile when you look at them," and things that are even worse). I asked my friends who were real Internet pros if there was any way to identify the liar who whipped up that rhetorical excrescence using my name and they said that, in theory, there was, but in practice, no. Because there is nothing easier than erasing the footsteps of rhetorical frauds, injecting lies and tricks of that kind. I could try to, of course, but it would take me a lot of time and, without a doubt, some money. It would be better to forget the matter. That's what I did, of course.

Until a year or two later, when I received a call from a journalist at *La Nación*, in Buenos Aires, the newspaper that published my articles in Argentina. He was asking me, surprised, if I was the author of a text, signed with my name, called, "Yes, I'm Crying for You, Argentina," a ferocious diatribe against Argentines that was making the rounds on the Internet. In this case, the text attributed to me was despicable, but was not stupid. The falsifier had concocted it with careful astuteness, taking phrases that I had, in fact, used at one time, for example to criticize the policies of President Cristina Fernández de Kirchner or of President Hugo Chávez, in Venezuela, and peppering them with vileness and pestilent vulgarities of his own making ("the unhinged pariah, troglodyte beast of the extinct and very dear Republic of Venezuela," "Peronism is the party of the most aberrant embittered, full of hate, visceral resentment, fanatics, fascists, ill with inexplicable rage," and beauties of that sort).

I went to see a lawyer. He explained to me that regarding an author's rights, in copyright, the digital world is still a confusing forest, the object of multiple negotiations in which no one can come to an agreement, and that, although in principle, through a long and costly investigation, they could arrive at the source of the fraudulent text, the effort would probably be useless, since the falsifier or falsifiers would have taken the necessary precautions to erase their traces, having posted the slanderous article not from his own computer, but rather from one that can be rented in any cybercafé. So there was nothing to be done, then? In reality, no. Or, rather, yes: take it as a joke and forget about it.

And here we arrive at the most serious and transcendental part of the matter, more permanent than an anecdote. The audio-visual technological revolution, which has pushed communications like never before and given modern society instruments that allow it to bypass all censorship, has also had the perverse and unforeseen effect of putting in the hands of the political and intellectual scoundrel, of the embittered, the envious, the one with complexes, the imbecile, or, simply, the bored one, a weapon that allows him to violate and manipulate what until now seemed to be the last sacrosanct sanctuary of the individual: his identity. Technically it is possible today to revise someone's real life—what he is, what he is like, what he says, what he writes—and start subtly altering it until it is completely changed, causing, along with it, irreparable damages. Probably the worst cases of these criminal operations don't even come from a political conspiracy, or a business or cultural conspiracy, but something more pedestrian, from poor devils who try to combat tedium and the frightening lack of excitement in their lives. They need to entertain themselves somehow, and isn't it a fun sport to vilify or make ridiculous or cause scandal for others, if, besides, they can perpetrate this with the most absolute impunity?

As such, the valuable efforts that Philip Roth makes in defense of his identity as a writer and citizen, so that he is allowed to continue being what he is and not a caricature of himself, although admirable, are probably totally useless. We live in an era when that which we thought was the last bastion of freedom—personal identity, in other words, what we have come to be through our actions, decisions, beliefs, that which crystallizes our life's trajectory—no longer belongs to us except in a very provisional and precarious way. Just like political and cultural freedom, our identity can also be snatched away from us, but in this case by invisible tyrants and dictators, who, instead of whips, swords, or canons, use keyboards and screens and rely on the ether, on an immaterial and surreptitious fluid so subtle and powerful that it can invade our most secret intimacy and capriciously rebuild it.

Throughout history, human beings have had to confront all kinds of enemies of freedom and, with great sacrifices and leaving the battlefield strewn with countless victims, they have always managed to defeat them. I think that, in the long run, we will also defeat this last one. But this victory, I greatly fear, will be a long time coming and neither Philip Roth nor myself will be here to celebrate it.

Madrid, October 12, 2012

The Students

Words can also become worn with use. *Freedom, democracy, human rights, solidarity* often come to our lips and mean almost nothing anymore because we use them to say so many things or so few that they become devalued ghosts of themselves and merely noise. But, all of a sudden, social and political circumstances recharge them with content and truth, impregnate them with feeling and reason, and it is as if they were resuscitated and again express the feelings of an entire people.

That is what we are living in these days, in Venezuela, listening to student leaders and opposition leaders, to ordinary men and women who were never before involved in politics and now are, risking their jobs, tranquility, freedom, and even their lives, compelled by the consciousness that, if there is no national democratic shock to awaken and mobilize it, their country will go to ruin, to a totalitarian dictatorship and the worst economic catastrophe of its entire history.

Although the process has been a long time coming—the last elections saw the gradual growth of opposition to the Chavist regime—the qualitative change took place at the beginning of February of this year, in San Cristóbal, Tachira State, when the attempted rape of a young woman at the University of the Andes led students to call for a huge march against personal insecurity, food insecurity, kidnappings, murders, and the systematic restriction of citizens' freedoms. The regime decided to react harshly. The National Guard and paramilitary forces—armed individuals with guns, knives, and clubs, riding motorcycles with their faces covered—attacked students, beating and shooting them, killing several of them. The dozens detained were taken to far-off barracks where they were tortured with cattle prods, beaten, sodomized with sticks and rifles, and the women raped.

The repressive ferocity was counterproductive. The student mobilization was extended throughout the country and in all of Venezuela's cities and villages, gigantic popular protests that expressed repudiation for the regime and solidarity with the victims. All around, barricades went up and the entire country seemed to be living through a libertarian awakening. The five hundred volunteer attorneys who had made up the Venezuelan Penal Forum and were to defend the detained and denounce the murders, disappearances, and tortures had developed a report that documented, in detail, the savagery with which the heirs of Commander Chávez tried to face that formidable mobilization that has changed the correlation of forces in Venezuela, attracting an unequivocal majority of Venezuelans to the ranks of the opposition.

My impression is that this movement is unstoppable and that even if Maduro and his accomplices try to crush it in a bloodbath, they will fail and massacres will only serve to accelerate their fall. Freedom has won the streets of the country of the real Bolívar (not the caricature that Chavism made of him), and the proclamation of "Twenty-First-Century Socialism" is mortally wounded.

The sooner it goes, the better for Venezuela and for Latin America. The way that the regime, in its frenetic effort to collectivize and convert the nation into one where the state controls everything, has impoverished and destroyed one of the world's potentially richest countries and will remain an emblematic case of the insanity to which blind ideology can lead in our time. Besides having the highest inflation in the world, Venezuela is the country with the least growth on the entire continent, the most violent, the one in which bureaucratic suffocation is so quickly reproduced to the extreme of keeping almost all of public administration paralyzed. The regime of controls, "fair" prices, and state intervention has emptied all the warehouses and markets of products, and the black market and contraband have reached dizzying extremes. Corruption is the only area in which the country is making giant leaps.

Disconcerted by the student-led popular mobilization that it cannot manage to crush through repression, Maduro's government, with the complicity of ALBA countries (Bolivarian Alliance for the Peoples of Our America), tries to buy time by opening peace talks. The opposition has done well in turning to them, but without demobilizing, and demanding, as proof of governmental good faith, at least the release of political prisoners, starting with Leopoldo López, who, by being imprisoned, has turned, according to the latest polls, along with María Corina Machado, into Venezuela's most popular political leader. I have met his mother and his wife, two admirable women who, with unusual courage, face harassment for being among the vanguard of a peaceful battle that the opposition is fighting to prevent the disappearance of the last opportunities for freedom still remaining in Venezuela.

But I would like to once more highlight the very central role that students play in the great quest for freedom in Venezuela. The Chavist revolution must be the only one in history that managed, from the beginning, to deserve the nearly widespread hostility of intellectuals, writers, and artists, as well as that of students, who, in this case, proved to be much more lucid and have better political instincts than their Latin American brethren did in the past.

It is stimulating and revitalizing to see that idealism, generosity, openhandedness, a love for truth, and courage are alive among the youth of Venezuela. Those who, frustrated by how inane are the political struggles in their commonplace and routine democracies, become cynics, have contempt for politics, and adopt the philosophy of "the worst is the best" should take a stroll through the Venezuelan *guarimbas*, for example, the one on Avenida Francisco de Miranda, in the middle of Caracas, where young women and men have been living together for several weeks already, organizing conferences, debates, seminars, explaining to passersby their projects and hopes for a future Venezuela, when freedom and legality return and the country awakens from the nightmare it has been living through for the last fifteen years.

Those who have reached the depressing conclusion that politics is a nasty pastime for thieves and the mediocre, and that, as such, they should turn their backs to it, should come to Venezuela, and by speaking to, listening to, and learning from these young people they will learn that political action can also be noble and altruistic, a way of facing barbarism and defeating it, of working for peace, coexistence, justice, and freedom, without shooting anyone or planting bombs, using reason and words, like philosophers and poets, and creating, every day, gestures, shows, and ideas like artists do, that move and educate and bring others along on the libertarian project. Hundreds of thousands, millions of young Venezuelans are giving an example today to Latin America and the entire world that no one should give up on hope, that a country, no matter how deep the abyss into which demagoguery and ideology have thrown it, can always come out of that trap and redeem itself.

Some of these young people have already been imprisoned and suffered torture, and some of them may die, like the nearly fifty companions that have already lost their lives at the hands of the hooded assassins through whom Maduro seeks to quiet them. They will not be silenced, but it is not fair for them to be so alone, that democratic governments and organizations do not support them and instead, at times, join in the cause with their executioners. Because the most important battle for freedom in our days is happening on the streets on Venezuela and has a young face.

Caracas, April 2014

Part V

José Donoso; or, A Life Made into Literature

He was the most literary of all the writers I have met, not just because he had read so much and knew everything there was to know about the lives of, deaths of, and gossip surrounding literary fairs, but also because he had modeled his life like fiction is modeled, with the elegance, gestures, insolence, extravagance, humor, and arbitrariness shown off by the characters of English novels, his favorite ones of all.

We met in 1968, when he was living in the Mallorcan heights of Pollensa, at an Italian country house from where he contemplated the strict routines of two Carthusian monks, his neighbors, and our first meeting was preceded by a theatrical quality I will never forget. I arrived in Mallorca with my wife, my mother, and my two very small children, and Donoso invited all of us to lunch, through María del Pilar, his marvelous wife, the gardener of his neuroses. I accepted, delighted. The next day, María del Pilar called to explain that when he got to thinking about it, Pepe believed it preferable to exclude my mother from the invitation since her presence could encumber our first encounter. I consented, intrigued. On the eve of the arranged day, another call from María del Pilar: Pepe had asked for the little mirror, and lunch should, perhaps, be canceled. What little mirror was this?

The one that Pepe asked for on those afternoons when he felt fate closing in on him, the one he obstinately pored over waiting for his final breath. I replied to María del Pilar that, lunch or no lunch, little mirror or no little mirror, I would go to Pollensa either way to meet that raging madman in person.

I went and he seduced my whole family with his brilliance, his anecdotes, and, especially, with his obsessions, which he displayed before the world with the pride and munificence with which others display their collections of pictures or stamps. During that vacation we became very good friends and never ceased to be so, despite the fact that we never, I believe, coincided in our literary tastes and distastes, and that I managed, several times, in the years that followed, to drive him crazy by claiming that he praised *Clarissa*, *Middlemarch*, and other similar duds simply because his professors at Princeton had forced him to read them. His knuckles would turn white and his eyes red, but he didn't wring my neck, because that lack of moderation was inadmissible in a good novel.

He was writing at that time his most ambitious novel, *The Obscene Bird of Night*, and, heroically supported by María del Pilar, he relived and personally suffered the obsessions, traumas, delirium, and baroque eccentricities of his characters. One night, at Bob Flakoll and Claribel Alegría's house, he had about twelve of us dinner guests hypnotized as we listened to him refer to, no, rather interpret, sing, and mime like a biblical prophet or wizard in a trance, true or supposed stories of his family: a great-great-grandmother who crossed the Andes in a Homeric mule cart, leading whores to the brothels of Santiago, and another, with a fixation on wrapping and packaging, who saved her nails, hair, food leftovers, everything that ceased to be useful or to be used, in exquisite little boxes and bags that took over closets, wardrobes, corners, rooms, and, finally, the whole house. He spoke with so much passion, gesticulating, sweating, flames coming out of his eyes, that he infected everyone with his fascination and, when it was over, like someone watching the curtain fall at the end of a

Ghelderode play or at the end of *The Obscene Bird of Night*, all of us felt so sad, despondent for being forced to abandon that apocalyptic delirium for mediocre reality. I say all of us, and I lie; in reality, present in the room was also Claribel's brother-in-law, a Norwegian marine biologist who didn't understand Spanish. He spent the whole night pale and huddled up on the edge of a seat, shaking; later, he confessed that at many points of that memorable, incomprehensible, and noisy soiree, he thought he was not going to survive, that he would be sacrificed.

Everything in José Donoso was always literature, but the best quality, and without mere affectation, superficiality, or frivolous representation. He put together his characters with the care and delicacy of the most refined artist painting or sculpting and later transubstantiated himself in them, disappeared in them, re-creating them in their minor details and taking them on to their final consequences. As such, it's no wonder that the most bewitching character he invented was that moving old transvestite from *Hell Has No Limits*, who, in that world of truck drivers and semiliterate brutes, disguises himself as a typical Spanish lady, a *manola*, and dances flamenco even though it might mean his life. Although he wrote stories that required more effort and were more complex, this story is the most complete of his, in which that confusing, neurotic world of rich literary imagination is most perfectly feigned, at odds to the end with the traditional naturalism and realism of Latin American literature, made in the image and likeness of its creator's impulses and most secret ghosts, who leaves his readers.

Among the many characters Pepe Donoso embodied, several of which I had the luck of meeting and enjoying, I am now left with the aristocrat, a Giuseppe Tomasi di Lampedusa type, from the years he lived in the mountains of Teruel, in the little village of Calaceite, where he rebuilt a beautiful stone house and where my sons' pranks and those of his daughter Pilar brought him the story in his novel *A House in the Country*. The village was full of widowed little old ladies, which ended up charming him, since old age had been, along with illness, one of his most precocious vocations—describing its evils and symptoms, he arrived at levels of inspiration bordering on a genius that not even his stories of arteriosclerotic old men and women surpassed—and he had one sole doctor, a hypochondriac like him, who, every time Pepe went to tell him about his illnesses, stopped him short, saying woefully, "My head, my back, my stomach, my muscles hurt more than yours." They got along marvelously, of course.

The first time I went to spend a few days with him in Calaceite, he informed me that he had already bought himself a tomb in the cemetery because that landscape of rugged roughness and lunar mountains was the most appropriate for his poor bones. The second time, I confirmed that he had in his power the keys to the churches and sacristies in the entire region, over which he exercised a sort of feudal guardianship since no one could visit them or go to pray in them without his permission. And the third time, that, besides being the supreme pastor or super sacristan of the region, he also served as judge, since, seated at the door of his house and stuffed into espadrilles and a beekeeper's suit, he settled the local conflicts neighbors put to his consideration. He represented that role marvelously, and even his physical appearance, his shock of gray hair and unkempt beard, the deep stare, the paternal gestures, the good-natured funny faces, the faded wardrobe, made of him a timeless patriarch, an absolute lord and master of bygone times.

The time period in which I saw him the most was in Barcelona, between 1970 and 1974, when, due to a conspiracy of circumstances, the beautiful Mediterranean city became the capital of Latin American literature, or something like that. He describes one of these meetings—at Luis Goytisolo's house—in his personal history of the "boom" that marks those exciting years in which literature seemed so important to us and so capable of changing people's lives, and in which the abyss separating writers and Spanish and Latin American readers seems to have been abolished, and in which friendship seemed unbreakable, with a nostalgia that shines through the lines of his prose so insistent on keeping an English circumspection. It is a night I remember very well, because I lived it and then relived it reading his book, and I could even add a comment about something he left out, that anecdote he used to tell when he was swept away and feeling at ease—and he told it in such a way that it was impossible not to believe him—about when he was a shepherd in the solitude of the Chilean Magallanes, and he would castrate rams in the primitive way, in other words, bite by bite ("Like this, zas, zas!") and then spit out the jewels sixty-some feet away. At some point, I heard him boast of having made short work, he alone with his teeth, of the virility of at least a thousand defenseless rams in the remote Magallanes.

The last two times I saw him, last year and a few months ago, in Santiago, I knew that this time, literature was not at play, or rather, that this was realistic literature, pure documentary. He had gotten very, very thin and could barely speak. The first time, in the clinic where he had just received an operation, he spoke to me of Morocco and I understood he had confused me with Juan Goytisolo, of whom he had read a book recently. When I said goodbye to him the second time, he was lying nearly breathless on his bed. "Henry James is shit, Pepe." He pressed my hand to force me to lower my head until it was at the same level as his ear: "Flaubert, more so."

Pepe, my dear: this is not a tribute. It is just an article. The real tribute comes now, when, alone, I will read from beginning to end, with that attentive, intense, and somewhat malevolent gaze with which good literature should be read, your *Conjectures on the Memory of My Clan* that I bought in the Madrid airport a week ago, that was piled up on my night table among books to be read, but that I have decided to move to the head of the stack.

London, December 8, 1996

Cabrera Infante

Humor, word games, movies, and a persistent nostalgia for a city that might have never existed are the main ingredients in Guillermo Cabrera Infante's work. The Havana that appears in his stories, novels, and accounts, and leaves such vivid memories in the reader's mind, must surely be—like Joyce's Dublin, Svevo's Trieste, or Cortázar's Buenos Aires—a product more of the writer's imagination than of his memories. But there it is now, smuggled into reality, more real than the one that served as his model, living as he did almost exclusively at night, in the turbulent pre-revolutionary years, shaken by tropical rhythms, smoky, sensual, violent, journalistic, bohemian, sunny, gangsterish, in his delectable eternity of words. No modern writer in our language, perhaps with the exception of Macondo's inventor, has been capable of creating a local mythology with so much strength and color as this Cuban has.

Ever since I read *Three Trapped Tigers*, in manuscript form (the book was called "View of Dawn in the Tropics" at the time), in 1964, I knew that Guillermo Cabrera Infante was a great writer and I fought uncompromisingly for him to win the Biblioteca Breve Prize, on whose jury I sat. Two days later, in my office at Radio Television France, where I earned my living, the telephone rang. "This is Onelio Jorge Cardoso," the thundering voice said. "Do you remember me? We met in Cuba, last month. Listen, why did you give that prize, in Barcelona, to that dullard Cabrera Infante?" "His novel was the best one," I answered, trying to remember the speaker. "But you're right. I met him the night the prize was given and it's true, he seems like a real bore." Not long after, I received a copy of *In Peace as It Is in War* with the most uncomfortable inscription: "For Mario, from a certain Onelio Jorge Cardoso." Later, when fate would have it that, exiled from Cuba and kicked out of Spain, where he was denied political asylum, Guillermo went to seek refuge in London, in a basement located in Earl's Court, half a block from my house, he confessed to me that, because of me, he had never again jokingly assumed a false identity with any of his friends.

Naturally, this was a lie. Cabrera Infante has always been willing to earn himself any and all enemies, to lose all of his friends, and even his life, over a joke, a parody, a play on words, mental gymnastics, verbal jousting, because for him, humor was not, as it is for most mortals, a pastime of the soul or amusement that relaxes the spirit, but a compulsive way of challenging the world and of demolishing the certainties and rationale underpinning it, bringing to light the infinite possibilities of nonsense, surprise, and outlandishness, and that, in the hands of a skilled juggler of language as he is, can turn into dazzling intellectual fireworks and delicate poetry. Humor is not just the way he writes, in other words, it's something very serious, with which his existence is deeply engaged. It is his defense mechanism against life, the subtle method he relies upon to deactivate the aggressions and frustrations that stalk him daily, undoing them via illusions of rhetoric, games, and jokes. Few suspect that a good part of his most hilarious essays and chronicles, such as the ones that appeared in the late sixties in *Mundo Nuevo*, were written when he had become something of a pariah, confined in London without a passport, without knowing if his petition for asylum would be approved by the British government, barely surviving with his two small daughters—thanks to the love and strength of the extraordinary Miriam Gómez—and ceaselessly attacked by valiant gossip columnists who, by taking him on, were earning their credentials as progressives, when the whole world seemed to be ganging up on him. Nonetheless, from the typewriter of that harassed writer, whose nerves were on the verge of exploding, rather than lamentations or insults, guffaws, puns, ingenious absurdities, and fantastic rhetorical sleights of hand came forth.

As such his prose is one of the most personal and incredible creations of our language, an exhibitionist, luxurious, musical, and intrusive prose that cannot narrate anything without simultaneously narrating to itself, interjecting his bravado and linguistic somersaults, his disconcerting wisecracks, at each step, between what is told and the reader, such that the latter, often, dizzy, divided, absorbed by the frenzy of the verbal show, forgets the rest, as if the richness of the form itself became a pretext, the content an unnecessary accident. A learned disciple of those great Anglo-Saxon jugglers of language, such as Lewis Carroll, Laurence Sterne, and James Joyce (whose *Dubliners* he translated impeccably), his style is, nevertheless, unmistakably his, of a sensory and eurythmic quality that he, at times, in one of those fits of nostalgia for the land that was taken from him and without which he cannot live, nor, above all, write, insists on calling "Cuban." As if literary styles had a nationality! They don't. In reality it is a style that is only his, created in his image and likeness, the product of his phobias and affinities—his finely tuned ear for music and for spoken language, his elephant-like memory for the dialogue of movies he has liked and the conversations with friends he loved and enemies he hated, his passion for the great Latin American and Spanish art of gossip and delirious joking, and the oceanic literary, political, cinematographic, and personal information that he arranges to arrive every day at his book-, magazine-, and video-plastered lair on Gloucester Road, and that is light-years away from the other writers who are as Cuban as he is: Lezama Lima, Virgilio Piñera, or Alejo Carpentier.

Since he likes film so much, sees so many movies, has written screenplays and collected several volumes of cinematographic essays and criticism, many have the impression that Guillermo Cabrera Infante is closer to the so-called seventh art than to conventional literature. It is an explainable error, but a colossal one. In reality, and although he himself may not wish it to be so, and in case you don't know, we're dealing with one of the most literary writers in existence, in other words, more a slave to the cult of the word, of the phrase, of the linguistic expression, to such an extreme that this happy servitude has taken him to the extreme of creating literature that is essentially made of an exclusive and excluding use of the word before anything else, a literature that is so spellbound by words that, to fuel them, to turn them around, to squeeze them and put them on display and play with them, he often manages to dissociate them from what the words also represent: people, ideas, objects, situations, facts, a lived reality. Something that, in our literature, has not happened since the glorious times of the Spanish Golden Age, with Quevedo's conceptismo paroxysms or Góngora's labyrinthine architecture of images. Cabrera Infante has taken much more from the films that have served him, as Degas did with ballet, Cortázar with jazz, Proust with the marquesas, and Joannot Martorell with the rites of chivalry. To read his chronicles and commentaries on movies—especially that dazzling collection *A Twentieth-Century Job* (1963)—is to read a new genre, which seems like criticism but is actually something much more artistic and elaborate than reviews or analysis, a genre that partakes as much in storytelling as in poetry, except that its starting point, the material that makes it up, is not lived experience, or dreamed up by the author, but rather is lived by those animated fantasies that are the heroes of films and the hardworking directors, screenplay writers, technicians, and actors who bring them to life, raw material that stimulates

Cabrera Infante, fires his imagination and his words, and leads him to invent those precious objects that are so persuasive they seem to re-create and explain film (life), when, in reality, they are nothing more than (nothing less than) fictions, literature.

Cabrera Infante is not a politician and I am sure that he would subscribe without qualification to Borges's statement: "Politics is one of the forms of tedium." His opposition to the Cuban dictatorship has a more moral and civic than ideological reason—a love for freedom that is more than an adherence to some party-driven doctrine—and as such, although throughout his long life as an exile, definitive vituperation against Castroism and its accomplices have emerged from his pen and his mouth, he has always preserved his independence, without ever identifying himself with any of the tendencies of the Cuban democratic opposition, on the island or in exile. Despite this, for at least a couple of decades, he was an outcast to a great part of Latin America and Spain's intellectual class, bought off or intimidated by the Cuban Revolution. This represented infinite sorrows and, nearly, disintegration. But thanks to his vocation, his obstinacy, and, of course, to Miriam's marvelous company, he endured the isolation and harassment by his colleagues just as he endured the other exile, until, little by little, new developments in the political arena in recent years and a change in the atmosphere and ideological realities have at last made it possible for his talent to be recognized in broad sectors and returned to him his right to his city. The Cervantes Prize that was just given to him is not only an act of justice for a great writer. It is also an act of amends to a singular creator who, because of intolerance, fanaticism, and cowardice, has spent more than half of his life living like a ghost and writing for no one, in the most limitless solitude.

Berlin, December 1997

Welcome to Fernando de Szyszlo

I met Szyszlo in the middle of 1958 when he was getting ready to leave for Washington and I had my bags packed to travel to Europe. He lived in an attic built on the rooftop of a house on Avenida Arenales, a warm and rickety bastion that recalled Paris in its bohemian informality. In that brief encounter, we talked about the poet César Moro, a friend of his who had passed recently, whose unpublished poems and prose, the edition of which I was helping André Coyné prepare, had us going to Szyszlo for help. He did help us; in fact, one could write a very long history of poets and writers in need who, for more than half a century, like us that time, have gone knocking on the doors of Szyszlo's workshop and come out with the sketch, the engraving, the illustration, the subscription, and the encouragement they were seeking. But for me, that quick conversation, besides winning me a friend, also gave me an idea of a painter who, beyond painting very well, also knew about poetry and literature, cited Proust and Rilke, loved culture, and had ideas and reasons, in addition to instinct, institutions, and an artisanship that spanned the talent of all the painters I had met until then. Forty years later and after meeting at least two hundred more painters, I must confess that only a handful of them have given the impression that

Szyszlo does, of an exceptionally refined and intelligent creator who moves with ease in the world of knowledge and can skillfully opine on his trade and many other cultural matters.

You do not need to be refined or intelligent to be a great painter, of course, or to be gifted with intellectual lucidity and fully understand what you are doing with a paintbrush to later formulate it in writing. These are two different things. The history of art is full of great artists who didn't know what they were doing, although they did so marvelously well. The clearest example is Picasso, the great deranger of modern painting, the living border where the attitudes, ambitions, techniques, aesthetics of the past changed in nature and were transformed and dispersed into the thousand and one directions of contemporary art. No artist has marked his time and the artistic work of his era more than Picasso, whose discoveries, experiments, acrobatics, delirium, and games, besides producing masterworks, have planted the most diverse tendencies of modern painting, from cubism to pop art, from surrealism to abstraction and conceptual art. Picasso's genius was essentially intuitive, not at all intellectual; the daring and originality that burst through everywhere in his paintings and sculptures, nonetheless, can become the pathetic babbling of banalities or mere insolence on the few occasions on which he tried to theorize, to reason about what he was doing and explain it conceptually. And from a moral and political point of view, it is better to quickly turn the page, since the unquestioned genius of modern art died undisturbed by the horrific revelation of the millions dead in the Gulag when he paid tribute to Stalin and his regime, a regime that otherwise always considered Picasso's art as contemptible, because it was decadent and bourgeois. His case is not unusual: creators abound who express themselves on the canvas and become so completely consumed that they don't have, shall we say, the time, energy, or curiosity left over to take an interest in other aspects of spiritual life. And who, like a Picasso, act as if genius exonerated them from those ethical and civic servitudes that weigh over common mortals.

This is not the case of Fernando de Szyszlo. His, like a Tàpies or a Mondrian, is that of an artist in whom intuition and mastery have always been irrigated by a powerful intellectual energy, a rational knowledge, and a reflection about his own work, something that comes across in his oeuvre, adding a dimension that transcends the strictly visual. His paintings crackle with allusions and reverberations about other dimensions of knowledge, as Emilio Adolfo Westphalen observed, commenting on an exhibit of paintings by Szyszlo inspired by the anonymous Quechua elegy *Apu Inca Atawallpaman*, translated into Spanish by José María Arguedas. The artists I have cited are very different from one another, although all three of them have created non-figurative painting. But what they really have in common is that the Peruvian, the Catalan, and the Dutchman have been not only original artists but cultured men who reflect, whose sensibilities were refined by intense commerce with intellectual life, capable of creating and taking a critical perspective with what they created, permanent introspection that allowed them to explain what they did, place themselves at will within a tradition and vanguard that faced a tense dialogue in their work, and skillfully opine with good judgment about the phenomenon of art.

Szyszlo's oeuvre is one of those artistic islands on which we can take refuge today, when we feel overwhelmed by the proliferation of false idols, by successful tricksters whom frivolity puts on a throne and publicity passes off as great artists. In this work we are on solid ground and, from the first glance, we know what to expect regarding his quality and style, the unity that holds together all of the themes and designations that move him and the forms he expresses. Perhaps some who view these paintings do not like them or like them less than those of other creators: that is their right. But no one who stands before them and allows himself to be invaded by their communicative force, the sumptuousness and subtlety with which he combines colors in them to create spaces and themes that refer to one another until they constitute their own world, apart from the spectator's world and other worlds created by art, can help but respect it, or deny its vigorous singularity.

Szyszlo's painting, like that of other great creators, is made of dissimilar alliances to which he has added, of course, inventions of his own harvest. This is a generality, I formulate it only to add something that, based on evidence, seems notable to me: that the sources from which Szyszlo's art drinks reveal the universal man he is, the unrepentantly curious and varied person within him.

Of course it is still an instructive paradox that in a nonfigurative painter, ancient pre-Columbian cultures left a more memorable mark than on the so-called Indigenist painters, who loudly reclaimed, with a sincerity that should not be doubted, that tradition and were insistent on continuing it. But in reality, with scarce exceptions, the so-called Indigenism indulged and, frequently, caricaturized the motives of pre-Hispanic art, transferring them to their paintings because of their picturesque exteriors and without greater reworking. This art prowls like a ghost around Szyszlo's painting, "agonizes" there, shall we say, using a Peruvian expression, but it is not easy to circumscribe its presence, since it has dissolved in its context and is, like the food the body turns into blood, bone, and muscle, something transmuted, that has served the artist to erect his own mythology. Nonetheless, the legacy of the ancient artisans who, in the valley of Chancay, in Paracas or in Chavín, produced those objects from mud, those objects woven with feathers, the paintings and metal idols about which Szyszlo has written, on many occasions, with devotion, is unmistakably there, like sediment or an aura, in those realms that suggest the votive temple, the sacrificial chamber or the practice of magic by the prerational being of so many Szyszlo canvases, appearing, at times, in allusive forms such as totems, doors, curves, stairs, and a diversity of geometric motifs or a particularly violent burst of colors that, we notice immediately, lay a subtle bridge between this work so visibly placed in modernity and the dark and skillful trade of those remote maestros who created art without realizing it, thinking that, in making it, they adored their gods and exorcised the dreadful dangers of the world.

In Szyszlo's paintings, the ancient Peruvians shake hands with European cubism, in which the artist took his first steps, with a wide panoply of artists from three worlds, among whom some names, Rothko, Tamayo, Zadkine, Motherwell, and poets such as Octavio Paz, are essential to cite. The way that poetry has stimulated Szyszlo's artistic undertakings would provide material for a study. One of his first exhibits rendered tribute to two incorruptible figures: Rimbaud and André Breton. In 1950 in Paris, he produced a series of lithographs whose source of inspiration was the poetry of César Vallejo. Westphalen commented on the encounter thus: "Vallejo's convulsive, broken, and tender poetry had deeply moved Szyszlo's spirit and his creative impulses, thus aroused, resolved itself in images that spoke of the sadness and uncertainty of man in the face of a hostile world with a 'black sun' and constant anguish, but, also where, incredibly, love and luck bloom. The universes of Vallejo and Szyszlo could have been close, but they persisted in their independent fates, spinning in their own orbits."

Octavio Paz, whom Szyszlo met in 1949 in Paris, when he was writing *The Labyrinth of Solitude*, an essay that, according to his own confession, decisively helped Szyszlo to assume his condition as a Latin American, has been a continuous reference throughout his life. He has always admired Paz's poetry as well as his essays and critical texts, which have touched on, without exaggeration, all of the great artistic, literary, and political problems of our time. The influence of Octavio Paz's critical reflection on modernity and the Mexican past, as a continuity without pause, contributed, without a doubt, to reviving the passion that prehispanic art awoke in Szyszlo at a young age. In his own words, "I think that for Paz, who is deeply Mexican, as for a person born in any Andean part of the continent, it is a stimulating and intoxicating feeling to know that in these same places, many millennia ago, a completely autonomous civilization developed that invented agriculture through its own talent and then had the time to produce a vision of a surrounding world and, with it, develop religious theories and their inseparable component, art. This independence was always and still is present in the words of Octavio Paz, this certainty that he is a person who does not come from a colonial and derivative world, but from a group that had produced culture for centuries." It's obvious, in this citation, that, when speaking of Octavio Paz, Szyszlo is also talking about himself and about the fecund relationship between his vanguard art and the ancient cultures of Andean prehistory.

This theme of identity has always seemed dangerous to me, because unless it is enclosed in the exclusive sphere of the individual, I find it at odds with freedom. The only admissible identity is that which signifies self-creation, a continuous effort by the sovereign individual to make himself, defining himself in the face of those impositions and legacies of the environment in which he develops, the geography that surrounds him, the history that precedes him, language, customs, faith, and the convictions within which he was raised. But none of it is nature, an inalienable condition; it is culture, in other words, something that the reason and sensibility of the individual can accept, reject, or modify thanks to his critical conscience and as a function of his own inclinations, ideas, or devotions. An identity cannot be a prison from which an individual, due to the banal reason of having been born, is held captive and where he is sentenced to live identically to one's self and his companions in that confine, that homeland, that church, that culture outside of whose barbed-wire fence he would lose his soul, becoming no one, nothing.

Nonetheless, the concern for identity that, surely, comes from a hidden fear of freedom, from the obligation to have to create one's self, each day, choosing and rejecting different options, instead of abandoning one's self to the comfortable inertia of belonging to a supposed collective being, of which the individual would be a mere epiphenomenon, has been a constant of Latin American culture, at least since the start of the independent life of our countries.

According to the eras and dominant trends, Latin American artists have considered themselves white, Indian, or mestizo. And each of these definitions, Hispanicism, Indigenism, Creolism, has signified a mutilation, has excluded from our cultural personality some aspects that had as much right to represent us as the one that was chosen.

But despite the countless treaties, articles, debates, symposia about a matter that is never exhausted, because it is largely fictitious, that of our identity, what is certain is that each time we have the luck of finding ourselves before a genuine work of creation that came out of our environment, the doubt vanishes: what is Latin American exists, it is there, it is that thing we see and enjoy, that bothers us and exalts us and that, on the other hand, gives us away. That which happens to us with Borges's stories, Vallejo's or Neruda's poems, the paintings of Tamayo or Matta, also happens to us with Szyszlo's painting: this is Latin America in its highest expression, in it is the best of what we are and what we have. Because the whole world is buried in it.

To dig for the tracks of our identity in those disturbing paintings is dizzying, since they delineate a labyrinthine geography, where the most skilled explorer gets lost. The son of a Polish scientist and a Peruvian from the coast, Szyszlo is also divided regarding his artistic sources: pre-Columbian art, the European vanguard, a mosaic of North American and Latin American painters. But perhaps the landscape that has surrounded him for the greater part of his life—Lima's gray skies, his city, the deserts full of history and death from the coast, and that sea which appears with so much force in a time period of his painting—was such a determining influence in configuring his world as the legacy of anonymous pre-Columbian artisans whose masks, feathered cloaks, clay figurines, symbols, and colors quintessentially appear on his canvases. Or the refined audacities, denials, and experiments of modern Western art, cubism, nonfigurative art, the surrealism without which the paintings of Szyszlo would not be what they are either.

An artist's roots are deep and inextricable, like those of large trees, and if one insists on following them to their origins, he will discover that it is impossible to place them within a region, nation, or continent, since they flow, entirely free through all the territories of humanity, this universe. It is useful to study them, since they bring us closer to this mysterious center from which beauty is born, that indefinable force that certain objects created by man are capable of unleashing and that disarms and subjugates us. But knowing them also serves to know their limits, since the sources that feed a work of art never explain. On the contrary, they show how an artist always goes beyond everything that contributed to shaping his sensibilities and perfecting his technique.

The personal dark material made of dreams and desires, of feelings, reminiscences, and unconscious impulses, is as important in Szyszlo as the picturesque currents through which his work can be filtered, or that which he has admired or emulated. And in this secret stronghold of his personality lies that inaccessible key of mystery that, along with elegance and skill, is the great protagonist of his paintings.

Something happens in them, always. Something that is more than form and color. A spectacle that is difficult to describe although not to feel. A ceremony that sometimes seems to be an immolation or sacrifice, carried out on a primitive altar. A barbarous and violent rite, in which someone bleeds out, disintegrates, hands himself over, and also, perhaps, rejoices. Something, in any event, that is not intelligible, that you have to arrive at through the torturous path of obsession, nightmares, visions. Many times my memory has suddenly updated that strange totem, visceral by-product, or monument covered in disquieting offerings, spurs, suns, cuts, incisions, and antlers that have been recurring characters in Szyszlo's canvases for a long time. And I have asked myself the same thing countless times: Where does it come from? Who, what is it?

I know there is no answer to these questions. But that they are capable of resurfacing and being kept alive in the memory of those who come into contact with his world is the best credential for the authenticity of Fernando de Szyszlo's art. An art that, like Latin America, is lacking in identity because it encompasses all of them: it plunges into the night of extinguished civilizations and brushes elbows with the newest ones that have appeared in any of the world's corners. That is, it stands at the crossroads, avid, curious, thirsty, free of prejudice, open to any influence. But staunchly loyal to its secret heart, that buried and warm intimacy where experiences and lessons are metabolized and where reason is at the service of unreason for the artist's personality and genius to bloom.

Szyszlo's painting, like that of all major artists, has relied on everything within its reach to give shape to that particular need to express what moved him. When, following the conquest of his personal voice, those outside materials managed to be poured into concrete works, they ended up expressing only him. This is ultimately what is important for us to know when we fall under the spell of one of his canvases: that this intense drama that seems to be fighting to emerge, shot out of its violent stillness, from its belligerent immobility of colors and shapes, summarizes, in its unexplored anatomy, the task, fantasy, technique, and also the fears and dreams of a global citizen who, without ever breaking with the dirt feeding him, always practiced his artist's vocation fully conscious that what he was doing did not nor should not have any borders besides that of the human condition, that common denominator of the species, about which all genuine art is a testimony and which genuine art helps to endure all work and days.

To finish, I'd like to refer to the new academic's civic credentials. These are the items that, I know well, are not taken into account, or very rarely so, when a new member is elected in this type of corporation. (Let's also recognize that if they were indispensable requirements, we would have a rather low population here.) But since Fernando de Szyszlo is being adorned, another rarity on his résumé, why not mention them? Although he has never been too interested in politics, or been a politician, or participated in endeavors of this type except as a citizen committed to some ideals but without an interest in power, and has shown himself to jealously guard his independence in the face of it, one can say of Fernando de Szyszlo that in his whole life there is not a single episode, fall, or concession that tarnishes or twists his permanent defense of freedom, understood by its rejection of dictatorships and its defense of democracy. Which means that, in a country like ours, where democracy has been more of an exotic flower and authoritarianism a chronic illness, Szyszlo has spent his life, or slightly less, in the limbos of the opposition. Not even the right-wing dictatorships such as Odría's or the current one, the underhanded one of Messieurs Fujimori, Bari Hermoza, and Montesinos, or the left-wing ones, such as that of General Velasco, would be able to claim having bribed Szyszlo with their praises or intimidated him with their blackmail: he has always been there, defending with a clear voice a regime of legality and freedom for his unfortunate country, that is, of civilization, which, in Peru, once and again has been toppled every time it starts to flourish. If someday Peru manages to break that infernal cycle of long dictatorships and fleeting democratic periods, it will be due, above all, to those clean and persevering Peruvians who, like him, never lost hope or stopped fighting daily, in the humble measure of their powers and, with the example of their behavior, to bring that day closer.

Ever since I can remember, there has always been, in Lima, some figure that, due to his contagious enthusiasm, gift with people, love of culture and art, and his capacity for attracting like minds, has carried out the role of first-rate cultural promoter and, transmitting information, encouraging projects, others' vocations, and projecting in turn an auspicious, warm, stimulating environment, has embodied the life of culture in Peru like a sort of symbol. A person like that was Sebastián Salazar Bondy, a contemporary and fraternal ally or adversary in the youthful aesthetic battles of Fernando de Szyszlo. So too, in the same admirable and discrete way, was Luis Miró Quesada, the unforgettable Cartucho, whose absence has left in the country's intellectual and civic life, as well as in the lives of his friends, a great void. Like them and very few others, Szyszlo has, for many years now, been one of those symbols who makes it worth turning our gaze to Peru when we feel discouraged. With his way of being and acting, with his living work in perpetual renovation, with his generosity, his rigor, and his artist's ambitions, he gives us hope and reminds us that here also it is possible, like in the highest intellectual and artistic centers, to make a work that can be a paragon of the best and maintain, even in the most difficult circumstances, high morals and undefeated integrity.

By bringing him into its bosom, the Academy of Language rewards him and rewards itself. Dear Gody: welcome.

Rio de Janeiro, November 10, 1997

Friendship and Books

It happened to me a few years ago with Javier Cercas and now it just happened again with Héctor Abad Faciolince. When I read the former's extraordinary novel *Soldiers of Salamis*, not only did my body—and well, my spirit—retain that feeling of happiness and gratitude that the reading of a beautiful book provides, but I also felt an urgent need to meet him, to shake his hand and express my gratitude in person. Thanks to Juan Cruz, one of whose merits is inevitably being exactly where he is needed, not long after, on a strange night on which Madrid appeared to have been left deserted and as if lying in wait for nuclear annihilation, I met Cercas at a restaurant filled with ghosts. I immediately discovered that the person was as magnificent as the writer and that we would always be friends.

Rarely do I feel that urgency to personally meet the authors of books that move or amaze me. I've already suffered some deep disappointments in this realm and, generally speaking, I think it is preferable to maintain the ideal image one creates of the writers one admires, over risking a comparison with reality. Except for when you have the overwhelming suspicion that it's worth the effort.

After having read, a while back, *Oblivion: A Memoir*, the most passionate experience I've had as a reader in recent memory, I ardently desired that the gods or luck would grant me the privilege of meeting Héctor Abad Faciolince so that I could tell him in person how much I owed him. It's very difficult to summarize what *Oblivion: A Memoir* is without giving it away, since, like all masterpieces, it is many things at once. To say that it is a heartbreaking memoir about a family and the author's father—who was killed by an assassin—is correct, but petty and infinitesimal, because the book is also a shocking immersion in the inferno of Colombian political violence, in the life and heart of the city of Medellín, in the rites, the mundane, the intimacies and grandeur of a family, a delicate and subtle testimony of a son's love, a true story that is likewise a pretense, due to the way that it is written and built, and one of the most eloquent indictments against terror as an instrument of political action.

The book is heartbreaking, but not gruesome, because it is written in a prose that never goes too far in the outpouring of emotion; it is precise, clear, intelligent, educated; it skillfully manipulates the reader's mood without missteps, hiding certain details from him, and distracting him with the goal of exciting his curiosity and expectations, thus forcing him to participate in the creative task, hand in hand with the author. The ravines of the book are two deaths—that of his sister and of his father—one from an illness and the other through a work of political savagery, and in the description of both there are more silences than elocutions, an elegant modesty that curiously increases the sadness and horror with which the dazzled reader experiences both tragedies.

Contrary to what my description here might evoke, *Oblivion: A Memoir* is not a demoralizing book despite the devastating presence of suffering, nostalgia, and death on its pages. On the contrary, as always happens with successful works of art, it is a book whose formal beauty, quality of expression, lucidity of reflections, grace and refinement in portraying that warm and touching family who you would wish to be your own make it a book that lifts the spirit, demonstrates that even from the vilest and cruelest of experiences, the sensitivity and imagination of a generous and inspired creator can be used to defend life and show that, despite everything, besides pain and frustration, there is also pleasure, love, ideals, uplifting feelings, tenderness, mercy, fraternity, and laughter.

The gods or luck were benevolent with me and organized things in such a way that at the recent Hay literary festival in Cartagena, and, of course, thanks to the intervention of the ubiquitous Juan Cruz, I met Héctor Abad Faciolince in person. Naturally he was as noble as what he wrote. He was educated, likable, and generous, and speaking with him was almost as entertaining and enriching as reading his writing. After chatting for ten minutes at Cartagena's Fishing Club under a postcard-style full moon as the silhouettes of rodents prowled about the dock while we sat in front of a succulent plate of rice with coconut, I knew he would forever be a good friend and companion, and that to the end of our days we would have on our agenda the subject of Onetti, whom I like very much and who bores him. I hope to have time and enough lucidity to persuade him to reread texts such as *El infierno tan temido* or *A Brief Life* and that he discovers how close Onetti's world is to his own, because of the moral authenticity and the technical mastery they both share, as well as the impeccable in-depth study of Latin America that, without meaning to, each has outlined in his fictions.

In the three and a half hours that the flight from Cartagena to Lima lasts, I read Héctor Abad Faciolince's latest book: *Betrayals of Memory*. It contains three autobiographical stories, accompanied by photos of places, objects, and people who illustrate and complete the narrative. The first one, "Un poema en el bolsillo" (A Poem in the Pocket), is by far the best and the longest, and is, in a way, an indispensable complement to *Oblivion: A Memoir*. In the pocket of his father, who was killed in Medellín, the young Abad Faciolince found a poem manuscript that begins with the verse "We are already the oblivion we shall be." At first, it seemed the work of Borges. To confirm the exact identity of the author was a multiyear adventure, composed of trips, meetings, bibliographic searches, interviews, wandering and retracing steps, a truly Borgesian journey of learning and games, an investigation that, rather than being lived, could be called a fantasy of a writer "made rotten by literature," good-natured, mischievous, and with an abundance of displays of imagination.

This exploration at first appears to be a personal and private effort, one more way for a son destroyed by his father's terrible death to keep his memory alive and very close, to show him his love. But little by little, as he compares the opinions of professors, critics, writers, and friends, and the narrator finds himself vacillating between and bothered by contradictory versions, this search brings to light more permanent themes: the identity of the literary work, above all, and the relationship that exists, when it comes to judging the artistic quality of a text, between this and the name and prestige of the author. Respectable academics and specialists insist that the poem is no more than a crude imitation, but suddenly, an unexpected circumstance, a sudden intrusion, turn all the certainties upside down, until the proofs come to be decisive and unequivocal: the poem does, in fact, belong to Borges. The literary merit of the text shifts, increasing or decreasing its originality and importance as the search confirms or denies the possibility that Borges is the author. The text is read with fascination, especially when one has the feeling that, although everything being told is true, it is, or rather, has become, thanks to the magic with which it is told, a beautiful fiction.

This story and the two others—about the young scriptwriter who is half starving to death and trying to survive in Turin and the essay about the "future exes"—had the virtue of making me forget for three and a half hours that I was ten thousand meters high and flying at eight hundred kilometers per hour over the Andes and the Amazon, a feeling that always fills me with dread and claustrophobia. It's clear that I will spend the rest of my life in debt to this Colombian author.

Lima, February 2010

Fifty Years of the Latin American Boom

(Inaugural Conference of the "Canon of the Boom" Congress)

Yesterday, when I began to jot down notes for tonight's talk, I discovered with a certain sense of dread that I am one of the few, very few, survivors of what was called the Boom of Latin American literature. An anguished privilege, to be honest, but one that prevents me from speaking the way a critic would, with perspective, with neutrality, about a phenomenon or movement in which I participated, was an accomplice, and, in a way, was one of the protagonists. So my talk will be rather informal, the testimony of someone who was implicated in what was called the Boom and the recollection of a series of writers who were very important for our language, very important for Latin America, and of course, very important to me, personally.

No one knows how this word came about that designates this movement, the Boom. A few days ago, I saw in a newspaper that the authorship of the word *boom* is attributed to the critic and writer Luis Harss. It is true that he was one of the first, perhaps the first, to bring together in one book a series of writers and see in them common denominators, and that he was one of the first to contribute to the creation of what was called the Boom. But going over his book *Into the Mainstream*, even in the English edition, the blasted "little word" did not appear. I've read different attributions: that it appeared for the first time in an Argentine magazine that was called *Primera Plana*, that it was a university professor who invented it . . . In sum, why *boom*? *Boom* is a word that doesn't mean anything, it is an onomatopoeic word that links itself to the idea of an explosion. Does this mean that Latin American fiction came about in the sixties like an explosion? Of course not. I think that the Boom was, above all, a recognition that Latin America does not only produce dictators, revolutionaries, cowboys, the mambo, the *guaracha*, boleros; but that it also produces good literature, a literature that can be read in other languages, through other cultures, because it contributes something novel, original, and creative to modern literature. This is a discovery made outside of Latin America, I think initially in Paris, and almost immediately after in Barcelona, and from there is born the idea that there is a movement of Latin American fiction writers that is novel, that is important, and those fiction writers begin to be edited, read, and the famous Boom leaps toward Latin America and Latin America begins to discover its own fiction writers, who until then had lived rather obscure and marginal lives.

I think that many Latin Americans began to feel Latin American thanks to what was called the Boom. That was certainly the case for me. I was born in Peru, grew up first in Bolivia, and then in Peru. I discovered my vocation as a writer while very young, and I came of age, as I think many writers of my generation and previous generations did, reading above all translations of North American and European writers. I grew up mostly unaware of what was happening in the field of literature, especially in the field of fiction, in the countries neighboring mine. I met some Latin American writers who were icons, who were first-rate stars, such as Neruda, for example, whose poetry was read in all of Latin America, but practically, until I arrived in Europe, I didn't know Latin American fiction writers. An Argentine critic, Ana María Barrenechea, had passed through

Lima, speaking to us about Borges, and thanks to her, I read some of his stories, but it was, in fact, in Paris where I discovered that there was a very rich, very novel, very original Latin American literature, which I read—devoured—and from which I learned a lot. Among the things I learned were to feel Latin American, to discover that, in Peru, I was only a small part of a community that had very large common denominators, not just language but also history and social, political problems that, with rather minor variations, were being lived from one corner to another of Latin America.

The first Latin American writer I met, I met in Paris, and it was Julio Cortázar. It was in December 1958. I was studying at Madrid's Universidad Complutense. I was working toward my doctorate and had gone to spend a few weeks in Paris, and a Peruvian from UNESCO invited me to dinner and sat me, at his house, next to a very thin young man whom I thought was about my age. He spoke with a slight French accent and told me he had already published a book of stories and that Juan José Arreola was going to publish another book of stories of his in the Presentes collection, in Mexico. I told him that I had a book of stories that had won a prize in Barcelona and was coming out soon and that I was very excited about the idea of seeing a published book of mine for the first time. And later, at the end of the dinner, I discovered that that young man who appeared to be my age was twenty-two years older and was named Julio Cortázar. He was there with his wife, Aurora Bernárdez. They were the most asymmetrical couple in the world: he was very tall and she was very short, and between the two of them, there was a kind of understanding and complicity when they spoke that never ceased to amaze me. Every time I was with them, I was fascinated, bewitched by the manner in which they spoke. You had the impression that they had rehearsed their conversations, due to the elegance, the grace, the humor, and the way in which they complemented each other, telling anecdotes, speaking about what they had read recently about the exhibit they had just seen. They were two very important people to me in those first years in Paris; I was impatiently waiting to be invited to dine at their house, because dinners at the Cortázars' were amazing.

That Julio Cortázar, who was of course already a magnificent writer, later experienced a mutation, the most extraordinary one I've seen in my life, an absolute change in personality. The first Julio Cortázar was a character who was supremely courteous and supremely aloof; he had that courtesy that always keeps one distant. He could be very affectionate and sweet, and at the same time, one constantly felt that there was a secret dimension in him, surely the most important part of his personality, that which nourished his writing, which one would never be able to reach. He lived a very isolated life, hated big groups, hated politics; I once tried to introduce him to Luis Goytisolo and he said, "No, no. He's too political for me." He was interested in things that were rather strange. He once took me to a congress of witches, in Mutualité: palm readers, fortune-tellers . . . there were dozens and dozens of them. I confess that I was supremely bored, and I think that seldom had I seen him so excited, so enthusiastic about those characters: great hucksters, some very skilled hucksters, but for him, they opened the doors to a certain dimension of a reality that was mysterious, esoteric, and rationally uncontrollable, which, of course, fascinated him.

Going to an exhibit with Julio Cortázar was amazing because of the liveliness of his observations, the richness of his comments. At the same time, he was a very modest man who lacked social ambition, so natural in the world of literature. He had few friends, but he showed them they were truly dear, and possessed a very rich, opinionated, and original depth of literary culture.

I learned a lot from him, and among the many things I admired in him was his generosity: he was one of the first people to whom I took my novel *The Time of the Hero*; he made some very generous comments to me and tried to find me a publisher. Later

I worked with him and with Aurora at UNESCO, as a translator, and, I insist, their relationship was mutually enriching, they always seemed to have read the same books, they seemed up to date on literature, not what was new, but ultra-new, even what was to come. Julio Cortázar had something that I do think was one of his characteristics, one of the few common characteristics to writers of the Boom: he wrote in a language that seemed natural, that seemed like spoken language, everyday language; he laughed a lot at writers who put on a suit and tie to write. He and Aurora greatly mocked a phrase—though I do not know whether it was true or if they had invented it—from a novel by Eduardo Mallea in which a character walks into a room and turns on the light and they would say, "So-and-so enters the room and transforms the obstinate darkness into electric light."

Latin American literature of Cortázar's generation broke a bit with this "literary" language, which was pretentious, bombastic, full of itself, and which, thinking itself literary, distanced itself from common, everyday language, the language of the streets; a language that Cortázar knew how to convey marvelously in his writing, which gave his stories, and would later give his novels, their personality and charm.

In those years he was writing *Hopscotch*, and one of the things that most surprised me, me for whom it took a lot of work to write, was to see the ease with which he wrote such a complex novel, practically without a plan, without a script, without a previous outline. Many times, I heard him say, "Today, I don't know where the novel will go." What he most liked was precisely that feeling of risk, of insecurity, that was sitting down every morning without any preconceived plan, to move forward the novel he was writing, and which, as you know, made him enormously popular. I think, nonetheless, that at some point, Cortázar experienced a sort of trauma or interior revolution that completely changed his personality. This secret, intimate, private character, suddenly turned public, began to live on the streets, let an enormous red beard grow, began to show interest in the politics that he previously deplored, and became a young revolutionary when he was on the verge of turning sixty. And a problematic, belligerent, and, I believe, enormously naïve and simultaneously extremely pure revolutionary, without any of those stumbling blocks that often turn politics into an activity or task that corrupts and psychologically and morally degrades some of its devotees. I think that he was innocent, authentic, although I don't think he was always right in his political choices.

Our political differences did not in any way cast a shadow over our friendship: every time we saw each other, there was the old cordiality, and there were always reasons to maintain the admiration and affection I felt for him the first time we met.

In Paris, I also met Borges. I had read Borges, as I said, in Lima thanks to Ana María Barrenechea, and later I had continued reading him. And the wonder, the richness of his originality, of his intelligence, of his culture, broke all of the absurd prejudices I had against him due to the bad ideas I'd acquired by reading Jean-Paul Sartre, who had been one of my idols when I was young, the one who gave me the idea of literature, of the writer's commitment, of the function of literature within society, against which what Borges represented seemed indefensible. So I read Borges practically in secret, like someone committing a sin, but that admiration finally revealed itself. I think that there are only two writers whom, upon meeting them, I went mute with emotion. The first one was Pablo Neruda, whom I had read when I was still a boy. When I met him at the house of Jorge Edwards, I was so moved to be before that living myth that I lost the ability to speak; and the second writer was Jorge Luis Borges, in 1963, during a visit he made to Paris that was fundamental for him and for Latin American literature. I was working as a journalist at Radio Television France and I went to interview him; I always remember how moving it was to see that figure who was so fragile, so blind already, who spoke with that slowness and with that, shall we say, extraordinary literary information. He seemed to have read every book and to have retained them all in his memory. I still recall his response to some of the questions I asked him; I asked, "What is politics to you, Borges?" He said to me, "It is a form of tedium."

Borges amazed the French. Borges's conferences in Paris brought together a truly noble enthusiasm and admiration. He participated in a tribute to Shakespeare organized by UNESCO in which Giuseppe Ungaretti represented Italy and Lawrence Durrell Britain. Durrell presented a very brilliant talk in which he said that Shakespeare was the Hollywood of his time and that his works were like movies, Hollywood's blockbusters. Ungaretti read his Italian translations of various of Shakespeare's sonnets; and finally Borges went up with his cane, with difficulty, led by Roger Caillois, who had been his great promoter in France. He spoke for fifteen minutes but in antiquated French, in a French of an age past, with great perfection, and said things that were so original, so absolutely personal and intelligent about Shakespeare that I remember the thunderous ovation with which his presentation was received.

Later he spoke at the Sorbonne; and at the Sorbonne, in the audience, there were true luminaries of the French intelligentsia. Someone who never went out, who never went to conferences, Raymond Queneau, was there in the first row. And all of the writers who were in fashion, a fashion of which there is barely any memory today, the writers of the nouveau roman, of the objectivist or objective novel (Robbe-Grillet, Nathalie Sarraute, Claude Simon, Roland Barthes, who was the theorist of the movement of the objectivists), were also there listening to him, truly dazzled. He spoke about fantastic literature, and his speech, which he gave looking into the void, as always, and speaking with a slowness that made it seem like he would be interrupted at any moment, created a truly magical atmosphere. He told fantastic stories and went along drawing little conclusions, and with all of this, he was creating an atmosphere of surprise, of expectation, of delight and admiration.

That visit by Borges to Paris was definitive, first of all, for his glory: the most important magazines dedicated special issues to him: *L'Herne*, *La Nouvelle Revue Française* . . . His entire oeuvre was translated or retranslated, and ever since then, I think that, thank you, Borges, Latin American literature in France began to be seen and read with a respect that it had not obtained before.

At the same time that this was happening in France, in Barcelona—and I have to name Carlos Barral here, the poet and editor—Latin American books were being published. Seix Barral was a small publishing house making a huge effort to open the doors and windows of Spain to the most modern literature of Europe, of the United States. It engaged in Homeric battles to negotiate and avoid censorship, which was still very strong in Spain, and we have to be grateful to Barcelona and to the publisher Seix Barral for having been the first to build a bridge toward Latin America.

My first novel, *The Time of the Hero*, was published there, and Carlos Barral really fought for it to come out without too many cuts from the censors. The novel had a very decent distribution, I believe in large part thanks to the Peruvian military, who didn't prohibit it, but did publicly burn it. This awoke enormous curiosity regarding the book, and I have always wondered if the long life *The Time of the Hero* has had is due to its having been the victim of an Inquisition-like act or because of its own merits. But the truth is that Seix Barral began to publish Latin American authors, introduced Latin American literature in Spain, and, besides, made Latin Americans read their own authors, who, until then, I repeat, were seldom read or not read at all. With some exceptions: one of these was Carlos Fuentes.

Carlos Fuentes had published years before *Where the Air Is Clear*, a novel that was very widely read, one of those rare novels that broke the barriers confining Latin American books to their own countries and to very limited sectors within those. It was a very ambitious novel, a great fresco of Mexico City, a novel that made use of the novels of the lost generation; it was a novel that in some way had remote reminiscences, but not without losing its originality, of course, of the novels of Dos Passos about North American society, of Faulkner. And it is a novel that brought Carlos Fuentes's name to the forefront; he was one of the few Latin American writers, I believe, who was read outside of his country.

Later, with his second novel, *The Death of Artemio Cruz*, Fuentes became much more widely read. His books were translated, and in 1962, I met him, also because of my journalistic activities: Radio Television France sent me to Mexico, where there was a great French exhibit, and Claude Couffon gave me a letter for him.

I met him at the house of a Mexican filmmaker whose name I have forgotten; I entered and immediately recognized him: he was standing on a table, stomping his feet; it was a completely unusual vision, because Carlo Fuentes did not drink much and, above all, never made a ruckus, as many writers tend to. And there he was; he had drunk, I think, more tequilas than he should have, and he was stomping. Then I had an image of Carlos Fuentes that never again repeated itself. That same night, we became friends.

The image Carlos Fuentes immediately conveyed was that of a winner. He was a cosmopolitan Mexican, he spoke four or five languages, he had traveled all over before even being born, because his father was a diplomat. He had been through I don't know how many schools, was a citizen of the world, in addition knew everything happening in all the important cities, and was a source of the best information about cultural and literary developments. He was likable, fun, he was very good-looking: all the women fell into his arms; he reminded me of that famous *corrido* by Juan Charrasqueado: "He took the most beautiful women and left the valley without a single flower." He was a born seducer, but not just of women; he also enchanted men with his intelligence, with his brilliance. And at the same time, this person who seemed like an eminently social figure was a tireless worker, very disciplined; Carlos's personality was very contradictory, and the proof is the oeuvre of Balzac-like dimensions that he has left behind. He cultivated all genres: novels, essays, short stories, theater, and even, at some point, poetry. He gave conferences and, besides, was an extraordinary cultural promoter. I don't think that anyone contributed as much to bringing together Latin American writers, extending ties of friendship, and getting them to collaborate as Carlos Fuentes.

With him the idea was born that never came to fruition—although, in a way, indirectly, it did—of a group of writers each writing a story about our dictator. I was going to write about General Manuel Odría, García Márquez was going to write about Rojas Pinilla, Cortázar was going to write about Perón, Roa Bastos was going to write about Dr. Francia. It was a very nice idea, and because of it we had many meetings, but in the end, nothing came of it, nobody wrote his story, but almost all of us ended up writing novels about our dictators, and in some way, these novels came about at Carlos's initiative.

I did not meet García Márquez, another one of the main characters, protagonists of what was called the Boom, in person until some years later. We first met via letter.

Lack of communication within Latin America was so great at that time from a literary point of view that when I worked for Radio Television France, I once received a book to comment on, an edition published in France, translated from Spanish by one Gabriel García Márquez, called *Pas de lettre pour le colonel*, or *No One Writes to the Colonel*. That is how I discovered the existence of a Colombian writer named García Márquez, with the prose that is so clean, so clear, so precise. The translations came out easily and the book, the little book, I was about to say, because it is a book of few pages, received very good reviews in France and I loved it, it seemed to me a wonder of precision, of synthesis, of expressive beauty. And then I tried to find out who he was and to see how I could obtain books of his in Spanish, since there were almost none, I must say as an aside: his editions had been published in very small runs, almost as if for friends and family. And thus I came into contact with him via correspondence, we had a very long correspondence and even planned to write a novel between the two of us about the thirty years' war between Colombia and Peru in the Amazon. He was going to write the novel from the Colombian point of view and I was going to write from the Peruvian point of view; we had even exchanged guides and outlines for that novel that never went anywhere.

In reality I met him in another city that played a very important role in the history of the Boom, which was Caracas. This was in the years of the "Saudi Venezuela" and there were constantly congresses, literary encounters being organized there, and at one of them, when the first Rómulo Gallegos Prize was being awarded, we met. He had published *One Hundred Years of Solitude* shortly before and was bothered, really bothered by the extraordinary success of that novel. It was the first work written by an author of the Boom that everyone and their mother read. It was a work that, for several reasons, of course, came to be read by everyone, by the most rigorous readers, most demanding, and also by the crudest reader, the most common and ordinary reader who sees one point and latches onto it. Because one of the extraordinary virtues of this book is that it has something for every kind of reader. It can be read very easily, very directly, or it can be read more complexly and rigorously because the book does all of these things at once. He wasn't expecting it, he had not been recognized except by very small groups of readers and suddenly, from one day to the next, he found himself at the center of a tension that spilled out not just across Latin America, Europe, but reached everywhere; translations appeared and in all these places it was immensely successful with critics and the public. At that moment, we met, and I think the first person we talked about was Carmen Balcells.

Carmen Balcells, as you know, the literary agent, played a role almost as important as that of Carlos Barral to turn Barcelona into one of the main centers of the Boom. Carmen Balcells, once she knew of García Márquez's existence, had taken a plane to see him in Mexico, had become his literary agent, and had convinced him to leave Mexico and live in Barcelona. And Carmen Balcells is so persuasive, so brutally persuasive, that García Márquez went to live in Barcelona.

One or two years later, Carmen Balcells landed in London, where I was living. After Paris, I went to live there, I was teaching at the university, I had a job I liked, I liked teaching literature; I liked London a lot. And one fine day, Carmen Balcells, a true tornado in a skirt, came into my house and said to me, "Today, you will resign from the university and go live in Barcelona," and when Carmen Balcells orders something, you either kill her or you obey, and so I then went to live in Barcelona and I will never regret it. These were, I think, the five most beautiful years of my life, and I am sure that they were for all Latin Americans who found ourselves there at the beginning of the seventies. García Márquez was there and José Donoso was already there.

José Donoso, a Chilean writer who was very well-known in his country, was also beginning to be known outside of Chile. I think we were the first three Latin Americans to settle in Barcelona, but other Latin American writers who didn't live there went very frequently, like Fuentes and Cortázar, and since Barcelona, thanks to the publishing movement and thanks also to being the city in Spain with the widest opening toward Europe and the rest of the world, culturally speaking, attracted many people, and it went on attracting more and more young Latin American writers. It was very moving to see how they arrived—young men, young women, Colombians, Mexicans, Peruvians, Argentines who went to Barcelona as we had gone to Paris before, because you had to be there, because that was the place where a writer could succeed, because there were editors there and because, if one was edited in Barcelona, books came out and could be distributed throughout Latin America. This was one of the most positive consequences of the Boom.

In regard to literature, Latin America and Spain had turned their backs on each other at least since the Spanish Civil War. I think that in Spain we were unaware of all the Spanish writers of the time and the same thing happened with Latin Americans. When I came to Madrid as a student in 1958, I was surprised by the almost complete unawareness in Spain regarding Latin American literature. That began to change dramatically in the sixties because Barcelona became, after Paris, the literary capital of Latin America. And there, again, writers of the Spanish language from both sides of the Atlantic met, formed very intense, very deep friendships, and in addition we had the feeling that we all belonged to the same homeland, an enormous, common homeland that encompassed twenty-some countries and had the formidable denominator of a shared language. Of course there was also a history, a tradition, that united us, but a language, that language that we now saw revitalized, living, beating in original, novel works, that was reaching a larger public every day, that deserved interest and the curiosity of other languages was something that united us and made us live truly exciting shared experiences.

It was very clear that Spain, sooner or later and probably much sooner than later, would change, that the dictatorship would disappear and that the Spain to come, the new and democratic Spain, would be a Spain in which culture, in which literature, would play a central role. I think that gave life, and literary work, in Barcelona in those years a special flavor: one had the feeling, writing in those years, that he was not only seeing through a vocation, he was fulfilling himself by accepting responsibility for it, but rather what he did, if it turned out well, if it went straight to a reader's heart, then in some way it was going to contribute to change, to the reforms, and make life better.

Many writers who had already written, at least, their most important works were rescued thanks to the Boom, and they soon came to a much larger public in the new situation. Among them, for example, the Cubans, the admirable Cuban writers. Alejo Carpentier had published his first novel in 1930-something, a regionalist novel, *¡Écue-yamba-O!* But in the forties, he published an absolute masterpiece, a small gem—because it was brief—one of the most original, richest, and most difficult novels to write in his time, *The Kingdom of This World*. It's a novel that I have read many times, that I've had occasion to teach at universities and that has never ceased to appear richer, more complex, more difficult to conceive. It's a novel that narrates the entire historic period of the first years of Haiti's independence, not in a realist way, but through myths, through legends, using a language that is mythical, that is legendary and that makes us feel not just the events, some of them incredible, that marked this whole period, but that makes us feel it from the perspective of those who were living through this myth and believed in those myths and legends thanks to an extraordinarily worked-over prose that, in the antithesis of a Cortázar or a García Márquez, did not pretend at all to be like spoken language. It was a bookish, expert, pretentious prose, but at the same time was enormously persuasive, coherent, and functional. He had written *The Lost Steps*, *Manhunt* . . . He had written half a dozen stories and really admirable novels, and in those years, Carpentier's work had a sort of renaissance. In those years, Guillermo Cabrera Infante also began to be known.

Guillermo Cabrera Infante had written a book of revolutionary stories, *In Peace as in War*, but he later wrote a magnificent book, a book that absolutely corresponded to what the spirit of the time was, renewing, experimental, that owed a lot to reading the best novels of his time, in his case, English and North American ones, especially; and that was at the same time, profoundly original because in it appeared Cuba, Havana, the night in Havana above all, humor, the way of speaking in Havana. I'm referring to *Three Trapped Tigers*, one of the eminent books of those years. I think there was also great recognition in those years of José Lezama Lima, who had been admired and read in Latin American literary circles as a poet, but who published in those years an exceptional novel, exceptionally difficult to read, hermetic, esoteric, but that greatly compensated the intellectual effort that reading it signified: *Paradiso*.

I met Lezama Lima on one of those trips I made in the sixties to Havana. He had left Cuba only once in his life, on a trip to Jamaica, which is very close, and which had motivated that marvelous poem called "To Get to Montego Bay," a trip that seemed like Ulysses's return to Ithaca due to the luxuriance, the imaginative richness with which he had camouflaged that minor migratory experience. Lezama Lima was a very fat man, a very slow man, and a man who himself lived within myth. He lived in a rather modest house, but when he started describing the objects he had in that house, the chairs, the little portraits, the small, insignificant objects started becoming, all of them, due to the way he described them and linked them to anecdotes or people, mythical objects, truly wondrous objects, and he knew how to create around him an atmosphere of extraordinary baroqueness, and everything became steeped, as in Borges's case, in literature, because they were all literary references. He was also one of those people who seemed to have read every book and to have them all present in his memory, and to understand life through the books he had read. He was a man who spoke like he wrote.

I think that what the Boom signified, in other words the recognition that Latin America had a literature that deserved to be read, was very important from the sociological point of view because it made Latin Americans discover a literature that until then, save for insignificant minorities, they were unaware of. I think it helped many Latin Americans, writers, to break with an inferiority complex and dare, as Borges, Carpentier, Carlos Fuentes, and Lezama Lima did, to be universal and to take risks with universal themes and to come out of their own milieu and invent and create stories on the basis of others' experiences, ones that were foreign to their own historical or cultural worlds.

We must also point to the Brazil that was part of the Boom. João Guimarães Rosa is the author of an absolutely extraordinary novel, *The Devil to Pay in the Backlands*, and thanks to the Latin American Boom, I think that novel broke the confines of Brazil and was translated into other languages. It's very difficult to translate because its linguistic complexity is no less than *Paradiso*, but that truly extraordinary novel was revived (it had been published many years before) thanks to what was the Latin American Boom.

How long did the Boom last? I think that all the exaltation, the friendship, the cohesion, the shared enthusiasm, the fraternity, didn't last more than ten years, and if you have to pinpoint a time at which this experience in some way ends or at least enters into a certain dénouement, it's with the Padilla case. I think it was politics, the enormous division that the Padilla case caused among Latin American writers, which in a certain way started undoing the ties that kept us so close to one another, so united and feeling like we were participating in a common task. Not only because the political rupture, as tends to always happen in Latin America, also signified the rupture of friendships and even relationships, but also because a kind of fragmentation came that not only politically affected an entire intellectual world, but had very direct effects on the literary work itself, and in some way a certain distance was created between those who had been a part of this common experience. I am not, in any way, saying that, with this, Latin American literature entered a recession, nor anything of the sort; I'm saying that the vital experience, besides the literary one, of the Boom, probably ends when the Padilla case happens, and from then on, what had been a common enterprise comes to be an individual task. But something did remain; a literature that had come into its own remained, a literature that had opened some doors that had previously been closed, and in addition, the stimulus remained, an example that was taken full advantage of by the writers of later generations.

To begin to write, to discover that one has a literary vocation and to want to turn it into a way of living, as you must, I wouldn't say that it is easy for a Peruvian, Colombian, Paraguayan, or Chilean writer today, but what I can say is that it is less difficult than when we, fifty or sixty years ago, discovered that we had a literary vocation and looked around us and saw a huge wasteland that wanted to dissuade us and steer us in different directions.

Today, the young Latin American writer knows that if he works hard, if he pays the price that has to be paid, he can, in some way, realize his vocation and not become thwarted in the early stages, as happened so frequently before the Boom. I think that the young writer in Spain, in Argentina, in Brazil participates in a reality that is not circumscribed by borders and feels that there is a common homeland that has to do with language, that has to do with certain shared experiences, and that, with it all, a literature can be made that reaches a much larger audience than in his own city or his own country. And without a doubt, so that this could be possible today, the experience of the Boom was worth something.

The Boom is already history and I think that the greatest proof is this meeting that we begin today. To all of the writers who have come, some from very far, to talk about the Boom, I would ask you to keep in mind that the Boom was not only the good books that were written then, the presence that Latin America gained before the rest of the world, the importance that the world began to give this beautiful language that is ours, that beautiful language in which we write; but also remember that other part that I have tried to evoke through certain anecdotes, the relationships among the protagonists of the Boom.

Friendship is beautiful, it is beautiful to have the experience of sharing aspirations, of sharing dreams, and above all, to undertake together this common fight for fiction, for literature, for culture, that, as you well know, is much more than entertainment or pleasure, although it is also that, and in a compelling way: it is the means of fighting against what we don't like, against that which disgusts us in the world.

Nothing has contributed as much as literature in Latin America, and, of course, in Spain, to opening our eyes regarding what is going poorly. Nothing has contributed as much to reminding us that life is poorly made, that the world is insufficient for placating our longings, our dreams, our appetites, our desires; some dreams, some longings, some appetites, and some desires that good literature inspires more than anything else. Literature helps us to live, without a doubt; literature produces an extraordinary experience of pleasure, but also, at the same time, good literature helps to keep alive society's dissatisfaction with the world, with reality, and that is why you can say that literature is also an extraordinary source of civilization and progress.

I really appreciate your attention and I wish much success to the symposium beginning today and that all who participate in it, when they leave, take along good memories of these days.

Thank you very much.

Madrid, November 5, 2012

Index